Metaphors, Maps and Mirrors:
Moral Education in Middle Schools

Contemporary Studies in Social and Policy Issues in Education: The David C. Anchin Series

KATHRYN M. BORMAN, SERIES EDITOR

Minority Education: Anthropological Perspectives
edited by Evelyn Jacob and Cathie Jordan, 1993

Reinventing the University: A Radical Proposal
for a Problem-Focused University
by Jan Sinnott and Lynn Johnson, 1996

Schoolteachers and Schooling: Ethoses in Conflict
by Eugene F. Provenzo, Jr., and Gary N. McCloskey, O.S.A., 1996

Social Reconstruction Through Education:
The Philosophy, History, and Curricula of a Radical Ideal
edited by Michael E. James, 1995

In preparation:

The Minority Voice in Educational Reform: An Analysis by Minority
and Women College of Education Deans
Louis A. Castenell and Jill M. Tarule

Metaphors, Maps and Mirrors:
Moral Education in Middle Schools

Carol K. Ingall
The Jewish Theological Seminary of America

Ablex Publishing Corporation
Greenwich, Connecticut
London, England

All names of institutions, educators, students, parents, and place names used in this account are pseudonyms.

Printed in the United States of America

Library of Congress Cataloging-in-Publication Data
Ingall, Carol K.
    Metaphors, maps, and mirrors : moral education in middle schools / Carol K. Ingall.
        p.   cm. — (Social and policy issues in education)
    Includes bibliographical references (p.) and index.
    ISBN 1-56750-301-2 (cloth). — ISBN 1-56750-302-0 (paper)
        1. Moral education (Middle school)—United States—Case studies.
    2. Values—Study and teaching (Middle school)—United States—Case studies.   3. Heroes—Study and teaching (Middle school)—United States—Case studies.   4. Role models—Study and teaching (Middle school)—United States—Case studies.   5. Middle schools—Social aspects—United States—Case studies.   6. Cross-cultural studies—United States.   I. Title.   II. Series.
    LC311.I54   1997
    370.11'4—dc21   96-52274
                                                                                   CIP

Ablex Publishing Corporation
55 Old Post Road #2
P.O. Box 5297
Greenwich, CT 06830

Published in the U.K. and Europe by:
JAI Press Ltd.
38 Tavistock Street
Covent Garden
London WC2E 7PB
England

To my hero Michael, whom I followed into the wilderness

Contents

Acknowledgments

Many people made this book possible.

The real heroes of this study are: the four moral educators who shared their classes, their time, and their reflections with me;

My immediate family: my husband, Michael; my children, Marjorie and Andrew; and my extended family: Belleruth and Art; Michael and Sandy; Bess and Tom; Gilda and Sam; and Nancy and Joel, all of whom encouraged and supported my decision to resume my studies and to write this book;

My friends and colleagues who found sources for me, clarified fuzzy thinking, and helped me out in numerous ways: Elizabeth Cohn, Ann Webb, Judy Rothenberg, Russell Faux, Miriam Goldberg, David Cappella, Suzanne Cane, Ruth Page, and Edy Rauch;

My skillful editor, Karen Feinberg;

And Sue Tauer, who invariably asked the right questions and, like a true friend, kept pushing me until I answered them.

This book is about teachers and their power to influence. I became the person I am largely because of the teachers in my life. I have to thank my first teachers—my parents, the late Olla and Harry Krepon, who taught me by example the values of integrity, perseverance, and caring; past teachers, such as Mollie Stein Glanz, Rabbi Joel H. Zaiman, William Damon, and Philip Tate; and my current teacher, Rabbi Alvan H. Kaunfer. I owe a particular debt to my academic mentor, Kevin Ryan. The Talmudic tractate Avot offers the following advice: "Get yourself a teacher; find a friend; and judge each person with merit" (1:6). Kevin Ryan modeled all three qualities for me. He is a *mensch*, and I am truly grateful for the experience of studying and working with him.

Preface

Concern about a crisis in values has raised questions about the nature of contemporary education. It has also caused a renewed interest in the function of moral prototypes—loosely defined as heroes and role models—in the process of schooling. What part do moral prototypes play in shaping character and defining values? Some critics look to traditional cultural icons to replace a patriotism lost in the Vietnam era; others turn to new heroes who embody more timely values such as multiculturalism and feminism. Some theorists opt for "quiet" or "ordinary" heroes, or for personal exemplars—role models instead of heroes.

In this book I focus on four middle school teachers who care as much about teaching moral values as about content. Through detailed portraits based on observation and interviews, I hope to analyze the place of moral prototypes in their teaching. I compare their understanding of heroes and role models with moral education theory. In addition, I investigate the cultural context provided for the teachers by their schools, by their administrators, and by students and their parents. Finally, I examine how students in these teachers' classes understand heroes and role models, and how their views compare with the research on adolescents and moral prototypes.

The four teachers in this study teach diverse subjects in a variety of settings. They are a teacher of religious studies in an Orthodox yeshivah, an American history teacher in an urban multicultural school, a mathematics teacher in a girls' independent school, and a literature teacher in an affluent suburban school. Although their definitions of moral education are shaped by their backgrounds, their institutions, their perceptions of their students' needs, and their disciplines, all of the teachers consider moral education to be central to their work. For all four, the moral prototype serves as an appeal to the students' imagination, an opportunity to build connectedness and, most important, an invitation to young people to transcend themselves. Each tries consciously to serve as a moral model for students through interactions with them inside and outside the classroom.

These teachers are remarkably successful. The students' exemplars closely parallel those that their teachers espouse. They overwhelmingly admire their parents and parent surrogates, including teachers. Celebrity heroes are not prominent in their lists. The girls' exemplars differ from site to site, but their choices are generally more restricted than the boys'. Factors such as race and socioeconomic class raise questions about conventional notions of young people and those they admire.

This study suggests that educators can influence their students through moral prototypes. To do so, they must create school environments rich in heroes and role models as well as opportunities to introduce their students to exemplars across the curriculum. Teacher educators must include moral education in their course offerings. They should seek out candidates who view teaching as a calling and who are committed to serving as moral models for their students. Finally, school reform efforts cannot overlook what Cuban calls "the power of pedagogy" in producing young people who know, love, and do the good.

1

Introduction

SHAPING MORAL BEHAVIOR

Who are America's heroes? Do young people have heroes? Are they the same as role models? What part do heroes and role models play in shaping moral behavior? Questions about the place of heroes and role models in contemporary American life arise in public and private conversations, in print and electronic media. The fall of national idols from grace, the cult of celebrity heroes, and whether minority athletes are role models are topics of discussion in homes and workplaces across the United States, and in academic circles as well.

Contemporary social critics are concerned about the place of moral prototypes in American life. I use the term *moral prototypes* to refer to those figures, real and symbolic, who inspire others to better themselves. These prototypes range from the larger-than-life hero to the role model. Sometimes the differences between the two are blurred. The hero is traditionally a cultural icon who legitimates a virtue deemed necessary by a given society. Character educators such as William Bennett (1991) decry the absence of heroes. Those who share his view, including Kilpatrick (1992) and Wynne and Ryan (1993), link the unraveling of traditional American values to the demise of the heroic. Other observers of the social scene view traditional heroes as irrelevant. Walter Truett Anderson (1993) asks, "Heroes: Who needs them?" He and others like him believe that our nation would be better served by down-to-earth leaders than by mythic heroes.

The saga of O. J. Simpson that has unleashed an avalanche of type (and hype) on the power of the media and the corporations to create heroes. These observers deplore the use of the word *hero* to describe a celebrity (Lasch, 1978). They ask for a restoration of the classical definition of the hero: the timeless, larger-than-life icon, rather than the image captured by the relentless eye of the camera and made smaller than life through its projection on television screens throughout America.

1

The need to rethink the heroic to include women and minorities represents a third area of concern about the hero. In *Eve's Daughters: The Forbidden Heroism of Women*, Polster (1992) analyzes why women shrink from heroism and then invites them to take up the challenge and become heroes. Polster and numerous multicultural scholars have no quarrel with the iconic or metaphoric aspects of heroism. Their intent is to make the concept of the heroic more inclusive, adding an ethnic or female aspect to a traditionally male image.

Still another group of theorists rejects heroes as moral prototypes and advocates role models instead. Feminists such as Brown and Gilligan (1992) lament the absence of role models for young women. Their discussion of moral education is rooted in personal connectedness rather than in identification with the abstract; in their view, the role model, close by and therefore observable, is a far more compelling moral prototype than the distant hero. The Center for Educating African-American Males similarly calls for more male role models in order to change the destinies of male inner city black youth (Holland, 1991). Still other educators insist that role models are no substitute for heroes and believe that moral education requires both (Epstein, 1991; Singer, 1991).

Heroes

The use and understanding of moral prototypes, which include both heroes and role models, is the subject of this book. Long a staple of moral education, heroes embody a culture's values (Bennett, 1991; Eliade, 1963). In classical, traditional societies, heroes were connected to virtue, notably the virtue of courage (MacIntyre, 1984). Heroes not only symbolize and legitimate the abstract virtues that bind a social group, they also provide transcendental meaning to individuals. They are potent emblems of a life worth living, affording glimpses of the immortal (Becker, 1973). Because heroes enable ordinary people to become extraordinary, they have always played an important part in moral education.

In classical antiquity, some of the first heroes were teachers. The life of the teacher/hero served as the subject of study for those disciples who wished to emulate his greatness (Greek: *arete*). Hadas and Smith (1965) trace aretalogy, the genre comprising studies of these lives, to the histories of Philo and The Gospel According to Luke, written in the first century of the common era. Classical biographies, such as those of Plutarch and his successors, although not aretalogy, are its descendants: attempts to use the hero both to inspire and to elevate.

Elders of diverse religions and ethnic groups have long recognized the power of the hero to transmit their moves to the young. American educators have used heroes in character education since the emergence of Horace Mann's common school. The common school, the dream of educational reformers in the first half of the 19th century, promised universal, free public education. The curriculum of the common school was created by the brothers McGuffey (Minnich, 1936), whose textbooks, the *McGuffey Readers*, dominated American classrooms. The American Book Company, the successor to the first publishers of the series, estimates that more than 122 million copies of the readers were sold between 1836 and 1920 (Mosier, 1965, p. 168).

The heroes of the *Readers* represented rugged individualism, the dignity of labor, and the basic virtues of thrift, honesty, and charity—what later was referred to dismissively as "middle-class morality" (Mosier, 1965). These heroes also exemplified the patriotism that the authors were eager to teach the hordes of new immigrants who flooded American shores. While bringing to life the abstract values of the United States, heroes also provided an antidote to the radical ideas that millions of European immigrants brought along with their samovars, feather pillows, and priceless photographs.

McGuffey Readers featured patriots such as William Penn, Benjamin Franklin, Patrick Henry, John Marshall, and, above all, George Washington, who was lionized as the American Cincinnatus. Mere mention of Washington's name conjured up images of courage, sacrifice, and leadership, qualities sorely needed by the fledgling republic. (Semioticists refer to this capacity as *onomasticism*, the powerful relationship between the name or sign and that which it signifies [Makolkin, 1992].) Such heroes were essential components of the ideals that, to use Arnold Gehlen's term, formed the "background" (Berger & Kellner, 1965) of American life for well over 100 years. These values were "taken-for-granted knowledge" (Berger, 1990): unquestioned beliefs promulgated by the schools through their curricula as instruments of socialization.

Role Models

Role models have performed a different function: transmitting the details of behavior and attitude appropriate to a given societal, occupational, or gender role (Jung, 1986). Parents and parent surrogates traditionally have been expected to act as role models, teaching by example the aspects of life appropriate each child's status, sex, and function.

The idea of role models is not new to moral education. The teacher has always been expected to serve as an object of emulation for students. In Tractate Shabbath 114a, the Babylonian Talmud states that a teacher is forbidden to appear in public with a spot of grease on his clothes. The teacher in the 19th-century common school was hired for her moral character as much as for her academic mastery (Herbst, 1989). She was far more likely to lose her position for a moral infraction than for a mistake in subtraction. In addition to teachers, schools relied on older students to serve as role models. Dickens's schoolboys, whether in private academies or in dens of thieves, were taught as much by the old boys as by their teachers. Therefore, in addition to looking at heroes, I examine the dual use of role models in four middle schools both as a part of the formal curriculum (the plan of instruction) and as a part of the informal curriculum (the instruction itself).

In traditional societies, the hero and the role model were distinct; today they are not. The confusion about these terms recently became obvious to me when I studied published curricula that use heroes to convey values. I discovered that the heroes of my childhood—noble, white, male, and nearly immortal—had vanished. The heroes I remembered looked much like those featured in Blaisdell and Ball's (1915) American history book, *Heroic Deeds of American Sailors*. These heroes fit MacIntyre's (1984) description of the traditional, classical hero. They embodied courage and self-sacrifice: They appeared on the scene—usually a battlefield—without thought of personal risk, to save the imperiled. The values they espoused—humility, charity, self-control, persistence, responsibility, and industry—represented a "civic religion" promulgated by American schools through their curricula for nearly a century (Yulish, 1980). These values provided the structure necessary to enculturate generations of immigrants. Moral exemplars, embedded in the amber of these curricula, reflected American ideology (Apple, 1990).

Curricula are promoting other values today. Self-esteem is one value that attracts a great deal of attention in the contemporary literature of moral education. The need to build self-esteem echoes throughout the research on the education of minorities and women (*A.A.U.W.* Report, 1992; J. A. Banks, 1993; Brown & Gilligan, 1992). The emergence of Afrocentric schools with Afrocentric curricula featuring African and African-American heroes is only one example (Poinsett, 1988). The growing body of research on the education of girls has engendered a number of curricula featuring strong women as role models or exemplars. The prospectuses of independent girls' schools routinely refer to the research on adolescent girls and the need to build their self-esteem through positive role models (National Coalition of Girls' Schools, 1992).

Accordingly, the heroes of contemporary curricula are very different from those assembled by Blaisdell and Ball (1915). They too reflect ideology—the forces of multiculturalism and feminism—but today's social studies textbooks have expanded the heroic pantheon to include African-American heroes, such as Frederick Douglass, and women, such as Amelia Earhart. Others texts include contemporary heroes—for example, César Chavez, Martin Luther King, and Sally Ride (Cook, 1993; Russell, 1988).

The Giraffe Project (1991) has created a character education curriculum for grades 6 through 12. The curriculum is built around "giraffes": people who stick their necks out for what they believe. "Giraffes" are:

> real life heroes—men, women and children worthy of admiration and emulation . . . . Giraffes span all age groups, ethnic, religious and political backgrounds. They are students, retirees, truck drivers, forest rangers, doctors, lawyers, housewives, cops. And they work on every issue from homelessness, pollution, and drugs to decaying cities and failing schools. (p. iii)

The heroes of The Giraffe Project are not larger than life, but everyday people whom the authors of the curricula hold up as role models.

When the word *hero* is used in contemporary curricula, it is often qualified. "Local heroes," "ordinary heroes," "little heroes," "real-life heroes," "unsung heroes," and "everyday heroes" are the scaled-down embodiments of contemporary ideology (Berkowitz, 1987; Dunn, 1991; Facets, 1985; Gerzon, 1982; Giraffe Project, 1991). In fact, these heroes are not heroes in the classic sense—cultural icons who serve as anchors for a national culture—but what Colby and Damon (1992) call "moral exemplars" or paragons of social commitment. Unlike the heroes in the Blaisdell and Ball curriculum, the heroes of The Giraffe Project come in all colors, sizes, and ages.

The authors of *Giraffes in Schools* (Giraffe Project, 1991) compare their heroes to the heroes of mythology. The hero of fairy tales undertakes a perilous journey, venturing into the unknown and conquering evil so that the land can be reborn (p. 23). For Giraffes, evils are pollution, urban decay, divisiveness, suspicion, and cynicism (p. 23). These heroes no longer serve as "carriers" (Berger & Luckmann, 1966) of national values such as patriotism and respect for authority.

Those values were discredited by the events of Vietnam and Watergate. As Kevin Ryan pointed out to me in a personal conversation, the new "ordinary heroes" represent a set of values about which there is consensus, namely the new values of social concern. Today's heroes are less lofty; they are localized moral exemplars who live virtuous lives, inspiring those whom they encounter. *Hero* has come to mean many things: the classical hero of mythic proportion, the new ethnic hero, the celebrity hero, the moral exemplar, and the role model.

I was curious to learn whether these trends that I had noted in commercially printed materials were also true in the informal domain, in what is said and done in the classroom. Is the notion of the hero changing, as classroom materials and observers of the social scene would suggest? To answer this question, I decided to study the use of moral prototypes in four middle schools, two public and two private. The public schools are an urban multiethnic school (grades 6–8) and a middle- to upper-middle-class suburban school (grades 6–8). The private schools include a middle- to upper-middle-class Quaker girls' school (N–12) and an Orthodox Jewish day school (*yeshivah*) (pre-K–12) in urban settings. In all four sites I visited either a seventh grade, an eighth grade, or a seventh-eighth grade elective. The teachers in the public schools teach history and literature; the independent school teacher teaches mathematics; the Jewish day school teacher teaches Biblical and rabbinic texts.

How do four teachers who consider themselves moral educators use moral prototypes to convey values and to shape moral behavior? How do they make meaning out of the range of moral prototypes? My intent was to try to understand how teachers, using their instruction and curriculum, hope, in Socrates's words, to make children good as well as wise.

I chose the middle school for a number of reasons. Most important, it appears that the need for intervention is critical for this age group. Societal indicators reflect a startling rise in antisocial behavior, such as pregnancy, suicide and violence, in middle school youths (McEwin & Thomason, 1989). In 1993, for example, the City of New Haven began to make condoms available to fifth-grade students. Also, a poll commissioned by *Newsweek* and the Children's Defense Fund reveals that when asked what they fear most, 56% of children this age respond that it is violent crime against a family member ("Growing Up Fast and Frightened," 1993). In fact, four months after I interviewed one of the students in my study, his brother was killed in a shoot-out with the police.

Middle school spans the fifth to the eighth grade; this period includes two of Erikson's (1985) tasks of ego formation, industry and identity. If (as Erikson contends) young people define themselves through their work in school, then the commitment of a middle school to moral education is particularly crucial and timely. If (as Erikson maintains) the next developmental stage, early adolescence, is characterized by trying on identities like so many different hats, then early adolescence is ripe for character education.

My decision to study this population stems from my personal interest, both as a teacher and as a curriculum writer, in bar/bat Mitzvah education (Ingall, 1993). The choice of early adolescence as the point of entry into the adult Jewish community apparently was made for good psychological reasons. The rabbis of the Talmud clearly did not view 13-year-olds as true adults. They recognized, however, that these young people were ready to participate in a community in which identity was defined as engagement with texts, texts that conveyed insights on how to live a holy life. Therefore one of the sites I chose for my research is a Jewish day school, an Orthodox yeshivah.

My interest was further piqued by the compelling literature about young adolescent girls and their evolution from self-assured, spunky 11-year-olds to self-effacing, passive 14-year-olds (A.A.U.W. Report, 1992; Brown & Gilligan, 1992). I intentionally chose an independent girls' school in order to investigate this phenomenon at close range.

Finally, as a former history teacher, I was curious about the use of heroes in contemporary history classrooms. Before ethnicity became fashionable, I taught in a homogeneous middle-class suburb. Thus I was eager to learn how an American history teacher uses heroes in the multicultural 1990s. Throughout my teaching career I have been interested in the nexus between heroes and history. Thirty years ago I assigned Carlyle's (n.d.) *Heroes and Hero Worship* to my European history advanced placement class. What role do heroes play in history curricula today?

PARAMETERS AND LIMITATIONS

As Maxwell (1992) reminds his readers, qualitative studies can be generalized to only a modest degree. I can make no sweeping statements about the larger institutional settings that surround these classrooms. Nor can I generalize about heroes, role models, young adolescents, and moral education. This study is limited to the interplay of heroes and role models in four classrooms in four schools. It is bounded by the idiosyncrasies of place, time, and persons.

Place is significant because I am convinced that each community has a character of its own, and that character is bound to play itself out in its schools. The site of three of the schools I investigated, the city of Springfield, is a metropolitan center of 155,000. It is socially more conservative than a major urban center and far less susceptible to the nuances of popular culture. It might be easier to shut out the effects of popular culture in Springfield than in Beverly Hills or in Midvale, an affluent suburban community 50 miles from Springfield, and the site of my fourth school. Yet it is also more difficult for the Orthodox Jewish residents of Springfield to create a self-contained community than for the Jews of Crown Heights and Borough Park in Brooklyn. A yeshivah in Springfield does not represent the totality of the yeshivah world. Nor does an urban middle school in Springfield represent those in Bedford-Stuyvestant.

I also have not examined how family influences the students' and schools' choices of heroes and role models. I tested the waters of home-school congruence through telephone interviews with parents, but in-depth research on the students' families is beyond the purview of this study. I discuss, in a limited way, how the parents perceive the school's efforts to teach moral education, and I elicit their views on the role of moral prototypes in that education. I also do not explore how students respond to their teachers' messages. Whether or not the students' lives are changed by their teachers' concern with the good and the true is far too large a topic for this study. Here I discuss only how the students understand the notion of moral prototypes.

The study is limited by the short time—six weeks to eight weeks—that I spent in each classroom. Perhaps I came upon unusually topical material merely because of the idiosyncrasies of the calendar. I joined the yeshivah class when it was studying the narrative of the 12 spies in Numbers, which opened up a rich discussion of leadership and collective responsibility. Had I come at another time, I might have encountered a much drier discussion of case law. Visiting a teacher while he teaches a class titled "Heroes and Sheroes" was bound to give me a different perspective on the importance of moral prototypes than if I visited "Art and Architecture," another of his classes.

The composition of the classes also sets limits. Each of my teachers mentioned that the classes were different from those of previous years. The yeshivah class had an unusually large number of children from observant families and contained no children, such as Soviet émigrés, who had yet to be enculturated into Jewish tradition. The teacher in the urban school stated that in the current group it was safe for African-American children to do well; it would not be perceived as "acting white," as in other years. The teacher in the girls' independent school noted that the current pre-algebra students were unusually bright, feisty, and outspoken. The literature teacher in the suburban school told me that the current students were more receptive than those in previous years to the idea of the conventional hero. Thus I can make no claims for all the classes taught by these teachers—only for those I observed during the time when I observed them.

Another set of limits is imposed by my presence as a researcher. My visits to the school may have changed the very culture I was hoping to record. The participants knew I was interested in heroes and role models. Therefore, consciously or unconsciously, they may have generated moral prototypes in the hope of pleasing me. My being a woman may have made the male teachers I visited more sensitive to the issues of role models for girls. Certainly my femaleness raised questions for the yeshivah teacher that he had not considered before. Also, my religious background may have elicited more discussion of spiritual and religious issues with my collaborating teachers and their administrators.

My research is limited as well by the personalities of the teachers I worked with. I tried to record faithfully their views about moral prototypes. My study is about the teachers, and only peripherally about the schools in which they teach. Consequently, I can make only modest generalizations about the place of moral prototypes in the schools I visited. Although I followed a student in each school throughout a typical day, my discussion is based on one teacher in one classroom in each of the sites.

This study is also limited by the interview format and by my reliance on self-reported data. To some extent I was able to counter this tendency through member checks and triangulation of data with other sources, but the likelihood of misunderstanding one's informant, and his or her natural tendency to remember selectively, are always present in this methodology. What I learned from the teachers and their sites has been filtered through me, the primary research instrument. In Chapter 3, where I describe my methods, I have delineated my assumptions as a researcher and my attempts to counter these assumptions.

As Henry (1993) points out, a classroom or a school, like any culture, is a living thing. To be alive is to be subject to change. The classrooms I depicted then are not the classrooms that exist today. The teachers, the students, the subjects taught, the school, the society at large, and the research instrument—the researcher—are in constant flux. I attempt here to capture a moment in time—with all of the concomitant limitations.

Moral education is a hot topic. Mutual interest brings together odd bedfellows: those who decry the loss of civic virtues, or of safety in schools and in the streets; standard-bearers for academic excellence, who blame the decline in test scores on the self-esteem movement; both religious and secular educators, who look to the transcendent as an antidote to the narcissism and greed that characterize a culture based on impulse. However, the many, often diverse voices calling for moral education, from traditionalists like Bennett (1993) and Kilpatrick (1992) to reconceptualists like Purpel (1989) and Noddings (1984), can agree on an interest in moral prototypes.

A first step toward enhancing this agreement is an understanding of what terms such as *hero* and *role model* mean to those concerned with moral education. As demonstrated in the next chapter, however, the subject of moral prototypes has been addressed only peripherally.

2

Of Moral Education and Middle Schools

Ideas, like heroes and role models, are socially constructed. In the words of a sociologist of knowledge, these constructions then "act back on their producer" (Berger, 1990, p. 3); they are used to shape the society that shaped them.

Just as the Founding Fathers were inspired by the models of classical antiquity, the Virginia patriarchs became the models for later generations of Americans (Fears, 1990). The mythology surrounding George Washington is one such example, as mentioned in Chapter 1. The myth of Washington, as American icon and national savior, was nurtured by historians and folklorists in order to heal the wounds of the Civil War (Rabinowitz, 1978). This hagiography not only helped to reunite the fragmented Union but also (as stated earlier) functioned as an integrative force for a nation of immigrants, many of whom had no experience with republicanism.

Arnold Gehlen (1980), another sociologist of knowledge, claims that the dominant characteristic of a modern society is the shattering of the uniformity of language, religion, and culture. In a modern society, public agreement on values is replaced by multiple, personal views. The subjective replaces the objective; privately held views command the authority once wielded by official norms. Sociologists of knowledge call this process, in which "taken-for-granted knowledge" is challenged and dethroned, delegitimation (Gehlen, 1980). Delegitimation results in instability, which is expressed in the transformation of symbols and ceremonies. According to some sociologists of knowledge, heroes have become privatized. The products and producers of a national culture have been replaced by personal role models.

RECENT TRENDS IN MORAL EDUCATION

Like the hero, moral education is a social construction that reflects the attitudes of a larger cultural and political world. Yulish (1980) describes the hegemony of the character education movement, America's civic religion, from 1890 to 1935. Challenged by scathing reports by Hartshorne and May and colleagues (1928, 1929, 1930), which questioned the efficacy of character education, the movement crumbled in the wake of new interest in psychology and the self. Moral education in the 1940s and 1950s turned inward and stressed life adjustment skills (Bullis & O'Malley, 1952; Stratemeyer, Forkner, & McKim, 1947).

During the 1960s and 1970s, values clarification swept the schools, replacing older techniques (Simon, Howe, & Kirschenbaum, 1972). Sharing the stage with Simon and his followers was Lawrence Kohlberg, the pioneer of the cognitive-developmental school of moral education. Kohlberg and his followers urged teachers to help their students analyze their stages of moral development. They encouraged teachers to use moral dilemmas to elevate their students to increasingly more universalized stages of moral reasoning (Kohlberg, 1983). Heroes played no role in either of these approaches.

Kohlberg was criticized by feminist theorists, who noted two moralities or at least two voices of moral concern: the masculine concern with universals and justice, and the feminine concern with context, connectedness, and care (Gilligan, 1982; Noddings, 1984). Propelled by the feminist critique and by a concern for ethnic and racial equity, educators sought to include nontraditional exemplars in the school curriculum as heroes and role models in order to raise the self-esteem of women (Tomin & Burgoa, 1986), African-Americans (Poinsett, 1988), Hispanic-Americans (Tinajero, Gonzalez, & Dick, 1991), and others through pluralistic curricula.

Recoiling from the turmoil of the late 1960s and the relativism of the 1970s, observers blamed the nation's malaise on the failure of moral education in the schools. Values education had come to be regarded as antiestablishment, promoting alienation and self-centeredness (Junell, 1969). Values educators were accused of separating moral thought from moral behavior (Sichel, 1988). Therefore educators and social critics called for the teaching of virtue along with values (Damon, 1988; Harmin, 1985; Sommers, 1984).

Moral education in the 1980s and 1990s is as diverse as it has ever been in the history of this country. Moral educators who focus on pluralism have evoked a spirited response from others who fear the balkanization of America (Ravitch, 1990; Schlesinger, 1992). They are joined by those who blame our present moral paralysis on the failure of values clarification and the cognitive developmental approach. These critics call for a return to the Great Tradition of character education, which stressed conduct, authority, reinforcement, person-to-person interaction, and society's mission to civilize and perfect human behavior. They urge the teaching of common values—content, not process (Bennett, 1991; Kilpatrick, 1992; Wynne & Ryan, 1993).

Damon (1988) maintains a middle ground, noting that children have an innate moral sense which can be nurtured by parents and schools. Much like his predecessor, Dewey, Damon suggests that moral development is a result of the interaction of psychological and social forces. The affective and cognitive aspects of the child's personality are tempered by relationships with parents and other adults at home and in school. Relationships with peers also play a part in the child's moral development.

Other supporters of moral education note the importance of narrative for confronting moral questions. Parr (1982), Coles (1989), and Vitz (1990) make the case for using literature as the great repository of moral ideas, whereas Tappan and Brown (1989) and others prefer to use the students' own narratives to effect moral growth through dilemma-based deliberations. This discussion recreates the content/process schism of previous decades in the history of moral education.

HEROES AND ROLE MODELS: THEIR PLACE IN MORAL EDUCATION

Jacques Benninga (1991) refers to the content approach as *direct moral education* and the process approach as *indirect*. This categorization is tempting, but too simplistic. The Great Tradition is not about content only; it has always encouraged the process of reflection. The newer ethnic, feminist, and Afrocentric curricula are every bit as rich in content as the older character education they replaced. Tappan and Brown's (1989) approach could be characterized as indirect, but how do we categorize curricula such as *Giraffes in Schools* (1991), which encourage students to spot "ordinary heroes" and then emulate them? Perhaps it is time to borrow Gage's (1989) suggestion and call a truce in the paradigm wars of moral education.

The Objectivist View: Hero as Tribal Totem

Emile Durkheim (1973), the father of modern sociology, is the chief exponent of an objectivist, or "outside-in" (Eisner, 1985) view of moral education. His concern is about the transmission of values and norms, not about self-fulfillment. He observes the power of the school to mold human beings who can help to improve the social order. "The school is the only moral agent through which the child is able systematically to learn to know and love his country" (p. 79). The school, not the family, prepares the child for society.

Durkheim recognizes the importance of the hero for society and for its handmaiden, moral education. Individuals, by definition, are limited. True heroes are moral beings, by whose example individuals transcend themselves.

> We consider them to be heroes not only because they are great men— that is to say persons like ourselves although endowed with more tal- ent; but because in our minds they identify themselves with the impersonal ideal that they embodied and the great human groupings that they personified, we see them as raised beyond the condition of human beings and transfigured. This is why popular imagination, if it has not deified them, has nevertheless felt a need to set them apart and to identify them as closely as possible with divinity. (Durkheim, 1973, p. 93)

In Durkheim's system, the hero would be a potent tool for build- ing nationalism. As religiously-based myths toppled around him, Durkheim imagined that the myth of the state would serve as a sub- stitute, binding a people through shared history, symbols, and rituals. The hero would become a secular icon, inspiring the believer to tran- scend himself or herself (Goethals, 1978).

If the hero provides homogeneity to a nation, he or she then em- bodies national ideals. Because homogeneity is crucial for a nation of immigrants, contemporary American historians and social studies edu- cators show significant interest in the hero as a vehicle for civic educa- tion.[1] For these educators, the hero's power lies in his or her ability to transform; the hero is inseparable from the mythos of the nation. These educators ask that the hero do what Eliade (1963), Norman (1969), and Campbell (1971) claim the mythological hero always does: to serve as a symbol of what a culture expects its people to become.

Edward Wynne, a contemporary heir to the Durkheimian, objec- tivist position, believes that moral values do not develop, but are transmitted by the Great Tradition. Wynne (1986) points to the *McGuffey Readers* (which rely heavily on heroes) as an effective and artistic means of character education. For Wynne and Ryan (1993) and

---

[1] Brodbelt & Wall (1985), Parsons (1986), Shugar (1988), Butts (1988), and Frisch (1989) argue an objectivist case as they call for a reconstruction of American icono- graphy in an attempt to restore America's collective memory. Morgan (1985) asks his readers to rethink American heroes. His primary goal is not inclusion, but redefinition: downplaying the military hero and promoting the "peaceful hero."

for Kilpatrick (1992), heroes offer an opportunity for "loving the good," an emotional appeal to transcendence and an opportunity to concretize abstract virtues such as courage, duty, and perseverance. Their hero-based education echoes that of Sidney Hook (1955) a generation before. "Reinforced by folklore and legend, this variety of early education leaves a permanent impress upon the plastic minds of the young" (p. 8).

The curriculum writers at the Nebraska Curriculum Development Center (1968; Unit 80) describe the changes in the literary hero, from demigod to antihero, in language that resonates with the shift from hero to role model.

> The eighth grade units deal exclusively with heroes: men placed between men and the Gods who define a culture's, or a person's, conception of what it is to be 'ideal man'—half man–half god, a creature more-than-man to whom men may raise their eyes. (1968, p. xviii)

The Nebraska team includes an excerpt about Achilles to exemplify courage, a selection about Aeneas to depict courage plus control, and stories about Sir Gawain and Lancelot to teach courage and justice. The authors explain the disappearance of the classical hero as follows:

> As society becomes more complex, the literary audience is divided and the artist can no longer depend on a uniform reaction to his work. He no longer can represent the ideals of the whole group in his work, but of only a small part of the group—or perhaps just his own. Not only the tone of his work but also the traits of his heroes change. . . . The stature of the hero is reduced; he seldom has national or cultural scope, and he tends to be more realistic and *psychological* [emphasis mine]. The character of the hero loses its exemplary qualities as it gains psychological depth. Since the artist cannot rely on the values of the group to sustain or support his hero, he must construct a value system of his own. This system may or may not happen to support the morality of a large section of his society. . . . The modern realistic hero embodies the ideals of the artist who creates him—ideals that may conflict with the code of contemporary society. . . . When an artist starts with a national or cultural ideal and works towards a man, he creates an Achilles or an Aeneas; when an artist starts with a man and works towards his own ideal, he creates a Henry Fleming (*The Red Badge of Courage*) or a Santiago (*The Old Man and the Sea*). (p. 9)

The classical hero of literature is thus replaced by the antihero. In the words of the acerbic social critic Andrei Codrescu (1990), "After Don Quixote, heroes have been either too big or too small until they became, one sad day, the author" (p. 80). The modern hero no longer functions to serve society, but to define the self. To be heroic is to be admired. The replacement of the hero by the role model in moral education reflects a similar process on a larger scale—the psychologization of our age.

The Subjectivist View: Role Model as Personal Guide

The subjectivist or "inside-out" school of social theory is concerned with the individual rather than the collective. If sociology maps the terrain for the objectivist school of moral education, psychology does so for the subjectivist school. All of the disparate moral educators in the subjectivist camp are united by the claim that the curricula of American schools lack role models for the disenfranchised.

Mead (1948), Sears, Rau & Alpert (1965), and Bandura (1977) posit that the rewarding of imitation is the key to socialization. Observational learning and the taking of roles modeled by important adults, whether real or symbolic, form the basis of what is now known as social learning theory. Symbolic models offer vicarious experience through which young people learn (Bandura, 1977, p. 81) and thus contribute strongly to young adolescents' development. These models allow young people to "transcend the bounds of [their] immediate environment" (Bandura, 1986, p. 47) and serve "as guides for future behavior" (Bandura, 1977, p. 13).

Multicultural curricula featuring images of powerful women and members of minorities may play an important role in self-definition. Borrowing from Adrienne Rich, Bruner (1990) captures the significance of such role models: "When someone with the authority of a teacher describes the world and you are not in it, there is a moment of psychic disequilibrium, as if you looked into a mirror and saw nothing" (p. 32). Muuss (1988), whose handbook on adolescence is a classic, acknowledges the need for role models among minorities: "[T]he demand of radical groups that black students be taught by black teachers—since black children tend to identify better with black teachers—seems to receive some implicit support from social learning theory" (p. 298).[2]

Two studies involving Puerto Rican adolescents (Costantino, Malgady, & Rogler, 1988; Malgady, Rogler, & Costantino, 1990) emphasize the role model instead of the hero as a therapeutic tool. Therapists

---

[2] Since the 1970s, numerous curricula and school programs haved used African-American role models (Ascher, 1991; Division of Instruction and Child Advocacy, New Orleans Public Schools, 1975; Poinsett, 1988; Simmons & Grady, 1990.)

introduce Puerto Rican folk tales to at-risk teenagers to help raise their self-esteem. Tinajero, Gonzalez, & Dick (1991) direct their efforts at Hispanic girls, the group most likely to drop out of school. Working with mothers and their daughters, they rely on role models— Hispanic women students at the University of Texas, El Paso—to convey personal values such as self-esteem, self-discipline, and academic responsibility.

Many social observers claim that all young female adolescents are at risk, not only members of ethnic minorities. In "A Gender at Risk," Shakeshaft (1988) sounded the alarm when she called for more attention to women in curricula and in the classroom. Her warnings have been repeated by Sadker & Sadker (1989), Stern (1991), the much-heralded *A.A.U.W. Report* (1992), and in Mary Pipher's (1994) best-seller, *Reviving Ophelia*.

Why is adolescence such a critical time in girls' lives? At that time, "girls are in danger of losing their voices" (Gilligan, Lyons, & Hanmer, 1990, p. 25). In *Meeting at the Crossroads*, Brown and Gilligan (1992) chronicle the phenomenon of tough-minded girls becoming wishy-washy adolescents. In this book, a longitudinal study consisting of interviews with girls at Cleveland's Laurel School, the authors record the voices of young girls, which fade from confidence to caution.

One remedy for this cultural "laryngitis" is available via the formal curriculum, "the central message-giving instrument of the school" (*A.A.U.W. Report*, 1992, p. 61). To redress the imbalances of a male-dominated curriculum, numerous educators have constructed curricula and have written reports designed to increase sensitivity to gender issues and to offer role models for early adolescents.[3] In these new curricula, written after the social and cultural revolutions of the 1960s, role models tend to replace heroes; metaphors are replaced by mirrors. In their study of heroes and heroines in 31 secondary school textbooks, Brodbelt and Wall (1985) note that 65% of them do not use the term *hero*. If heroes do appear, their larger-than-life qualities are played down. Fowler, Glover, & Gore (1980) title their multicultural curriculum *A Hero Ain't Nothing But A Great Big Sandwich*. The title may be playful, but its message is serious; like *The Giraffe Project* (1991), this curriculum maintains that anyone can be a hero. The goal of *A Hero* is not to convey values but to clarify them. The authors ask students to discuss their perceptions of heroes, defined as people who

---

[3] These suggestions cut across disciplines: history (Styer's *Exploring Women's Political Careers through Biographies*, 1981; Tomin & Burgoa's *A Multi-Cultural Women's History Elementary Curriculum Unit*, 1986), reading (Rigg's "Those Spunky Gals: An Annotated Bibliography," 1985), and mathematics (O'Brien & Tracy's 1991 research on female role models for girls who are studying algebra).

inspire admiration, and to compare them with the heroes of other classmates and other cultures. The hero is no longer a beacon for the social order, as in the Durkheimian ideal, but a looking-glass in the search for the self.

Adolescence: A Time for Heroes and Role Models

Adolescence is the prime time for such a search. Csikszentmihalyi and Larson (1984) claim that this is the time to forge "a life theme"; Gilligan calls it "a crucial time for moral education" (1987, p. 71). According to Erikson, the adolescent arrives at self-definition by projecting his or her self-image on that of someone else. Seeing it reflected on another, the young person clarifies his or her own identity (1983, p. 420). "The adolescent looks most fervently for men and ideas to have *faith* in, which also means men and ideas in whose service it would seem worthwhile to prove oneself trustworthy" (p. 417). Adolescence is a time for ideology building. "Ideologies offer to members of this age-group overly simplified and yet determined answers to exactly those vague inner states and those urgent questions which arise in consequence of identity conflict" (Erikson, 1962, p. 42). For both objectivist and subjectivist thinkers, heroes and role models help adolescents to resolve their critical ego task (Erikson, 1985): forging an identity, both as a member of a group and as an individual.

"Ideal Person" Studies: Who Are Young Adolescents' Heroes and Role Models?

Nearly 50 years ago, psychologists Robert Havighurst and Hilda Taba (1949) built a theory of adolescence based on the concept of the "ideal self." The ideal self serves as an object of imitation for the developing child. Based on an image of the parents, it unfolds as the child grows, becoming a composite of parent surrogates, celebrities, and cultural heroes. The ideal self is the source of the child's moral authority.

As part of their Prairie City study, Havighurst and Taba (1949) asked 16-year-olds to complete the phrase, "The person I would like to be like . . ." (p. 71). From a sample of 100, 14 chose a parent or other relative; 5, a glamorous adult; 3, a peer; 15, an attractive and visible adult admired by the community; 57, a composite or imaginary character. Six responded with answers that could not be classified (pp. 71–72). None of them chose a hero he or she read about or studied, such as "Abraham Lincoln, Florence Nightingale, General MacArthur, or Madame Chiang Kai-Shek" (p. 71).[4]

Simmons and Wade (1983) replicated the Havighurst-Taba study with adolescents, 820 15-year-olds from six schools in the English Midlands. The teenagers completed the sentence, "The sort of person I would most like to be like . . ." (p. 19). The authors found that 19% rejected all models; these young people prefer to remain themselves. A small proportion (2%) nominated family members; 25%, a smaller percentage than their American counterparts, chose celebrities (p. 31).

These findings may suggest that adolescents, or at least adolescents in the English Midlands, are more impervious to popular culture than we think. Duck's (1990) study with Australian youths proves otherwise, however. Duck compared a group of 313 young people, from grades 5 to 9, with a pretelevision study conducted in 1962. Interviewing the children about the person they would most want to be like, she discovered that 50% to 75% chose media figures as opposed to people whom they knew personally (p. 24). Comparing her findings with those of the 1962 study, Duck noted "a marked shift away from the dominance of parent and parent surrogates as ideals towards the predominance of media figures" (p. 26).[5]

Duck also found that children with lower self-esteem are more likely to gravitate towards fantasy ideals (p. 24), and that stereotyped sex differences linger (p. 27): Girls still yearn for good looks, while boys want to be strong and tough, and to protect the weak.[6]

Since 1980 *The World Almanac* has conducted an annual survey of American students from grades 8 to 12. In this survey, "Heroes of

---

[4] In his dissertation, Wechter (1981) reviews the findings of Havighurst over several studies of the ideal self, or in Freudian terminology, the ego ideal. His results replicate those of Havighust. Wechter hypothesized that the level of ego ideal development in his subjects corresponded to their level of psycho-sexual development (p. 72). Once again, his findings corroborate those of Havighurst. Children younger than eight were more likely to choose parents or parent surrogates as ego ideals; 8- to 16-year-olds were apt to choose glamorous or famous adults or attractive, visible adults in the community. Only adolescents could construct abstracted ideals (p. 98). Reinforcing Erikson's observations on adolescence, Wechter notes that his findings for adolescents are murky because of the fluidity of their images of the ideal self (p. 97); teenagers' heroes seem to change weekly.

[5] Duck's findings about adolescents hold true for their parents as well. Both Dotter (1987) and Hakanen (1989) note a shift from traditional to nontraditional heroes. Rock performers, once considered countercultural heroes, are now mainstream.

[6] Balswick and Ingoldsby (1982) questioned 1,092 Georgia high school students about their heroes and heroines. They discovered that adolescents, no matter what their sex or race, still overwhelmingly selected heroes, rather than heroines, to admire.

Young America," students are asked to select those individuals in public life whom they admire most. The teenagers are also asked to name selections in other public categories, such as movie stars, television performers, athletes, and writers. From 1980 to 1990 the top hero was either an athlete or a performer, and always male (*World Almanac*, 1990, p. 33). A woman rarely appeared as the winner in the other categories. In 1991 the top hero (or heroine: the survey asked students for the first time to choose a "hero or heroine") was Paula Abdul, followed by Michael Jordan, the 1990 top hero (*World Almanac*, 1991, p. 32). In 1992 the top hero was Norman Schwartzkopf, followed by Julia Roberts (*World Almanac*, 1992, p. 32). It is unclear whether the inclusion of women was due to the change in the wording of the survey or indicated that the monopoly by males is tottering. No survey was included in the 1993 *World Almanac*.

In 1990 Adams-Price and Greene expanded on gender and ego ideals. Surveying students from grade 5 through the second year of college, the authors queried the informants about their favorite celebrities and asked the "magic wand question": "Imagine that there was a magic wand that could suddenly transform you into a person close to your favorite celebrity and you could choose your relationship. Who would you most like to be?" (p. 190). The celebrities chosen were overwhelmingly male. The boys in the survey generally wanted to be the celebrity; the girls wanted to be *romantically linked* to the celebrity (p. 192; emphasis added). These results add credence to Gilligan's (1982) finding that relationships are crucial to young women. Adams-Price and Greene conclude that "theoretically, at least, secondary attachments provide a safe context in which both male and female adolescents can experiment with alternate identities in the search for a consolidated sense of self" (p. 189).

This conclusion corroborates Erikson's view: Heroes and role models, whether peers, celebrities, parents or parent surrogates, or significant adults, serve an important function in the development of middle school-age youths.

THE ROLE OF THE TEACHER IN MORAL EDUCATION

Durkheim makes the loftiest statement about the function of the teacher as moral educator. Because he envisions the state as the successor to the church, the teacher is a secular priest: "Just as the priest is the interpreter of his god, the teacher is the interpreter of the great moral ideas of his time and of his country" (1956, p. 89).

Csikszentmihalyi and McCormack (1992) restate this position: So-ciety must transmit meaningful goals to the younger generation, and it is the teacher's task to do so (p. 43). Citing social learning theory, they claim that teachers who project mastery possess enormous power to influence their students. In fact, 58% of people whom they queried credit at least one teacher with influencing them to be the kind of peo-ple they became (p. 44).

Wynne and Ryan (1993) devote a chapter in their book to teach-ers as moral educators. In their view, the teacher who takes her man-date seriously models moral behavior indirectly through a concern for standards, both her own and those of her students. She models moral behavior directly by saying and doing what is right (pp. 112–133).

Recognition of the teacher as role model, however, is not limited to objectivist, "outside-in" social theorists. Scholars across the spec-trum agree that the teacher plays a significant role in young adoles-cents' moral education. For those moral educators whose primary concern is self-esteem, a curriculum that features symbolic role mod-els is only one solution. Another, perhaps more significant, interven-tion is the teacher, a living role model who can provide the observability that Jung (1986) describes as essential for those who wish to change their lives.

All of the policy recommendations regarding the education of African-American youths mention the teacher's potential as role model (Ascher, 1991; Poinsett, 1988; Simmons & Grady, 1990). As-cher (1991) reminds her readers that all Afrocentric programs are based on an assumed lack of appropriate male models for African-American boys. Because 80% of their teachers are women, these youths need positive images of African-American males (p. 11). Thus many Afrocentric schools rely on an all-male faculty (Holland, 1991).[7]

Feminist educators similarly cite the absence of appropriate role models as eroding young female adolescents' self-esteem. Brown and Gilligan (1992) blame teenage girls' loss of "voice" on adult models:

> It was first with a sense of shock and then a deep, knowing sadness that we listened to the voices of the girls tell us that it was the *adult women* in their lives that provided the models for silencing themselves and be-having like "good little girls." (p. 221)

---

[7] The all-male environment has raised concerns that these programs are anti-feminist and promote an atmosphere of woman-bashing. They further the charge that African-American women are succeeding at the expense of African-American men (Ascher, 1991, pp. 14–15).

Another feminist, Nel Noddings, asserts that the teacher as role model is central to an ethic of caring. Using the image of the mother-child relationship, she describes teaching as *engrossment*—nonselective attention to the other (Noddings, 1988, pp. 219–220). The recent emphasis on intellectual goals and technical skills diminishes the dialogue that is essential to teaching and learning, essential to an ethic of care (Noddings, 1988, 1992). Dialogue implies respect for the other; the teacher must model such respect if the student is to become a caring person.

Peace education also calls for the teacher to model the values of the curriculum. In an attempt to deemphasize the military hero, some moral educators have created curricula that emphasize peaceful heroes (Morgan, 1985; Shatles, 1992). Shatles (1992) names the teacher as one of the "men and women who are peacemakers [who] need to be presented to children as role models to emulate" (p. 4).

The Teacher as Role Model: The Middle School

Like the other moral educators cited above, Beck (1987) stresses the teacher as role model, specifically in the junior high school. He emphasizes the importance of a faculty that respects young people and that models "teachers and students learning together" (p. 211).

In the same vein, 25 of the 30 middle school teachers interviewed by Lanckton (1992) consider themselves important role models for their students. They teach moral education both implicitly and explicitly by demonstrating promptness, honesty, responsibility, kindness, critical thinking, politeness, humor, self-acceptance, respect for others, openness, achievement, political activism, fairness, and tolerance (pp. 150–159). Nineteen of these 30 teachers believe that one aspect of being a role model for young adolescents is telling them the right thing to do (p. 164). The teachers in suburban schools tend to characterize themselves as facilitators of students' understanding of what is right, rather than as preachers (p. 164).

There is a profound need for the teacher to be a role model for middle school students. The literature on African-Americans shows that black males' achievement declines by grade 4 (Ascher, 1991, p. 10). According to the research on female students, girls' performance in mathematics also begins to decline at this time (O'Brien & Tracy, 1991; Sadker & Sadker, 1989). As students lessen their reliance on their parents for moral guidance, the teacher can "facilitate the development of a conscience and moral judgment" (McEwin & Thomason, 1989, p. 21). All children need teachers who are willing to be moral exemplars; it may be even more important for youths who are struggling with self-definition. Theorists claim that the teacher is the most important influence in middle school students' lives (Stevenson, 1992). McEwin and Thomason (1989) state unequivocally that "middle grades teachers should have strong self-concepts and present reliable role models" (pp. 11–12).

Lanckton also observes the failure of teacher-training institutions to prepare preservice teachers for their role as moral educators. This theme is echoed in a study conducted in Norway by Bergem (1990) and repeated by Ryan (1990). Because this subject is omitted in teacher education, individual teachers must decide whether they are responsible for serving as role models for their students. Bergem found that prospective teachers' implicit theories about teachers' roles affect their attitudes toward moral education. The more traditional the prospective teacher, and the more religiously observant, the more likely that he or she will embrace the responsibility of being a role model (p. 98).

The Culture of the School

In Lanckton's study, 10 of the 30 respondents cited the importance of the school environment in creating a climate for moral education (1992, p. 228). Moral education extends beyond the walls of the "egg-crate" classroom; any research on the use of heroes and role models in the curricula must take the total school environment into consideration. What roles are played by the principal, other faculty members, and students in shaping this ethos? Who are the school's heroes, living or dead? How are they used to communicate a vision, to transmit values, and to shape behavior?

Several classic studies found unequivocally that schools can make a difference. Rutter and his associates (1979) were the first to call attention to the importance of school ethos. In a study of 12 high schools in inner-city London, they concluded that students' performance differs from school to school, independent of factors such as socioeconomic class and school size. The ethos of the school made the difference: A positive school environment is characterized by cohesion between students and teachers, by a strong academic emphasis, by teachers' positive expectations of students, by positive rewards, and by consistent, shared values and standards. Schools that demonstrate these qualities produce students who perform well academically, and who have good discipline and attendance records.

In her review of school ethos and its impact on minority students, Ascher (1982) reiterates Rutter's findings. She comments on the need for a "conspiracy of concern" that permeates the total institution (p.

2). The RAND study, *High Schools with Character* (Hill, Foster, & Gendler, 1990), confirms the importance of school ethos, which consists of clarity of rules and mission, school pride, an atmosphere conducive to learning, care for students, equitable treatment, the push for learning, and future orientation.

The "good high schools" depicted in Lightfoot's (1983) well-known study benefit from "strong, consistent and inspired leadership" (p. 323). The principal defines the vision of the school; this vision is often concretized in heroes and role models. Lightfoot's observations about permeable and impermeable boundaries suggested research questions for my study (pp. 316–323); she notes that religious institutions are much more successful than public schools at resisting outside influences, and that they create an alternative environment in which to effect moral education. One form of resistance is to set up a competing pantheon of heroes and an alternative array of role models.

Grant (1985) portrays a school that temporarily lost its vision. In his view, a school with a positive ethos communicates its message through its written goals, through a faculty consistently committed to those goals, and through rituals and ceremonies. Grant, Lightfoot, the authors of the RAND study, Ascher, and Rutter and his colleagues conclude, as did Aristotle, that the conduct of moral education requires a moral community (cited by Green, 1988, p. 133).

THE PLACE OF LITERATURE AND NARRATIVE THEORY IN MORAL EDUCATION

Lamme, Krogh, and Yachmetz (1992) have written a literature-based moral education curriculum for the elementary school. They have done what *The Art of Loving Well* (Boston University, 1988) has done for the middle school, and what Parr (1982) did for the college. Each of these curricula creates a classroom context in which to confront moral myopia and impotence by reading and reflecting on great works of literature. Lamme and her colleagues (1992) reason:

> Sometimes it is hard to find models of moral behavior, especially child models to whom children can readily relate. You may have to wait all day for a real example of a child who solves a problem peacefully or someone who reaches out kindly to others. Literature provides many such models. (p. 15)

Parr (1982) hopes to offset "the fantasy world of easy solutions" (p. 8) in which her students live. Her position combines that of the objectivists who would transmit society's norms, and the subjectivists who would transform the individual:

> By exploring the power of values and the complexities of moral choice within the literature they read, students will be better able to recognize and understand the possibilities for responsible action and self-realization within their own lives. I also hope that by seeing themselves as part of a rich, ongoing culture they will decide that moral choice is not only desirable, but also possible within their own worlds. (p. 9)

Both the objectivists and subjectivists use narrative as a tool of moral education, and both base their rationale on the recent thinking of Jerome Bruner. Bruner (1986) maintains that there are two modes of thought: Paradigmatic thought is propositional, logical, and scientific; narrative thought deals with imagination, consciousness, and intentionality. Both camps—the objectivists and the subjectivists—the "outside-in" and the "inside-out"—attest to the transformative power of narrative. Coles (1989) captures the essence of that power: "A compelling narrative, offering a storyteller's moral imagination vigorously at work, can enable any of us to learn by example, to take to heart what is, really, a gift of grace" (p. 191).

Vitz (1990) argues an objectivist case by claiming the efficacy of literature in teaching children to love the good. Reviewing the moral development literature, he demonstrates that stories can promote prosocial behavior. According to Vitz, narratives are effective because they are accessible to children; they are a staple in the history of the Great Tradition; and, contrary to the findings of Hartshorne and May, they can be effective in teaching virtues (pp. 716–717).

Like Vitz, Kilpatrick (1992) borrows from Bruner, grounding his views in the narrative rather than the paradigmatic mode of thinking. He states: "Morality needs to be set within a storied vision if it is to remain morality. Conceived of as rule keeping or refraining from wrongdoing, it never works for long" (p. 197). Kilpatrick is so strongly convinced of the power of the story to affect the readers' moral capacities that he includes in his book a bibliography of almost fifty pages, a "Guide to Great Books for Children and Teens." Bennett's *The Book of Virtues* (1993) and its successors offer compendia of stories designed to create moral literacy. It is important to note that Bennett's anthology includes not only the classics of the perennialists' canon, but also selections by and about women, ethnics, and people of color.

The subjectivist moral educators also cite Bruner's case for the potency of the narrative mode. They take issue with the objectivist position, which they describe as a vicarious arena for exploring moral choices and resolving moral conflicts. The subjectivists believe that the purpose of literature is to help the individual make meaning out of his or her life. Barthes, whom Bruner (1986, p. 5) names as one of his sources, expresses this view:

> Narrative does not show, does not imitate; the passion which may excite us in reading a novel is not that of a "vision" (in actual fact, we do not "see" anything). Rather it is that of meaning, that of a higher order of relation which also has its emotions, its hopes, its dangers, its triumphs. (Barthes, 1977, p. 124)

By turning his attention to the making of meaning, Bruner leaves behind the cognitive revolution of the 1950s, when psychologists tried to understand how human beings process information, and when the operative metaphor was the computer. In shifting his focus, Bruner (1990) stands the older psychology on its head: "It is culture and the search for meaning that is the shaping hand, biology that is the constraint" (p. 23). By asserting the primacy of "folk psychology," he rejects the positivist model of social science and psychology; that model was formulated by William Wundt, who happened to be Durkheim's teacher.

For the reductionism of the cognitive revolution, Bruner substitutes the significance of multiple meanings. His description of discourse is the literary equivalent of the description of modernity rendered by sociologists of knowledge (Berger, Berger, & Kellner, 1973). For Bruner, discourse entails presupposition (implicit, rather than explicit meanings), subjectification (depiction of reality through particular filters of consciousness), and multiple perspectives. For the sociologists of knowledge, modernity is characterized by the challenge of monistic authority by secularism, resulting in delegitimation, subjectivization, and pluralism.

The concept of multiple meanings underlies the philosophy of the thinkers I call the subjectivist or "inside-out" wing of the narrative theory school. This group uses literature to develop a moral conscience through decision making. According to Tappan and Brown (1989), the power of narrative lies not in its ability to transmit values but in its potential to cultivate a child's innate moral sense. These authors claim that telling stories of one's own moral conflict is an even more effective moral tool. Tappan and Brown contend that by "authoring" their own moral stories, children assume authority for their moral behavior. Their stories become texts, demanding a hermeneutic analysis and the exploration of multiple meanings by their classmates and teacher.

Tappan and Brown (1989) base their thinking on Gilligan (1977, 1982). Unlike Kohlberg (1983), who used artificial dilemmas to explore moral development, Gilligan listened to her informants' own stories. Narrative became the cornerstone of her theories of moral voice and moral development. Tappan (1991) ascribes the acquisition of a moral voice to the internalization of the many voices a child hears when he is growing up.

Tappan and Brown, wary lest the "multiple voices/multiple meanings" approach evoke the criticism leveled at values clarification, note that the perceived similarity lies only in the emphasis on process rather than on content. In contradistinction to the highly individualistic values clarification, Tappan and Brown point out that their narratives approach is communal, requiring "a connection between author and audience" (p. 198).

Unlike the functionalist supporters of the Great Tradition, advocates of multiple meanings reject the idea of narrative as social transmission. The purpose of stories is not to transform society, "because the principles and directives of society are by and large unreasonable" (Tappan & Brown, 1989, p. 200). The danger of the Great Tradition, according to Tappan and Brown, is the danger of indoctrination. In contrast, their use of narratives "promises a measure of freedom from the arbitrary imposition of culturally bound values and conventional stereotypes, as it seeks to encourage students to authorize their own voices and moral perspectives" (pp. 200–201).

Day (1991b) also rejects the approach of the Great Tradition to narrative. Asking teachers not to discount their students' experience, he states that "rehearsals of lessons already learned by educators, whether taught in narrative or other forms, are no substitute for the moral experiences that students bring with them from their daily lives" (p. 167).

For Day, as for Tappan and Brown, the notion of audience is crucial to one's moral voice:

> For Porter, Sandy, and Kim, (three moral storytellers) morality is relational and, in being so, is necessarily storied; for all of them, morality has to do with being accountable, which leads inevitably to a kind of theatrical rehearsal of the conduct that will later be judged, if only in the mind of the actor, by someone else. (1991a, p. 35)

Day's notion of moral development as rehearsals of moral conflicts before an audience resembles Tappan's concept of moral authorship

(Tappan, 1991). Important for my study is Tappan's belief in the efficacy of a "process [which] provides a unique perspective on the development of moral authority, particularly in adolescence" (p. 19).

For both the objectivist and subjectivist theorists, narrative offers enormous potential for the moral development and moral education of middle school children. Both groups rely on narrative to produce meaning in a seemingly inchoate world: for the objectivists, the meaning of the social order that sustains the individual; for the subjectivists, the meaning by which a regenerated individual can change that social order.

3

The Research and the Researcher

This is a study about process. It focuses on the "how" of moral education, a process approach. In each of my sites, I asked the following questions: How does the teacher use heroes and role models to teach children to love the good? How does the principal communicate to the faculty his or her vision of schooling as a moral enterprise? How does the environment encourage the enterprise? How do students and parents make meaning of the teacher's efforts?

This study also focuses on context. Firmly grounded in the belief that the setting in which schooling takes place affects the behavior of the individuals in that setting, this study is a classically qualitative enterprise. In deciding to observe classes and spend time in the school site, I recognized the appropriateness of an ethnographic methodology to do justice to the cultural context surrounding each of the four teachers.

Finally, this study explores how people make meaning of symbols. If human behavior is affected by the setting of education, surely the meanings that the actors derive from that setting are affected as well. Because this is a study about understanding, an attempt to comprehend phenomena not on the basis of the researcher's perspective, but that of the participants (Maxwell, 1992), a qualitative methodology seemed appropriate. For this reason, I chose a methodology that relied on interviews.

My goal is not to produce any sweeping principles about human behavior, nor to survey the importance of moral prototypes in middle school classrooms. I explore how classroom communities understand the place of moral prototypes in their worlds. I hope to take snapshots of moral education in four settings, to gently tease out some commonalties, and to generate some hypotheses. I do not purport to test or prove theory.

A methodology must suit the subject of its inquiry. As Bolster (1983) suggests, classroom inquiry must be compatible with teachers' perspectives. Teachers tend to be particularistic; they firmly believe that each class is different. Therefore, this study is grounded in description, process, context, and meaning (Bogdan & Biklen, 1992). It generates word pictures from classroom observation and interviews with teachers, principals, students, and parents. The end product is a series of descriptive portraits; the numbers I use are for illustration only. The portraits are drawn from the rich detail garnered by observation and interviews, by "hanging out" in schools and classrooms, by talking and listening to the people who are affected by the goings-on in a given classroom.

Teachers also recognize that their enterprise is holistic, that what happens in their classrooms is multidimensional. They claim that classroom instruction depends on multiple causation and is infinitely greater than the sum of its parts. Teachers, of all people, know that they can never have everything under control; teaching always must take account of the unexpected (Bolster, pp. 298–299). A proper methodological approach for the study of teachers and teaching allows for the idiosyncrasies of the profession, making room for the particularistic, the holistic, and the unanticipated contingencies of the classroom. Qualitative research is such a methodology.

PERSONAL BACKGROUND
AND THEORETICAL APPROACH

The literature of qualitative research reiterates the contention that the researcher *is* the research instrument (Bogdan & Biklen, 1992). My experience, assumptions, and biases inevitably color this study. Maxwell (1992) notes, "As observers and interpreters of the world, we are inextricably part of it; we cannot step outside our own experience to obtain some observer-independent account of what we experience" (p. 283). Acknowledgment of the researcher's assumptions is critical in an approach that assumes an interaction with informants and a sharing of emerging theory. Mills (1959) demands that qualitative researchers be reflective about their background:

> You must learn to use your life experience in your intellectual work: continually to examine and interpret it. In this sense craftsmanship is the center of yourself and you are personally involved in every intellectual product upon which you may work. To say you can "have experience" means, for one thing, that your past plays into and affects your present, and that it defines your capacity for future experience. (pp. 196–197)

Such reflectivity avoids what Peshkin (1991) so aptly calls being "caught red-handed with my values at the very end of my pen" (p. 287).

As a graduate of a women's college, I was introduced to the tenets of feminism before Betty Friedan gave the movement a name. My appreciation for the education I received predisposed me to attend to the issues being addressed by contemporary feminist theorists. This perspective made me very comfortable when I observed the independent girls' school, but I had to keep it in check during my research in the male-dominated Orthodox yeshivah.

I am a committed, practicing Jew, and I have been a Jewish educator for nearly 25 years. I had to self-consciously filter my observations through Jewish lenses. For example, I had to examine and then put aside the knowledge that the Shaw School had a reputation at one time for being anti-Semitic. If I occasionally felt "too Jewish" at Shaw (at the Vespers service, for example), sometimes I felt "not Jewish enough" at Springfield Torah Institute. When I wished my collaborating teacher a good Sabbath in modern Hebrew rather than the Yiddishized version common to that milieu, it was clear that I was an outsider.

I am an advocate of both public and private education, having taught in both settings and having sent my children to both types of institutions. As a former PTO president in a public school, with both volunteer experience and liberal proclivities, I am concerned about the future of public education. I was both embarrassed and pained by the economic gulf between the inner-city children of the Pierce School and the suburban children of the Smith School.

My views have been shaped by my recent experiences at both Boston University and Brown University, where I studied with several of the thinkers whose views I cited in Chapter 2. I am aware of my predispositions and have taken care to build into my study the opportunity to share my observations with others: the teachers in the study, whom I view as collaborators; members of the school community, and friends, relatives, and colleagues, whom I have directed to let me know when my values are showing at the end of my pen.

One of my assumptions is the belief that we must learn to live with ambiguity. I am accustomed to an approach based on the notion of multiple perspectives. A typical page from *Mikraot Gedolot*, the classic Jewish source for Biblical exegesis, consists of a small rectangle of Bible text surrounded by rabbinic commentaries—each different, each explaining that text. Geertz' (1973) description of doing ethnography resembles Biblical exegesis: "Doing ethnography is like trying to read (in the sense of 'construct a reading of') a manuscript—foreign, faded, full of ellipses, incoherencies, suspicious emendations, and tendentious commentaries ..." (p. 10). What Mills (1959) describes as the sociological imagination—the shift from one perspective to another in order to understand the subject at hand—might as well be used to describe the exegetical imagination.

The same is true of the historical imagination. As an undergraduate and graduate student I was trained in history, particularly historiography. Historians such as Tuchman, Schama, and McCullough do what Geertz advises ethnographers to do: "The aim is to draw large conclusions from small, but very densely textured facts; to support broad assertions about the role of culture in the construction of collective life by engaging them exactly with complex specifics" (1973, p. 28).

My studies with Kevin Ryan of Boston University introduced me to moral education. His approach to character education and literature is very comfortable for a religious educator; it allows me to quickly translate a concern about religious values into a concern for secular values. I also studied with Peter Berger, whose views on the social construction of knowledge I find quite compatible with my own. They have shaped my understanding of the history of moral education in this country, as well as the changing nature of the hero and the increase in attention to the role model in place of the hero. In addition, I studied at Brown University with William Damon, whose writing on child development filled a void in my background and whose belief in the power of moral prototypes I share.

RESEARCH DESIGN

According to Jackson (1990), classroom life is too complex to be studied from any one perspective. My intention was to study moral prototypes in middle schools from multiple approaches.

Multiple Case Studies

This research was based on ethnographic study, which gave me the opportunity to enter the conceptual world of others. If a case study is a detailed examination of one setting, or of a single subject, or of a single depository of documents, or of one particular event (Merriam, 1988), then this research, which is based on four settings, subjects, document sets, and events, can best be characterized as a multiple case study. My study of four classrooms is research on four "bounded systems" (Merriam, p. 9); my goal is to build what Glaser and Strauss (1967) call "grounded theory." The theory, based on multiple data sources, attempts to explain the place of moral prototypes in four middle school classrooms.

Field Notes

Field notes were the first of my data sources. My notes recorded what I saw, heard, touched, and sometimes smelled (after all, I was observing 13-year-olds) in the classrooms and schools I visited. They contained both descriptive and reflective comments. Upon returning from the field, I transcribed my jottings, raising questions for future observations or creating emergent theory that I tested later in the field and through artifacts, interviews, surveys, and questionnaires.

Artifact Collection

I increased my understanding of the teaching and learning in the four sites by analyzing both internal and external documents that related to the subject. Internal documents are those communications that follow a hierarchical, or top-down, course: materials generated by the principal, the superintendent, or the school board. These include written curricula, goal statements, and self-study documents. I also studied external documents, those items generated for public consumption: yearbooks, newsletters for parents, school histories, and handbooks for parents and students. I studied bulletin boards for fliers and students' artwork, student-produced newspapers, and journals.

Semistructured Interviews

I conducted at least two semistructured interviews with the teacher in each of my sites. The first elicited biographical data, the teacher's views of moral education, and ideas about the role of moral prototypes in the shaping of values. The second allowed me to check my observations with those of my teacher-collaborator. The semistructured interview is best suited to eliciting information about a specific subject area (Merriam, 1988). It sets the parameters for the discussion but allows the participants to pursue their mutual interest without the constraints of a set order or exact wording of questions.

For the interviews with the teachers, who were the focus of my study, I followed Seidman's (1991) suggestion and arranged at least two interviews, one to one and one-half hours long, one to three weeks apart. (The interview questions are included in the appendix.) By spending six to eight weeks in each classroom, and making at least six to eight visits, I tried to establish a relationship built on mutual respect and trust. I spoke with each teacher several times and met them in their sites twice before I began my school visits in earnest. Because the teachers volunteered to be a part of the study, I was able to build a trusting relationship quickly.

I interviewed the principal and other administrators (if necessary) for about an hour each, again using a semistructured format. By engaging in what Spradley (1979) calls a "friendly conversation," I was able to contextualize the classroom and to learn how much institutional support the school offered the teacher. The semistructured interview provided me the most possibilities for acquiring this information. Seidman (1991) reminds us that the purpose of the interview is to elicit stories. The word *story* derives from the Greek *histor*, one who is wise, and stories are intended to make us wise (Seidman, 1991, p. 1). If a story is to do its work, to make us wise by providing meaning for the events we observe, then the interview must be free enough to allow the respondent to tell the story in his or her own way. If an administrator's story or a teacher's story raised questions in my mind, I followed up with further questions. (The questions that served as a basis for the interviews with both principals and teachers can be found in the appendix.)

Focus Group Interviews, Questionnaires, and Surveys

To learn how the students understood moral prototypes, I used a focus group interview (Morgan, 1988), which Bogdan and Biklen (1992) claim is "useful in bringing the researcher into the world of the subjects" (p. 100). My intent was to interview eight students and thus to enter their world. The students were selected by the teacher for diversity as to academic standing, gender, race, ethnicity, and parents' involvement in the life of the school. I interviewed them for about an hour, hoping to learn more about their heroes and role models and about whether their class had affected their choices in any way.

From an earlier pilot study, I had learned the value of asking a group of teenagers, who are susceptible to peer pressure, to answer a questionnaire before participating in a group interview; this approach is also recommended by Anderson (1990). The questionnaire not only prepared the students to think about the questions we would pursue in the focus group, but also gave the more diffident youths an opportunity to express themselves. This two-pronged approach also enabled me to uncover inconsistencies in the teenagers' answers, which I could follow up later.

In addition to the questionnaire, I used a brief survey in which students were asked to identify 10 icons of popular adolescent culture. The list included rock groups, a brand of clothing marketed to teenagers, television programs, athletes, models, and actresses. (The survey is included in the appendix.) By noting the students' ability to identify the terms on the survey, I could determine how immersed they were in popular culture. All of the teachers in my study mentioned the influence of popular culture on their students, so this gauge helped me to understand the background of the adolescents in my study.

Telephone Interviews

To learn about the parents' support for the teacher's efforts, I created a 10- to 20-minute telephone interview to use with three of the parents of the eight students who formed the focus group in each school. I asked the teachers for names of parents who were involved significantly, moderately, and nominally in the life of the school. I suggested that each teacher consider academic, ethnic, racial, and gender differences in supplying parents' names. This interview, like those with the students and the principal, allowed me to ground the teacher's message in the community in which he or she works. (It, too, can be found in the appendix.)

Consent Forms

I prepared consent forms for all of my participants, in which I specified what they were being asked to do. I explained that I ensured the participants' confidentiality by using pseudonyms for the names of all persons involved in the study and for the school. I also promised to refer to the school only in the most general way, giving as few geographic clues as possible.

The teachers, after consultation with the principal, asked the students to participate in the focus group. I made it clear to the teachers that no student had to participate unless he or she wanted to do so. I asked the students' parents to sign, as well as the students, and included an abstract of my study with each consent form. (Sample consent forms are included in the appendix.)

Sampling

My interests and inclinations directed me to choose certain sites. As a religious educator, I sought out a sectarian religious institution. As a former history teacher, I wanted to observe a history class in a multiethnic public school. As a graduate of a women's college with an interest in feminist pedagogy, I was eager to include a girls' school that claimed a commitment to producing self-assured young women.

Qualitative researcher Joseph Maxwell (1992) argues that purposeful sampling gives the researcher a clearer understanding of the phenomenon she is studying. Purposeful sampling helps "to make sure one has adequately understood the variation in the phenomena of interest in the setting, and to test developing ideas about that setting by selecting phenomena that are crucial to the validity of those ideas" (p. 293).

Seidman (1991) recommends purposeful sampling to allow for maximum variation, which he says "allows the widest possibility for readers of the study to connect with what they are reading" (pp. 42–43). His argument, which deals with the question of audience, is a more pragmatic one than Maxwell's.

Wishing to cast as wide a net as possible, I considered both Maxwell's and Seidman's views in my research design. My net included public and private schools, sectarian and nonsectarian schools, multiethnic urban and well-to-do suburban schools, coeducational and single-sex institutions. I was also eager to spend time with teachers in different content areas: literature, American history, mathematics, and religious studies. Each domain has its own moral concerns. Literature teachers shape their students' values by exposure to the beautiful and the true; American history teachers are concerned with transmitting democratic values; mathematics teachers who instruct young women are concerned with issues of self-esteem and competence; religious studies teachers must transmit a vision of the good life as interpreted by their holy books. By making the sample diverse, I built in a check for my bias, ensured as wide a readership as possible, and produced more generalizability from a methodology whose claims in this realm are modest. Purposeful sampling "not only makes sense of the particular persons or situations studied, but also shows how the same process, in different situations, can lead to different results" (Becker, 1990, p. 240).

THE SITES AND GAINING ACCESS TO THEM

Springfield Torah Institute:
Rebbe Tuvia Kaplan, Teacher

The Torah Institute is a small Orthodox Jewish day school located in Springfield, a city of approximately 150,000 located in the northeastern United States. The school is about 50 years old, a more traditional institution today than its founding fathers could have imagined. Most of the students are from Springfield; all live within walking distance of the school. These 150 students, many of whom are children of Torah Institute faculty members, spend much of their lives in this building. Not only do they attend classes in this facility; on the Jewish Sabbath and holidays, they *daven* (Yiddish: pray) here as well. In addition to the Springfield residents, approximately 30 students come from outlying communities in which there is no Jewish day school.

Few of these children's parents would consider sending their children to public schools or nonsectarian private schools. A significant number of Torah Institute families do not own television sets; the wives of Torah Institute teachers and mothers of Torah Institute students cover their hair with ritual wigs, kerchiefs, or hats. Faculty children make up a substantial percentage of the student population, comprising one-third of the seventh grade. As Orthodox Jews, these families are the embodiment of *Am ha-Sefer*, the people of the Book; their lives are governed by Jewish law. Curriculum and life are one.

The key to living a "Torah-true life" is contained in Jewish texts— the Bible and its commentaries—and in rabbinic literature—the Talmud and law codes. Because the text is God's revealed word, study is elevated to paramount importance. Jewish folklore describes heaven as a yeshivah in which God and the heavenly host pore over religious texts. Prayer and study are interchangeable: The primary act of Jewish identification is engagement with holy books, and a Jewish child comes of age with a public reading from the Torah. Therefore Jewish learning is serious business.

Knowing that I wanted to include a religious school in my study, I approached the dean of the Springfield Torah Institute. Seidman (1991) encourages the inclusion of an extreme or deviant case in a purposeful sampling, and the Torah Institute is such a case. A right-of-center Orthodox school, it is as close to a total institution (Goffman, 1961) as I could find. A total institution is characterized by its encompassing character; it erects barriers to the world outside its walls. My study request produced a volunteer, Rebbe Tuvia Kaplan.

Rebbe Kaplan is not a rabbi. *Rebbe*, a term borrowed from the Hasidic lexicon, has been commandeered by other Orthodox groups to refer to teachers who serve as mentors and spiritual advisors for their students. Rebbe Kaplan, now 30, has been teaching in Jewish schools since his college days. A psychology major in college, he was enthusiastic about his involvement in my study.

Rebbe Kaplan saw me eight times over a six-week period, during which I sat in four times on his seventh-grade Bible and Jewish law classes. These classes met Monday through Thursday for two and a half hours, and for two hours on Fridays, when school was dismissed early.

Franklin Pierce Middle School:
George Stratas, Teacher

The Franklin Pierce Middle School, a public school, is also located in Springfield, a block away from the Torah Institute. Its history resembles that of many schools in the urban northeastern United States. Built in 1929 to accommodate a school population increased by the arrival of immigrants from Ireland, Italy, and eastern Europe, it is a stately three-storied square brick structure. Pierce Junior High School originally housed seventh-, eighth-, and ninth-grade pupils. It enjoyed a fine reputation for preparing students for the academically solid comprehensive high school in the neighborhood and for its rival, the downtown magnet school for the academically talented. In the 1950s, Pierce students garnered most of the first prizes in the citywide science fair; the orchestra won regional prizes.

Springfield's daily newspaper, *The Sentinel*, chronicles the ups and downs of Franklin Pierce in the 1960s and 1970s. The turmoil began when the City of Springfield reorganized its schools, changing Pierce from a junior high school of seventh-, eighth-, and ninth-grade pupils to a sixth-, seventh-, and eighth-grade middle school. The sixth-grade pupils came from a neighborhood school that included many of Springfield's African-American residents. *The Sentinel* from March to May, 1968, tells a story of neighborhood resistance and school department intransigence. The school finally was reorganized according to the superintendent's plan, despite sit-ins by parents. Many of the middle-class, white residents of the area turned to parochial and independent schools to educate their sons and daughters.

The first 15 years of the reorganized middle school were marked by turmoil, much like that chronicled by Grant (1988) in *The World We Created at Hamilton High*. Black pupils staged boycotts and walkouts to demand more black studies courses and black teachers. Vandalism, arson, and assaults on students, teachers, and administrators fill the pages of *The Sentinel* from 1969 to 1983. The establishment of a program for the gifted in another Springfield middle school offered yet another option for neighborhood parents who wanted an alternative to the turbulent Pierce School. The February 9, 1981, *Sentinel* report on Pierce is headlined: " 'Brain drain' at school upsets parents of students who remain." In 1984 the black principal who had been assigned to Pierce was reassigned; this change angered many of his supporters, white and black. His white successor was removed three years later.

The arrival in 1988 of David Stewart, a seasoned veteran of the Springfield school system, brought a certain degree of calm to Pierce. Stewart was trusted by the teachers and the neighbors. He held parlor meetings to woo neighborhood parents, hoping to convince them to send their sons and daughters to Pierce. Springfield embraced the suggestions made in the Carnegie Report (Carnegie Council on Adolescent Development, 1989), including team teaching, more advising, and greater input by parents. In the late 1980s and early 1990s an influx of new immigrants to Springfield and a crippling recession boosted the population from 500 to almost 600 students. A citywide option for early retirement in 1990 allowed many of the older teachers to leave. As one of the teachers told me, that offering cleared away the "dead wood."

Today Pierce is a quiet, orderly place. Signs in Spanish, Portuguese, and Khmer direct the visitor to the main office, which is labeled by a sign in English and Spanish. Students' drawings and holiday decorations adorn the walls. The room, furnished in Eisenhower institutional softened by burnished oak woodwork and chintz floral draperies, contains a photocopier and several desks for secretaries. The office staff is cordial, though not effusive. All visitors must sign in and wear a badge. (The principal's office next door, however, is no longer occupied by David Stewart; he was transferred in the summer of 1993. His successor, Allan Manderley, began his assignment in September, 1993. The assistant principal, Nick Nuñes, has remained.)

Students are bused to Pierce from all over the city in order to maintain ethnic and racial balance mandated by the Springfield school committee. Like Riverview High School, the school studied by Alan Peshkin (1991), Franklin Pierce is a school with no single ethnic majority. The school office provided me with information about the ethnic composition of the school for the 1993–1994 academic year; this is displayed in Table 1. As is the case with Peshkin's Riverview High, the neighborhood perception is that the African-American minority is larger than it is.

Table 1.
Franklin Pierce School: Ethnic Composition

Ethnic Group	Number	Percentage
Native American	6	1
Asian	80	13
African American	214	36
Hispanic	126	21
White	171	29
Total	597	100

I called the social studies supervisor, Jim Belladonna, a former high school principal with a reputation for responsiveness and competence, who was new to the position. When I asked him for the name of a middle school social studies teacher who thought of himself as a moral educator, Belladonna didn't hesitate. He recommended George Stratas, a teacher he supervised, the teacher Belladonna's daughter, a current student, idolized.

Stratas is in his late thirties, a former Marine whose no-nonsense style and quiet competence belies the fact that he has been teaching for three years only. Stratas' special love is American history. Coverage is the bane of history teachers. Since his seventh-grade American history course begins with a study of African and European history, Stratas' students get no farther than the drafting of the Constitution. Worried that his students would have no more exposure to American history until their junior year in high school, and knowing that a significant number of his students might drop out before their junior year, Stratas had lobbied for a two-year American history sequence. Stewart had approved his suggestion that American history be taught for two years, in both the seventh and eighth grades.

Stratas left for his summer vacation looking forward to a steamboat excursion down the Mississippi River and a visit to Civil War battlefields. In June he learned that he was required to take nine credits in English as a Second Language, that he would have to teach civics instead of the second year of American history, and that Stewart would be leaving.

I visited Stratas' four eighth-grade civics classes which met for 40 minutes each during nine visits to the school. I also sat in on a course elective in law that met Tuesday and Thursday afternoons. I made my first field observation during the 1992–1993 academic year and paid five subsequent visits during the 1993–1994 year.

Shaw School: Amy Medeiros, Teacher

The route to finding my third site, the independent girls' school, was convoluted. I began with schools I knew, asking students, parents, and faculty members whether these girls' schools made a conscious effort to deal with the moral development and education of their students. Since no one knew of any schools that fit the bill, I called Peggy McIntosh at the Wellesley Center for Research on Women. She echoed the findings of *The A.A.U.W. Report* (1992), on which she had collaborated. There were very few girls' schools that were working on the special issues of girls at the middle school level. A friend in Jewish education suggested I call someone he knew at Teachers College, who gave me a list of schools that might be suitable. I found a school that allowed me to do a pilot study there, but would not consent to my return. An acquaintance suggested the Shaw School, which boasts of a strong math and science department.

The Shaw School is an independent school for girls in Springfield. It evolved out of a number of private academies for girls, named after the various women who "kept" the school. After an unsuccessful attempt at coeducation with a nearby school for boys, the school reorganized in the twenties on a plot of land bought from the boys' school. Eventually named for John Singleton Shaw, a classics professor who taught at nearby Ivy University, the school is now over 100 years old.

The trustees resisted making any concessions to what a former headmistress referred to as "a tide of wild experimentation" during the sixties. According to Shaw's *Centennial Book*, it was known by its detractors as "the good, gray school." It also resisted a flirtation with coeducation in the seventies, when some trustees, worried about the future of single-sex education, suggested a merger with a nearby independent school for boys. The school is firmly committed to a feminist ideal. Banners stretched across the wide avenue that borders the school proclaim a host of programs and celebrations of achieving women: Lego Day, which invites the community to join Shaw students in building realistic and imaginative structures; National Girls and Women's Day in Sports; and Math/Science Day. Today there are over 300 girls enrolled in the school, which consists of 14 grades, nursery through grade 12. There are 85 girls enrolled in the middle school, grades six through eight.

Shaw is a Quaker school, although there is only one identified Quaker at Shaw, the African-American Head of the School, Barbara Burns. Burns assumed her duties in September, 1993. Fundamentals of Quaker education infuse the atmosphere at Shaw. The school espouses both individualism and community. This combination is most palpable during the weekly meetings in which silence is used as a means of worship. Every Friday morning the sixth to twelfth grades gather with their teachers in the school auditorium. For 20 minutes they sit in silent reflection, unless one of the members of the meeting chooses to share her thoughts. While Shaw has always stressed individual academic achievement, it requires its students to perform community service as well.

Shaw hosts an annual Math/Science Day which is open to the public. Aimed at middle school girls across the state, the program is designed to interest young women in fields that require mastery of mathematics and science. The brainchild of Mary Carparo, head of the middle school, the Math/Science Day of October, 1993, featured presentations by an environmentalist, a forensic toxicologist, a zoo keeper, a landscape architect, a physician, a roboticist, and others. When I called Carparo to ask if I could use Shaw as one of my sites, she was delighted. She suggested that I visit the class of Amy Medeiros, a vivacious woman in her mid-40s who teaches prealgebra and algebra in the middle school, as well as geometry in the upper school.

Amy Medeiros has been teaching for almost 20 years, having taken off a few years to care for her young children full time. She has been a member of the faculty at Shaw for seven years, having taught previously at a boys' independent school and in a public high school. She has served as the chair of the middle school math department for three years. She was initially concerned about whether or not her notion of moral education, a concern for academic excellence and perseverance, was "what I was looking for." After reading my proposal, she telephoned me and agreed to participate.

I observed Medeiros' seventh-grade prealgebra class, a 40-minute period, six times over six weeks' duration. I visited the school a total of ten times, attending Shaw Lego Day, Math/Science Day, the Hanukkah pageant, and Vespers program.

Roger Wolcott Smith Middle School: John MacDonald, Teacher

Finding my fourth school was easy. It was, in fact, the first site I identified. In the spring of 1992, a friend in charge of special education at Roger Wolcott Smith Junior High School in Midvale, a middle- and upper-middle-class suburb of a large metropolitan center, asked me about my research. Upon learning that I was interested in the subject of heroes, she suggested that I talk to John MacDonald, a colleague who was similarly concerned. I was delighted at the prospect of working within the Midvale system, a community known for the excellence of its schools.

Smith Junior High School opened its doors in 1956. There have been only five principals during its existence. From its very inception, the school diverged from the four other junior high schools in Midvale. Initially, its dissimilarity lay in its support of flexible grouping. By 1963, the differences were more striking. The school had defined itself as an alternative junior high school, characterized by governance through consensus and a commitment to student choice. Team teaching was commonplace. Students were given enormous latitude: They could determine when they wanted to come to school, how long they wanted to stay, and what they wanted to study. In 1967, the eight-week electives in social studies included The Rise and Fall of the Third Reich, The Struggle for Men's Minds, Advanced Economics, The Colonial Period in American History, Communism, The Vietnam War, Reform Movements in American History, The Music of Protest and Propaganda, Elizabethan History, Public Speaking, Music and War, The Rise and Fall of the Roman Empire, The Nineteen Twenties and Thirties, The Biography of the West, Renaissance Europe, African Studies, The Age of Jackson, Lewis and Clark, and The Negro in America. Teachers were expected to be facilitators, not instructors of skills or transmitters of information. The school was multigraded; seventh graders learned alongside ninth graders. Traditional report cards were replaced by evaluations of learning contracts made between the teachers and their students. By the seventies the school had a reputation as a wild and woolly place, where students hung out on the grass, smoking grass.

Smith has changed a great deal. When it was first built, the school consisted of the children of college graduates—predominantly Jewish, upper-middle-class families. Today, the Chins outnumber the Cohens. There is still a large percentage of Jewish students, but many of them are recently arrived Israelis or immigrants from the former Soviet Union. The school includes many for whom English is not their first language. Among the languages spoken in Smith homes are Hebrew, Russian, Japanese, Cantonese, Vietnamese, Spanish, Mandarin, Korean, Pushtu, Greek, Khmer, and Arabic. Thirty African-American students are bused in daily from the inner city. Table 2 displays the ethnic composition of Smith.

In the hopes of freeing up more classrooms for the graduates of Midvale's burgeoning elementary schools, the high schools incorporated the ninth graders into what had been a 10th- to 12th-grade program. The last class of ninth graders graduated from Smith in June,

Table 2.
Roger Wolcott Smith School:
Ethnic Composition

Ethnic Group	Number	Percentage
Asian	112	11
African American	70	7
Hispanic	21	2
White	785	80
Total	988	100

1981. With the loss of the ninth graders, the intellectual tone of the school changed. In September 1993, Smith became a middle school, with a population of one thousand sixth, seventh, and eighth graders. During the 1993–1994 academic year, the sixth graders have been treated as a school within a school. Some of the faculty members worry about a further dilution of the program once the sixth graders are fully integrated.

Although the school still functions with a high degree of faculty consensus, and there are numerous examples of team teaching, student choice has been severely curtailed. Students can select courses from a menu of offerings in applied and fine arts. There are electives in SS&E (social studies and English). Math, science, and foreign languages are required. Students are tracked, kept within grade groupings, and receive conventional report cards. Worried about what they referred to euphemistically "unstructured time," the school board tightened up on attendance, free periods, and off-campus privileges during the eighties. The school is a considerably more centrist institution today than it was twenty years ago.

John MacDonald teaches a literature-based course he calls Heroes and Sheroes to seventh and eighth graders. A beefy, jolly man in his late 50s, MacDonald is a seasoned veteran of teaching in public and private schools. He is known as a fixture at Smith, having taught there for 20 years. His principal describes him as the school's conscience, someone who keeps reminding the faculty of the founding principles of Smith. Heroes and Sheroes is one of a number of 12-week electives he has designed which weave the social studies and English disciplines around a theme. Others include an art and architecture course, Art and Esthetics, and Schools and Society. Smith faculty members informed me that students vie for slots in MacDonald's elective courses.

I contacted MacDonald in May, 1992. I was delighted when he accepted my request to observe his class in order to determine its suitability for my study. I asked the principal of the school, Janet Howell, for permission to visit and received it. After my visit, I knew I wanted to learn more about MacDonald and his class. I then wrote to the principal for formal permission to include the school in my study. I was directed to the assistant superintendent, who, upon receipt of an official request for permission to do research in the Midvale schools, granted me the right to do so during the summer of 1993. Ironically, although MacDonald was the first teacher I identified, he was the last I studied. Since his class is an elective and he teaches it on a rotating schedule, I had to wait for a year and a half for the class to be offered again.

The common denominators of the teachers in my study are that they teach middle schoolers; they are committed to moral education; and they have considered the place of moral prototypes, both formally and informally, in their teaching. All volunteered to work with me after being contacted by me directly or by their principals. What makes them different are the cultural contexts in which they teach: private vs. public schools; sectarian vs. nonsectarian settings; single-sex vs. coed populations. Another difference among them is the subjects they teach: religious studies, social studies, math, and literature. It is the commonalties and differences that make up the body of this book.

4

The *Godol*: Hero and Role Model

TUVIA KAPLAN, SPRINGFIELD TORAH INSTITUTE

Rebbe Kaplan's Classroom

I dress carefully for my first visit to Rebbe Kaplan's classroom. Although the temperature is in the eighties, I wear a jacket over a mid-calf-length skirt. I have to be dressed modestly, arms and legs covered, to be taken seriously in this institution. A woman displaying bare flesh or wearing pants is an infraction of right-wing Orthodox norms. I know not to shake hands with Rebbe Kaplan because physical contact between men and women, other than husbands and wives, is frowned upon.

A woman wearing a ritual wig and a long-sleeved, long-skirted dress takes me to Rebbe Kaplan's classroom. As we move through the corridors, I note the hall decorations. There is a bulletin board of student photos, which later will be replaced by a collage for the *Shavuot* (Hebrew: Pentecost) holiday. Commercially made posters on the importance of refraining from gossip, advertisements for Jewish books and services (including a woman who checks clothing for fibers permissible under Jewish law), and requests for funds to create a new Torah scroll decorate the walls. The hallway is spotless; there are no papers on the floor, nor graffiti on the walls or posters. We pass the general studies library. (The larger Judaic studies library is in the other wing.)

We find Rebbe Kaplan's room, and I begin the first of my four visits to his seventh grade. Rebbe Kaplan is not an ordained rabbi. *Rebbe*, a term borrowed from the Hasidim, is used by other Orthodox groups to refer to teachers, ordained or not, who serve as mentors and spiritual advisors for their students. Rebbe Kaplan defines the term as "mentor, teacher, instructor, role model. A person who represents certain religious values and instructs those religious values. For me personally, it means a person who [sic] I have an extremely close personal connection with."

A 30-year-old, chunky, bearded man with an easy smile and an outgoing personality, Kaplan is studying privately for the rabbinate. He talks quickly, gestures often, and laughs frequently. He interrupts himself as he tries to catch up with his thoughts. Dressed casually for a teacher in this institution, he comes to class wearing the traditional black skullcap, an open-necked shirt, and dark pants. Today he is wearing a white shirt; on other visits he wears a striped shirt or a purple shirt. Male teachers in the school generally wear black suits and white shirts; Rebbe Kaplan is the only male teacher pictured in the school yearbook without a jacket.

He peppers his speech with sports metaphors. The high school is "the big leagues." When he's on, he's "in the zone." He spends his spare time, which is truly spare as both a teacher and the informal activities director to the high school boys, in sports—following his favorite teams or playing football and basketball. Unlike many of his colleagues, Kaplan is a graduate of a secular university where he majored in psychology. He tells me that he does not come from a religious family; he became observant because of the influence of a teacher in his Jewish day school. Unlike many of the teachers, who come from cities with large Jewish populations, Kaplan grew up in a southern city with a few thousand Jews. He mentions that one-third of his seventh-grade students are faculty members' children. The fact that a number of his students are more observant than he is makes Rebbe Kaplan somewhat self-conscious: "All of them come from a home that was pretty much more observant than the one that I came from."

Kaplan compares this year's seventh grade with last year's eighth grade, a group that contained a substantial number of students who had arrived recently from the former Soviet Union. He reflects on how the nature of the class affected his instruction:

> That's the point I wanted to make about the eighth grade; there I felt like I was in my element. Here are kids who—that's the reason I went into teaching . . . to take kids—who don't have, because of their background or whatever the situation was, a deep appreciation of Jewish values, of Jewish heroes. . . . They don't have it. Then I felt like, wow, this is the kind of class I could do something with . . . so that by the end of the year they can come away with really positive feelings about Jewish values. They can come away with having seen certain practices that they might want to do—more importantly, the feeling, the approach, a love of, let's say, of *yiddishkeit* (Yiddish: traditional Judaism), of what it stands for. They can come away with a familiarity of Jewish figures that would be important and meaningful to them. Whereas with this year's class, I really felt the whole year that I was extremely limited in the amount that

I could accomplish in those areas. . . . With these kids there was very little that I could say that they weren't completely familiar with.

The cramped room is set up in four rows of hard chairs. I see no
graffiti on the functional furniture. Sixteen seventh graders, eight
boys and eight girls, are in attendance. The teacher's desk is in the
front of the room, between two bulletin boards. One bulletin board is
decorated with the students' writing samples from their general studies curriculum. They had composed "Explorer letters," letters that
might have been sent by Columbus, Magellan, Diaz, and Da Gama.
The students tried to make the letters look authentic by fraying the
edges and writing in a calligraphic script. The second bulletin board
displays letters that supposedly were written by Civil War soldiers.

A large bulletin board in the back of the room is divided into three
sections: two smaller ones, each about 2 feet across, flanking a middle
section about 6 feet across. This board is dominated by the Judaic
studies curriculum. The two smaller sections contain pictures of rabbis spanning the range of Orthodoxy. Rebbe Kaplan tells me he had
put them up to remind the students of the spectrum from the modern
Orthodox on the left to the ultra-Orthodox far right. When the class
studied an exegesis composed by one of these men, he pointed out the
author.

The largest part of the tripartite board is devoted to students' artwork depicting the holidays. During my visits the display includes
Passover and Shavuot drawings. A smaller bulletin board beside this
"triptych" contains students' posters promoting the patriots' cause on
the eve of the American Revolution. The display is titled, "Join or Die:
Be a Patriot." A part of the General Studies program, this display is
the only physical evidence that the students integrate their two
courses of study. The drawing of the Boston Massacre is captioned
"Boston Massacre Never Again," echoing the post-Holocaust slogan
"Never again." I see a few contemporary touches. One drawing depicts
King George III, holding his finger to his lips and saying, "Read my
lips. More taxes." Another portrays shows the king, crown and all,
with a red slash mark through his portrait.

Three shelves of books and supplies run across half the length of
the room; the books are arranged casually. Across the room, windows
overlook the street. Under the windows is a bank of shelves for storage.
On top of these shelves, in the corner, are a heap of books, scrap paper,
a wrinkled dictionary, a bottle of white-out, crayons spilling out of their
box, and a flier. An open closet contains a packed set of drawers. A
wastebasket overflows with papers.

As the students enter the classroom, they kiss the *mezuzah* (Hebrew: doorpost; a small container that holds a calligraphic parchment with several passages from the Torah), indicating their respect for God's revealed word. They repeat this gesture if they have to leave and reenter. The girls are dressed very modestly. Each wears a long-sleeved blouse and mid-calf length skirt. None uses makeup. All of the boys wear black *kippot* (Hebrew: skullcaps); only one wears the knitted *kippah* (Hebrew: skullcap), which is *de rigeur* among the modern Orthodox. The *tsitsit* (Hebrew: ritual fringes), which the Torah commands of all adult males, are visible on some of the students. I assume that the other boys wear them tucked in. Most of the boys wear shirts with collars; in my six visits to the school, I see only two wearing T-shirts (one bearing the logo of the Chicago Bulls). I notice no jeans at any time on anyone. Only the shoes, both the boys' and the girls', look like those worn by their counterparts in nonsectarian schools. Unlike their counterparts, each of these 16 youths has a Hebrew name either of Biblical or modern Hebrew derivation.

Tuvia Kaplan's Definition of Moral Education

Moral education, in any setting, is an idea of teaching people how to act correctly. Ethics. How to act to other people. How to act in society. How to have a productive life. *In the Jewish sense, I would say it's part and parcel of the education from the beginning, from Breishit (Hebrew: Genesis). Avraham Avinu, (Hebrew: our father, Abraham), Noah, Adom harishon (Hebrew: Adam, the first man)* [emphasis added]. How did they act when they did the right thing? We should copy them. When they did the wrong thing, we should learn from it what not to do. We should emulate their good attributes, their good characteristics, and so it's part and parcel of the system all the way through.

In his discussion of enculturation, Kaplan's theories are "outside-in" (Eisner, 1985). His definition resembles what Wynne (1986) calls "The Great Tradition." Like Ryan (1988), Bennett (1991), Kilpatrick (1992) and others who call themselves character educators, Kaplan fully believes in the importance of the school in shaping the individual's values and behavior. Like Durkheim (1956, 1973), he perceives teachers as the agents of the societies they represent, entrusted with the responsibility of socializing the next generation. Morality is superimposed on the child by the social order. He or she internalizes the rules, becoming a member of the social group and eventually an autonomous agent—that is, a member of the group who freely accepts its norms (Durkheim, 1973).

From the outset, Rebbe Kaplan differentiates between moral education at an institution such as the Torah Institute and in the secular world. He echoes the attitude of Pastor Muller at Peshkin's (1986) Bethany Bible Academy: "There are some very real differences between us and a public school. The primary distinction is going to be character; we develop character" (p. 7). Like Pastor Muller, Kaplan cannot imagine Jewish education without a moral dimension: "It's part and parcel of the education from the beginning." Moral education is the enculturation of young people into a religious and ethical system. Those students who are not so fully identified, who may come from less knowledgeable, less observant backgrounds, need "to develop a deep appreciation of *Jewish values, Jewish heroes*" [emphasis added]. In each of his discussions of moral education, Kaplan juxtaposes values, or values education, with heroes. Moral education is unthinkable without moral heroes.

Who Is a Hero?

Kaplan mentions Jewish and secular heroes in his exchanges. As a former southerner, he thinks of Martin Luther King in the latter category. He tells me of a Torah Institute controversy in which he found himself in the minority:

> Martin Luther King's birthday came up this past year and the secular teachers were going all out. There was going to be this special day, assembly, a talk about it, the bulletin board that's in the hall. . . . Classes were doing special projects. It was a big thing. I would say some of the teachers were a little uncomfortable with it. Some of the rabbis, and parents, some of the rabbinic parents who were not teachers in the school, maybe teachers in the high school, took really extreme views about this subject. It was striking to me because . . . I grew up with *"Martin Luther King's a great guy. He's a hero of mine"* [emphasis added]. So I [said], "Why are you guys getting upset about a man whose basic lesson is 'let's live together in peace and let's work together in harmony?' Let's not use violence." . . . I can't see anything wrong with the message here.

Kaplan explains his colleagues' expressed views at the schoolwide faculty meeting convened to discuss the subject. He tells me about those who disagree with him. One faction believes that if the school were "to really make a big deal about heroes, they should be traditional Jewish heroes." Another faction contends that Martin Luther King is unacceptable as a hero in the school because "this particular man showed a lot of moral lapses." A third faction argues "specifically that because he was a religious figure in his religion, that makes him totally unacceptable."

> Apologies were made and the issue was discussed, and at that meeting I very much got the feeling I was in the minority, saying, "Look, the guy had a good message, the guy sacrificed much. . . ." This is what I told people in conversation. "He went through a lot of sacrifices for this, and a lot of other people would have gone to violent methods, right? And [sacrifice; nonviolence] has its place." I felt like that was a minority position. I felt like the majority position would have been, "We could definitely do without this entire business," which is interesting.

Jewish heroes are different from secular heroes: we and they, Jacob and Esau. When Kaplan teaches II Samuel 22, David's song of thanksgiving to God, he asks his students to ponder the idea of a great general attributing his success to God.

> *Kaplan*: Imagine another general, Norman Schwartzkopf, Alexander the Great. What might that general's attitude be?
>
> *Sharonah*: Arrogant.
>
> *Kaplan*: "It's me. I've studied. It's me." It's a rare person who says *Hashem* [Hebrew: the name. Traditional Jews will use the Hebrew name for God only in prayer] gave me these skills. It's a rare attitude.

Kaplan teaches his class II Samuel 23:13–17, the story of a tired King David besieged by Philistines, longing for the water from a well in Bethlehem, his boyhood home. He sends out his men to bring him the water, thereby exposing them to great danger. Realizing that he has imperiled their lives for selfish reasons, David then refuses to drink the water; instead he pours it out to God as a sacrifice. Having created the background, Rebbe Kaplan says:
This story teaches about character. What does it teach you?

> *Devorah*: Dovid[1] will do anything for what is right.
>
> *Kaplan*: When it comes to crunch time, pained and thirsty, Dovid pours it out because it's the right thing to do.
>
> *Ruth*: Dovid admits he's wrong. Not embarrassed to say he made a mistake.

---

[1] Many Orthodox Jews pronounce Hebrew with an Ashkenazic (eastern European) accent rather than modern Hebrew, which uses a Sephardic (Spanish) accent. Ashkenazim say *Dovid* instead of *David*, *Doniel* instead of *Daniel*, *Shabbos* instead of *Shabbat*.

Doniel: He's going to be good even if it's controversial. He cared about *Hashem* (Hebrew: God). He's not like others who ask, "What will they think of me?"

Kaplan: Dovid is saying, "I value you so much I will not benefit from what I asked you to do, to risk your life for me."

Devorah: Why couldn't he drink it anyway? They risked their lives for nothing.

Kaplan: He's saying, "I appreciate your loyalty. Because I appreciate it so much, I can't drink this water." Dovid is different from a general who plans and doesn't care about the loss of his men's life. He doesn't just chuck the water; he pours it out to *Hashem*. This is sacred.

Kaplan rarely uses David's name without including *hamelekh* (Hebrew: the King). David embodies the ideal of the talented leader, whose qualities include the gift of humility and self-sacrifice. Similarly, when Kaplan mentions Moses's name, it is almost always with the epithet *Rabbenu* (Hebrew: our teacher); Abraham is *Avraham avinu* (Hebrew: our father). As Makolkin (1992) notes, the name wields its power through association. It is metonymic; mention of David's name conjures up images of all the kings of Israel and the suggestion of the Messiah. The shorthand simultaneously widens and compresses the image. The icon evokes multiple associations, but in doing so, it becomes depersonalized. Icons are two-dimensional; the process of iconization flattens and abstracts. David loses his human dimensions in becoming the embodiment of the monarchy, past and future. By its very nature, an icon is transcendent: elevated and remote.

The Hebrew term that Kaplan uses to refer to Jewish heroes captures the notion of distance and greatness. He thinks of them as *gedolim* (Hebrew: great ones). This is the term most often used by the faculty and parents at the Torah Institute. A hero is always, in the Dean's words, "spiritually an awesome power." A *godol* (Hebrew: great one) is not like you or me. A *godol* shares more with Blaisdell and Ball's heroes than with the local heroes of the Giraffe Project. Kaplan has decorated his classroom with pictures of *gedolim*, the rabbis who adorn the back wall. He uses the photos to make the point that *gedolim* could be found in every generation, across the spectrum of Orthodoxy. *Gedolim* are extraordinary individuals, people on a different plane or *madreigah* (Hebrew: level).

Kaplan comments on the historic function of idealized heroes or *gedolim*:

There is a certain fascination with this idea of the really high *madreigah. Jewish people attach their self-image to it* [emphasis added].

In other words, we didn't want to feel this guy's one of us. The opposite. We wanted to feel we can be proud . . ." My little wife in my little village, and little peasant, right? But look who *we've* got!" You know, the figure that towers above humanity. That's the way Jews have always thought. The Rabbi Akiva, the Rabban Gamliel, the *Yehudah ha-Nasi* (Hebrew: Judah the Prince, compiler of the Talmud) were not seen by the rest of the world. At that time the Romans might say, "Oh, there's the rabbi of the Jews." Some little figure and some funny clothing who studies some funny book, right? To the Jews this was the figure that towered above everybody else. This was *it*. And the opposite would be true. The Roman Caesar, or the Greek general, or whoever it was that the rest of the world was venerating, would basically be a person of not much esteem to the Jews. *In other words, their self, their identity was connected in what we've got. They didn't call it a godol; basically godol is kind of a modern term. We've got this great rabbinic figure and our national pride, self-identity is attached to that person* [emphasis added]. So that whole push is to make a person as high as possible, as lofty as possible.

In his analysis, Kaplan offers another, surprisingly contemporary explanation for Jewish heroes. He claims that they give an oppressed people an opportunity for reflected glory. This is also the rationale for the Afrocentric schools for young black males in dozens of cities across the United States (Ascher, 1991). In the language of the "inside-out" school of moral education, they build self-esteem.

The *gedolim* are not flawless, however. Kaplan muses about the material he teaches:

> *Shmuel Bes* (Hebrew: II Samuel) is packed with what we might think shouldn't be there. *Like you'd expect to always hear sugar-coated stories of this person did the right thing and lived happily ever after and got this reward and everything was great* [emphasis added]. The story of Batsheva and Dovid hamelekh, where he arranges to be with her and then sends out her husband to be killed in a war, that is a story that blows the class away. Any objective reader is smashed by the story.

One of Kaplan's greatest struggles is how to teach the story of David and Bathsheba in an intellectually honest manner. His integrity is at stake as he looks for what he calls "the *emes*" (Hebrew: the truth). In one classical exegesis, David, knowing he was sending his soldiers into a dangerous battle, asked all of them to give their wives the documents that constitute a Jewish divorce. This legal precaution would enable the wives to remarry in case their husbands died in battle without witnesses to their death. Therefore David is not guilty of adultery because Uriah and Bathsheba were already divorced. Landau (1993) comments on this interpretation, which Kaplan elected not to use.

> The Gemara (Talmud) says: "Anyone who thinks that David sinned is mistaken." For the Bible says of him elsewhere (I Samuel 18:14): "And David behaved himself wisely in all his ways; and the Lord was with him." Is it possible that sin should come his way if the Lord was with him? (pp. 179–180)

Kaplan observes that heroes must be presented in different ways, depending on the child's developmental level. With younger children, as in the fourth grade he has been teaching, he makes a case for the idealized hero: "You can't besmirch him that much before kids of an impressionable age." By the time students have reached the seventh grade, however, Kaplan claims that they can come to grips with flawed heroes.

Rebbe Kaplan's intuitive views seem to be justified by some of the research in developmental psychology. Donaldson and Westerman (1986) indicate that by the time a child is 10½, ambivalence can be tolerated. With his seventh grade, Kaplan refuses to whitewash King David.

> I don't know what to do. I've got the text and it says what it says, and they had choices to say it in different ways, but this is what it says. What do I make of it? Do I say he was such a *tsaddik* (Hebrew: righteous person) that he was totally above this? Do I, let's say, look for *m'forshim* (Hebrew: exegetes) that are gonna minimize his *het* (Hebrew: sin) to a little, tiny *het*? So I'm ambivalent about that. When I taught it, it was a tough challenge 'cause I wasn't sure how to teach it. I felt like it was right to say in the beginning, "We're about to study things about Dovid hamelekh that we cannot just take at face value."

Kaplan takes the gamble of presenting a hero with warts, even though he knows that he is on dangerous terrain. In fact, one of the parents, Rabbi Lifschitz, a faculty member, is somewhat troubled by his approach. Kaplan reflects on his teaching:

> I taught it the way I taught it, and the next day a student came to me and said, "My father would like to talk to you about the way you taught this." I thought [he meant], "My father wants to talk to you; give him a buzz when you get a chance," [but] it was, "My father wants to talk to you. He's right outside the door." I could see situations where it would be like a combination of trepidation and also indignation, like, "Who are you to come tell me how to teach this?" But it was a man who I have

[good rapport with] so I was actually enthusiastic, like I'd like to hear what he has to say. He said, "This is an incredibly difficult *myseh* (Yiddish: story) in *Tanakh* (Hebrew: Bible), and I like to use the following approach." He laid out certain guidelines and kind of left it in my lap, "Do what you want with it," which I felt was a good way to handle it.

Knowing the risks, Kaplan opts for a humanized, not an idealized, hero. He explains that the presence of flaws allows the students to make connections with King David, and from the connections, to find meaning—if not now, then sometime in the future.

The problem is this idealized picture of the hero which is separate from the person. In which case you just lost the effect it's supposed to have. If a hero is so put on a pedestal that there's no connection there, then you've lost it. It's like on some lofty plane 2,000 years ago, some person lived up to an ideal and wow, isn't that nice. Right. But not that those things have anything to do with me. For later life when these kids have to actually deal with life, reality, the mistakes that you make and making up for the mistakes that you make, it doesn't help you to know about some big *tsaddik*—we never heard of any mistakes that he made and who never had to do *teshuvah* (Hebrew: repentance). Right? *Then you need the lesson of Dovid hamelekh, down on the ground, crying over the kid that he lost and coming back* [emphasis added].

In teaching this story, Kaplan's use of the hero is very different than in the lesson of the noble David refusing to benefit from endangering his men. The *godol* offers his students an example of how to cope during the darkest moments of human existence. Kaplan uses the story in the hope of creating a lesson in personal endurance, a model to help his students face their own existential crises. It is the hero as source of personal meaning, not as avatar of cultural ideals. Once again Kaplan uses "inside-out" thinking to explain the place of the *godol* in his classroom. His view of the flawed hero with the "inside-out" orientation is not unique to him; it was shared by the dean, Rabbi Cahn. "Heroes are human in that they are capable of making mistakes. *'Ein tsaddik ba'aretz sheya'aseh tov v'lo yehta'* (Hebrew: There is not a righteous man upon the face of the earth who doeth good and sinneth not)."

According to Kaplan, there is a difference between heroes and role models, and moral education needs both.

The hero is more of a grand, an abstract idea. The role model is very practical. In terms of day to day, in terms of actual practicality, "How do I lead my life?" you need to see it in front of you. You need to have a role model.

Who Is a Role Model?

For Kaplan, *gedolim* are simultaneously heroes and role models, and thus are different from secular heroes. He notes that George Washington is most assuredly a hero, but (unlike a *godol*) not a role model. *Gedolim* teach behavior as well as embodying values; secular heroes only embody values. Kaplan discusses Genesis 18, in which Abraham greets the three messengers who will tell him of Isaac's birth. He is struck by the detail in the story. The details make the story. (In Hebrew, the root *s'fr* can mean *to tell* or *to enumerate*. It is detail which transforms a metaphor into a map, fleshes out an icon, turns an abstraction of hospitality into a blueprint showing how to behave like a host.)

> The Torah gives you so many details about *Avraham avinu*'s daily life that you can't idealize him too much. "Guys, please come in. I want to serve you. I want to help you." And he goes in. Details: Fix the bread, get the meat, put this down here. "Now I'm going to wash your feet." There's no way to take that person and idealize him out of the realm. . . . That's exactly the reason why the Torah has those stories there. Because let's say the Torah just said: *Mitzvah* (Hebrew: commandment): Thou shall visit the sick. Thou shall welcome guests. Thou shall be hospitable. *If you give people an idea without examples of how other people actually put it into effect and made it real, then the people don't know exactly what to do* [emphasis added]. They might follow it to a certain extent, but you'll never get the real modeling that you want them to follow.

Kaplan uses the Biblical material to exhort his students to behave morally. He overhears two of his students talking about the forthcoming Sabbath. One of the out-of-towners had asked to spend the Sabbath in Springfield with his classmate. The Springfield student refused.

> I said to the kid, "Is that how *Avraham avinu* would talk?" "Oh, *Avraham avinu*." There's no question in the kid's mind that he wants to be like Mikey, wants to be a little bit like *Avraham avinu*. We Jews don't get any higher than that. . . . And immediately in his mind is, "I do want to be like *Avraham avinu*, so I want to have the kid over for *Shabbos*, so I don't care what the problem is. We'll work it out."

Beside the exemplars from Jewish texts and tradition, the teacher also is a role model. This expectation is expressed in the six goals listed in the mission statement of the Springfield Torah Institute. The sixth goal is "to maintain a faculty which would serve as role models for those values and lessons which the school wishes to impart." Dean Cahn gives the example of the basketball-playing rebbe who swears as he misses a shot.

> I don't care if from today to tomorrow you speak about what our patri-archs and matriarchs went through, . . . but if what they [students] see is [that] the person that they have the closest contact with really just teaches those things but in their own life doesn't practice it, you basi-cally pulled the carpet out, in my opinion. They get this mixed message, and mixed messages when you're dealing with educating children are probably the most dangerous area.

The teacher is to be a living text, the personification of the norms of the group. Kaplan accepts this responsibility:

> I think the good rebbe feels like . . . I'm the little *Avraham avinu.* Like I'm gonna tell them about *Avraham,* and I'm gonna expect them to lis-ten. I also have to act in such a way that they're gonna look at me and say, "Rebbe Kaplan did this and this."

Kaplan knows firsthand the power of a compelling role model. Al-though he attended a Jewish day school as a youth, he was not per-sonally observant. As I mentioned earlier, he became observant in high school because of the impact of a teacher.

> The first guy who I consider to be my *rebbe* was a window to really im-portant stuff. What was he a window to? All of a sudden it hit me. If I'm around this guy enough to listen to him, I'm gonna hear about really really important things. I'm not even sure how it was clear to me, that all of Jewish tradition, thousands of years of sacrifice in Jewish tradition had meaning, and I could find out what it means through this guy.

This teacher was the first of many *rebbeyim* (Yiddish: mentors) for Ka-plan, but all were men with whom he could feel connected.

> It means a person who I have an extremely close personal connection with . . . I only pick *rebbeyim* like you'd pick a friend, a similar outlook, a sense of humor, a way of looking at things, easygoing.

The Dean too has a *rebbe.* He remembers when his *rebbe* taught him the true meaning of "Love thy neighbor as thyself":

> One year my *rebbe* visited me when I was living in Savannah, Georgia, and he lives now in Israel. We were driving to the airport and he said, "Pull over, pull over, there's a supermarket here. Please pull over." And

I did. So I said, "Does *Rebbe* mind if I come in with him? I'd like to see, you know." And he said, "No, no." We walked into the store, and I figure well he's going to buy some fruit or some cake to take on the trip. You know, going back to Israel from Savannah, Georgia. I see he heads for the household detergents, and he picks up three cans of Mr. Muscle. I am absolutely bewildered by this, and I didn't want to say anything so I got in the car, and he checks out with these three cans of Mr. Muscle which is an oven cleaner. We're in the car and I said, "You know, *Rebbe*, I'd really like to understand this." He says, "You know, in Israel we don't have self-cleaning ovens, and *Pesah* (Hebrew: Passover) is coming up. One of the toughest things that my wife has to tackle on *Pesah* is cleaning the oven. We don't have Mr. Muscle in Israel so I figured that this year to make that task easier. . . ."

You know, sometimes the people that you're closest to you take for granted, and sometimes an expression of love is not this big hug and kiss and taking-the-cruise-on-the-ship kind of expression. Sometimes the love of your fellow man is as simple as a can of Mr. Muscle.

Kaplan struggles with what it means to be a role model, when being so human, so real, in the Rogerian (Rogers, 1961) sense, is a detriment. Just as he struggles with the humanization of the hero, he struggles with the humanization of the role model.

I don't live up to that, I think, as much as other teachers do. . . . I got a lot of rough edges, right? The kids see me at gym or at sports or something like that in . . . the temper, the sweat, the running, maybe the use of questionable language once in a while, maybe getting upset. . . . Other *rebbeyim* are maybe more careful about that . . . because their nature is to be much more, let's say, controlled or disciplined, or always polite. In other words, they're more conscious of, "I'm always a role model to my kids." There are *rebbeyim* that the kids will never see except well-dressed, whereas the kids will see me on a Sunday in jeans and a crummy shirt and a dirty hat, running, jogging in the neighborhood.

My impression, as a visitor to the class, is that Kaplan's humanity was a plus for many students, The school yearbook contains an adoring tribute to him from the high school boys: "Words cannot express our admiration for him and our gratitude for all he has done for us." Students, male and female, hang around his desk after class. The boys talk about sports. Yitzhak, one of his students, telephones Kaplan on Sundays to invite himself over to play ball. Several of the girls flirt with him, making allusions to his bachelor status and asking him where he spent his Jewish holidays.

Kaplan knows he doesn't meet the needs of all of his students for role models:

I'm not obsessed with the fact that every individual teacher, every single year has to be a role model. There it's a matter of hoping that you have a mix of teachers, I guess, so that one year the guy who needs me gets me, and another year the guys who need the other kind of teacher get that other kind of teacher—which I think probably kind of works out.

Rochel, a student from an extremely observant home, finds Kaplan's human foibles a detriment. I first notice her in class—doodling, playing with coins, seemingly not paying attention. When I ask if she has a learning disability, Kaplan chuckles. In a conference earlier in the year, she told him, carefully and respectfully, that she found his personal style not to her liking. She conceded that she would learn vocabulary words and translations from him, but that was all. Rebbe Kaplan accepts her decision.

> The student is used to, from her own family, her own experience, the type of teacher that I am so "not" that I'm history. In other words, the only thing I've been effective with this student would be technical skills. That's it, because those things you can't change. So I taught certain skills, but as a role model? I'm out the door.

Despite his disclaimer that he doesn't worry about being a role model for everyone, Kaplan senses that the girls in the school don't have their fair share of role models. He knows that he spends more time with the boys. When the class breaks for recess, he goes off to play ball with them. The girls don't have women teachers for Judaic studies until they move on to the high school.

> . . . when they move to the high school, and they have a Mrs. Green or a Mrs. Levine teach them, and here is a woman standing in front of them who they know, who they see every day, who has an incredible, an unbelievable mastery, just tremendous teaching. That's a role model.

Kaplan worries about the lack of textual models as well. After the girls finish their studies of the matriarchs (Sarah, Rebekah, Rachel, and Leah), there are scant references to strong, achieving women.

> Post-Biblically, you're finished. . . . You can take your boys from Torah, from Prophets and Writings, through the *Geonim* (Hebrew: eighth, ninth century scholars in Babylonia). . . . They can talk about the scholars of the Mishnah, they can talk about the scholars of the Gemara. They can talk about the *Rishonim* (Hebrew: medieval Biblical commentators). Boys in just the seventh grade, relatively young, have heard about Rashi (11th-century commentator), have heard about *Ba'alei*

Tosafot (Hebrew: medieval French commentators), of the Rambam (Hebrew: Maimonides, a 12th-century commentator). They can come today to somebody like Rav Schach (contemporary Israeli religious leader), Moshe Feinstein (American halakhic [legal] authority who died recently). So they got this entire gamut of Jewish history at their fingertips. It's going to become, more and more, a tremendous system. The most the girls can do is to start out with some Torah figures, learn about some figures in Prophets and Writings, and then they're lost except for the occasional role model. Like maybe the one that started Beis Yaakov (a girls' seminary), Sara Schenirer, or a certain book about a certain *rebbetzin* (Yiddish: rabbi's wife). *The system is such that there's a tremendous gap* [emphasis added].

Echoing Bandura (1977), Kaplan implies that students are more likely to emulate people who resemble them. Most of the girls manage to accept the male role models. Others don't, and they feel shortchanged by a scarcity of strong female role models. Kaplan describes one of his fourth-grade girls who seems to challenge the absence of strong women in the Bible.

This little girl makes the case. She's like calling out without saying the words, "I need a female role model. I need it. I want it. I have to have it. Male role models are not enough for me."

Kaplan's observations resemble those of *The A.A.U.W Report* (1992) and the findings of Brown and Gilligan (1992) at the Laurel School in Cleveland. He worries about the absence of role models for the girls and about its impact. In choosing to discuss the question of self-esteem, Kaplan positions himself squarely in the "inside-out" camp.

Cultural Context

During our discussions together, Kaplan refers repeatedly to the support he gets from "the system." By "the system" he means the cultural context of the yeshivah. Kaplan echoes Jackson's (1986) definition of cultural context—"the awareness, presuppositions, expectations and everything else that contributes to its interpretation by the actors themselves and by outsiders as well" (p. 96).

Agreement on Values. One expectation shared by the Torah Institute community is the centrality of moral education. In the words of the title of Purpel and Ryan's (1976) book, "moral education comes with the territory." Each lesson is supposed to have a moral message. Kaplan tells a story about being observed by the Judaic studies coordinator, Rabbi Liebowitz. In filling out his lesson plan, Kaplan wrote "Not applicable" beside the line designated "Moral of the Lesson." Liebowitz pointed out the omission, reminding Kaplan, "You can't do that. Try to do it." Liebowitz smiles when recalling the exchange and informs me that indeed, every lesson should have a message, an ethical dimension.

Utility. Another aspect of "the system" is that knowledge is expected to be put to immediate use. I observe Rebbe Kaplan's seventh grade studying the labors that may not be performed on the Sabbath. Rebbe Kaplan lectures, or the students read and translate. They are required to memorize material on which they will later be tested. On the surface, this class hardly resembles student-centered learning, but the material is vitally important (for example) to the girl who wonders whether tanning herself on the Sabbath is forbidden, like the tanning of leather. This is not arcane lore she is studying, but information vital to leading a committed Jewish life.

Stories. "The system" includes the stories that convey its messages. Kaplan has a vast repertoire of stories: from classic Jewish texts, from Jewish history, and from the tightly knit world of contemporary Orthodox Jewry.

> The system is right there for you to use. Here's the value. Here's the man or the woman and this is how it's done. This is what they did. Here is the story. Here is how it's done. It's how to put the value into effect. We wouldn't have it without the specific stories about people.

Kaplan knows the stories, and he knows what works with his students. He sizes up the situation and finds the right story for it, demonstrating what Shulman (1987) calls pedagogical content knowledge. The stories work when they connect on an affective level. When they are meaningful to the students, Rebbe Kaplan sees what he calls "the gleam." The gleam appears when the stories are powerful and when the message and the medium are fresh. In remembering his lesson about King David and the water, Kaplan recalls that he saw the gleam:

> The water story happens to be one 'cause they had never heard that story before and the particular lesson it was driving at is off the beaten path in that sense. It's not the kind of thing that you're always being taught over and over again.

The payoff may not come immediately. Stories are seeds that allow values to grow:

So the hope is the seed is there to come back. Now I don't fool myself into thinking that all of the kids are gonna get all of the seeds, 'cause that's definitely not gonna happen. If some of the kids, some of the seeds come to fruition later on, I'll be a happy man. That's where it's at for me. That's a realistic goal for me.

Stories are rampant throughout the institution. During our interview, Dean Cahn would punctuate his remarks with narrative. ("Do you mind if I tell you a story?") The school yearbook contains messages from the dean, Rabbi Liebowitz, and the yearbook editor. Each uses a parable to convey a lesson on the value of friendship, the theme of the yearbook. As Bruner (1990) would have us believe, it is through the story that the self is defined. Jewish identity is conveyed through Jewish stories. These stories help the listeners or the readers, at the moment or perhaps in the future, make meaning.

Stories work for Kaplan himself. They help him make moral choices:

I know in my own life there are specific stories that I can point to, that resonate. I want to act a certain way or I'm in a certain situation and the story, it's just right there. You know, how we talk of *Avraham avinu's* hospitality. Wanting to do hospitality, when I've been in the situation where, let's say, I had somebody over and I had a choice of either saying, "Here's the stuff, make your own bed," or run in and make the bed for them. The thing that pushes me to do it wasn't just that *Avraham avinu* jumped up. It was the totality. The *Avraham avinu* stories. All of the stories put together, that *tipus* (Hebrew: personality), plus the emphasis on it, from hearing other stories about how Reb Chaim Brisker used to have people living in his living room. There are different stories told about him. . . . Seeing the way my mother treats guests. . . . That totality hit me and said, "Go make the guy's bed. Don't just give him the sheets."

The stories have created in Kaplan what Day (1991a) calls a "moral audience." Abraham's story and those of other moral prototypes prod Kaplan to action.

In discussing classical societies, MacIntyre (1984) states that "the chief means of moral education is the telling of stories" (p. 121). Kaplan's classroom and the larger world of the school depend on stories; the *godol* would not exist without his story. Like Coles (1989), Kilpatrick (1992), and Bennett (1993), Kaplan believes in the power of narrative. He uses the word *story* 84 times in a 1½ hour interview.

Role Models All the Way Down. In another story, perhaps true, perhaps apocryphal, an anthropologist asked one of his informants in the field for his view of the cosmos. The local respondent patiently explained that the world was held up on the back of a turtle. The researcher pressed further, wondering how the turtle supported himself. The answer was, "Another turtle." When the researcher kept probing, the native replied, with exasperation, "It's turtles all the way down." At the Torah Institute, another aspect of "the system" is that it's role models all the way down.

The dean, the faculty, and the high school students all serve as role models. In describing the school, Rebbe Kaplan alludes to the research of Konrad Lorenz (1970) and his geese: "The picture that I like is the baby ducks. It's inborn that they come out, they see the mother duck, and then they act like that. That, to me, is what we're trying to do." Rabbi Cahn corroborates Rebbe Kaplan's views. The school is full of mother ducks. Everyone is expected to be a role model: the dean for the faculty, the faculty for the students, and the students, even the youngest, for each other. Rabbi Cahn elaborates:

> It's not just looking at others. They in turn have to become, at their level, the same kind of thing for their classmates, the same kind of thing for the children in the lower grades, and so on. It's part of what I think makes moral education work, that every person looks at themselves as a potential model for others.

"*Middos* (Hebrew: values) are caught, not taught," quips Cahn. Even the building models a set of values. Rabbi Cahn says, "The walls are *rebbeyim*." He refers to the immaculately maintained lawn, the spotless walls and floors. Respect for property is a message about respect in general. Each of Rebbe Kaplan's classes ends with Kaplan urging his students to clean up around their desks. Rabbi Cahn insists, "In terms of conveying those values that you want the kids to play out in their own lives, the only way to do it is to get everyone and everything to be a role model in that process."

Parents. Mrs. Jacobs, like all of the parents I speak to, has chosen Springfield Torah Institute for her daughter because of its values. She, of all the parents, might have considered public schools; her family is the least observant of the group, and her daughter recognized 9 out of 10 items on my popular culture index. Mrs. Jacobs tells me that she sends Netanyah to Torah Institute because everyone knows the school "is strong on *middos*" (Hebrew: values).

In addition to the students, who are looking to their teachers for role models, parents at the Torah Institute expect role models as well. Mrs. Jacobs comments that her daughter looks to the teachers "and sees how these people comport themselves." Mrs. Schatz tells me that

Sharonah definitely "looks up to her teachers." For Mrs. Schatz, role models are more important than heroes in her child's moral education: "Heroes you put up on a pedestal. You can't really aspire to emulate them." It is behavior that matters, not ideology.

Kaplan tells me of a disheartening episode with a pair of seventh-grade parents who found him an unacceptable role model: too liberal for their taste. They had compiled a list of his offenses ranging from his comment in class that he watched football games on television on Sundays to his allusion to the lyrics of a rock song. He was astounded at the uproar that ensued because the parents were centrist Orthodox who owned a television set themselves. Had the furor come from a right-wing family, Kaplan would have understood:

> I would have been so at peace with it. Immediately I would have said, "I 100% understand and I feel it was inappropriate of me to say and I apologize," because it's true. A family that doesn't have a TV in the house has a right to ask the teacher not to glorify TV or music in the house.

I ask Rebbe Kaplan to try to explain the viewpoint of these parents. He says:

> I think it's a certain self-consciousness. "We [the parents] can't be the role models. We need this guy to be the role model, and because we're so dependent on him to be the role model, then we can't tolerate him."[2]

During my interview with Doniel's father, Rabbi Lifschitz, the rabbi differentiates between the heroes of Jewish tradition (the *gedolim*) and secular heroes. He says that observant Jews acknowledge that great people—for example, the heroes of American history—have faults. These faults can be studied and discussed, he adds, "but we're in much less a position to understand the faults of the *gedolim*. We ascribe a status to the sages which isn't like the authority figures in the secular world." *We* and *they*. It was Rabbi Lifschitz who came to Rebbe Kaplan's class to discuss Kaplan's teaching of the David and Bathsheba story, one which the Rabbi believed came perilously close to treating David like a secular hero.

Popular Culture. "The system," which differentiates between secular and religious heroes, also separates itself from the world of popular culture. In Rebbe Kaplan's words, "We don't reject modernity; we

---

[2] During the summer after our interviews, Rebbe Kaplan left The Torah Institute to become a teacher in a more centrist institution in a larger city.

reject the elements of modernity we consider to be antithetical to *yiddishkeit*." Heilman (1992) cites Rabbi Naftali Zvi Yehuda Berlin (1817–1893), who refused to allow secular learning into the Volozhin yeshivah, even though refusal meant that the yeshivah would be closed by the Russian government. Berlin explained his decision in his will: "[It is] necessary to separate between the sacred and profane, for it is the case that not only do all profane (i.e., secular) matters which become mingled with the sacred not become sanctified, but they also cause the sacred to become profaned" (p. 19). The Torah Institute offers secular learning, but it does not celebrate the world of television or Hollywood. The centrist Orthodox parents who complained about Rebbe Kaplan were worried about what Rabbi Berlin called "mingling."

During my visits to the school, I observe only a few references to popular culture. I notice a board game, designed by several of the students, intended to teach the laws regarding the seven weeks between Passover and Pentecost. It bears the title "Around the Omer in Forty-Nine Days." On my first visit, when a reference to mountain climbing triggers an association, Rebbe Kaplan sings the opening line of "Climb Every Mountain," one of the songs in *The Sound of Music*. As a student ponders a question, he also hums the theme from the television show *Jeopardy*.

I never hear students discussing rock music, television programs, or movies. In fact, Doniel announces proudly, "I don't watch TV and I've never seen a movie in my whole life." Doniel recognizes only 2 of 10 terms on my popular culture test, but other students recognize many more; Netanyah identifies 9 of the 10 terms correctly. The mean score on my measure is 5.25. These students live at the margins of popular culture, but they seal off that world when they enter the yeshivah.

One of the teachers tells me about a campaign that the school attempted, in the face of great resistance from some of the parents, to reward children who refrained from watching television. He is astounded when I remark that nonsectarian schools are also campaigning against television watching. Rabbi Liebowitz tells me he is opposed to television because it is the conduit to the worst in American culture. Television is appealing because it takes no effort, while withstanding the *yetzer hara* (Hebrew: evil impulse) takes work. If the school is to succeed, it must shut out the heroes and role models proffered by television and other mass media.

Who Are the Students' Heroes and Role Models?

For nearly 50 years, psychologists have been studying children's and adolescents' heroes and role models (Duck, 1990; Havighurst & Taba,

1949; Simmons & Wade, 1983; Wechter, 1981). This body of research is sometimes called "ideal person studies" since Havighurst and Taba (1949) asked the respondents to complete the phrase "The person I would like to be like is. . . ." The findings have remained essentially the same throughout the decades. Young people respond by listing parents or parent surrogates; glamorous adults such as athletes, celebrities, and media stars; attractive and successful adults known to the respondents; and composites or abstractions based on a number of people (Havighurst & Taba, 1949; Wechter, 1981). What has changed is the proportion in each category. In comparing 313 children with their counterparts 30 years ago, a pretelevision generation, Duck (1990) finds a larger number of celebrity heroes in the contemporary cohort: "There is a marked shift away from the dominance of parent and parent surrogates as ideals towards the predominance of media figures" (p. 26).

Eight students in Rebbe Kaplan's class participate in a focus group interview during class time. These three girls and five boys were among many volunteers; Kaplan selected them to represent levels of academic attainment, degrees of religious observance, locals and nonlocals, girls and boys. They speak about heroes and role models, about people they admire.

The students of the Springfield Torah Institute overwhelmingly admire their parents. All eight of the focus group members list one or both parents in response to my questions, oral or written. Akivah mentions a parent surrogate, a hockey coach. These students know who their heroes are; the *gedolim* who inspire Rebbe Kaplan inspire his students as well. Their list is studded with religious figures including Moses, Aaron, several Talmudic rabbis, and exegetes. Sharonah remembers the lesson about David and the water. In filling out her questionnaire, she writes that David is a role model for her: "He is brave, selfless, and is very thankful to G-d." (Just as traditional Jews will not pronounce God's name, except in prayer, they will not write it out in full.) In his discussion of moral prototypes, Doniel, the grandson of a *rosh yeshivah* (Hebrew: head of a yeshivah), names as a hero Rav Eliezer Schach, a spokesperson for the ultra-Orthodox community in Israel and the United States. Three students—one boy and two girls—list God as their hero. I am uncertain as to why God is a hero to these young people. They may understand the term *hero*, as the central character in a story, as do some of their peers at the other schools. Certainly God is the central character of the Bible, their primary text.

I am somewhat surprised that the students do not name their teachers as role models. Two mothers whom I interview claim that their daughters admire their teachers enormously, yet their children do not refer to their teachers as exemplars during our discussion or in their questionnaires. These two are among the more centrist Orthodox children whose families are less involved in the life of the school. Perhaps one explanation for the omission on the part of the more traditional, more heavily involved students is that four are rabbis' children; three of the four have parents who teach in the school. Their parents *are* their teachers. These parents go over lessons at home or may teach their own children in formal classes. (In Hebrew, the words for *parent* and *teacher* come from the same root.) Rebbe Kaplan has also warned me that these more traditional students are less admiring than last year's crop.

All of the ideal person studies mention the influence of celebrities or distant adults who appear glamorous or powerful. Ari and Yehudah refer to three sports figures: Roberto Alomar, Mo Vaughn, and Michael Jordan. Skin color or ethnicity is irrelevant to their choices. The boys admire the athletes' grace and skill, and call them "awesome." Two boys include secular heroes, political or military leaders: George Washington, Thomas Jefferson, Abraham Lincoln, and Claire Chenault. These heroes may not have the same cachet as the *gedolim*, but they are heroes nonetheless.

The success of "the system" is apparent. None of the students mentions anyone from the world of entertainment although some surely are familiar with the domain, as evidenced by their responses to my popular culture survey. The girls' lists show less variety than the boys'; this finding seems to corroborate Rebbe Kaplan's observations about the lack of role models for girls. The students' choices are overwhelmingly male. The only women who are included are the students' mothers, which is not a surprising result in an institution in which women rarely figure as authority figures. The students' choices of heroes, role models, and people they admire are shown in Table 3.

Table 3.
Springfield Torah Institute: Students' Exemplars

	Parents	Parent surrogates	Religious figures	God	Athletes	Peers	Political figures
Girls (3)	3 (both)	0	1 (M)	2	0	0	0
Boys (5)	5 (both)	1(M:Coach)	4 (M)	1	2 (M)	1 (M)	2 (M)
Total (8)	8 (both)	1 (Male)	5 (M	3	2 (M)	1 (M)	2 (M)

M = Male

In struggling to define heroes and role models, the students echo their teacher Rebbe Kaplan and the others in "the system." They differentiate between the two terms, and their understanding of the difference is related to distance. Heroes are remote, but role models are close: "someone who gives help and support"; "someone you can relate to and talk to"; "someone you can learn from." Heroes are cultural ideals. A hero is "a Bible figure"; a person "who can teach others"; "spiritually strong"; "close to God." A hero "does great deeds." Ya'akov offers the most concrete definition: "someone who saves your life." Yehudah offers the most sophisticated analysis.

Well, certain types of people from history are like role models. Like from American History, like the people like Thomas Jefferson and George Washington. They're not really role models; they're like heroes in a sense. *But you don't really look up to them for advice to see what they would do but like Moshe (Hebrew: Moses) or something. Even though he's dead, you still like look up to him and like the Rambam, (Maimonides) and like all these other great people* [emphasis added].

Like his teacher, Yehuda defines *gedolim* as both heroes and role models, thereby differentiating them from the heroes of American tradition. Yehudah mentions themes that appear as constants in the discourse about moral prototypes at the Torah Institute: that role models teach behavior and therefore require close scrutiny or observation; the translation of *heroes* to *great ones* or *gedolim*; and the uniqueness of Jewish heroes, teachers, and interpreters of God's revealed word, men who are both heroes and role models.

"Heroes and Role Models of Their Kind"

GEORGE STRATAS, FRANKLIN PIERCE
MIDDLE SCHOOL

George Stratas's Classroom

As I pass the stand of copper beeches that shade the green lawn of Pierce Middle School, I am impressed by the imposing building. A three-story brick edifice with a stone frieze proclaiming "Junior High School," Pierce simultaneously reflects the magnanimity and the parsimony of the Springfield city fathers in early 1929. The structure is massive and occupies a city block; coffers were full before the Great Depression, but not so full as to warrant carving a name permanently into a granite pediment when that name might be changed later. In fact, the school's name has been changed three times. When it was first built in 1929, it was called the Summer Street Junior High School. From 1930 to 1970, it was the Franklin Pierce Junior High School. Since 1970 it has been known as the Franklin Pierce Middle School.

Police cars sit in the back driveway alongside the school tennis courts. A substation is located on the grounds. The police do not patrol the school; they use it as a base from which to answer calls in the neighborhood. Even so, their presence has helped to calm a school that had a reputation for disorder and unrest 10 years ago.

Signs in English, Spanish, Portuguese, and Khmer direct the visitor to the office. I notice a large poster announcing that Pierce has been adopted by the regional telephone company as part of the adopt-a-school program. After signing the office register and obtaining a visitor's badge, I make my way down the wide, spotless hallways to the staircase, up to the third floor and George Stratas's classroom.

I pass a plaque memorializing the members of the Springfield Committee on City Buildings, the men who oversaw the construction of the school. Their uniformly Anglo-Saxon names contrast sharply with the names of the students who now occupy the desks in the spacious classrooms they built almost 70 years ago. Next to the plaque is a mural titled "Yesterday, Today, and Tomorrow." It was designed and executed by students named Shanté, José, Ernestine, Latoya, Tanisha, Leilani, Gina, Miladys, Xiong, and Zurbania. The hallways contain wooden vertical and horizontal display cases that attest to the multicultural nature of the school. One houses a diorama of Native American life. A collage of flags of many nations represents the origins of the school population. In a personal communication, the mayor of Springfield told me that English is the second language for 79% of the children in the schools.

George Stratas's third-floor classroom reflects the cultural diversity heralded on the first floor. Both his seventh grade in 1992–1993 and his eighth grade in 1993–1994 reflect the multiethnic composition of the school census (see Chapter 3, Table 1). The students are African-Americans; Asians, including Cambodians, Vietnamese, and Hmong; Hispanic students from Central and Latin America; and Caucasians of Anglo-Saxon, Jewish, and Italian ancestry. My field notes record the students' hairstyles:

> It is the hairdos that are most striking. The Hispanic girls pull their hair back so tightly it makes their eyes slant. They make a pony tail on top of their head and wrap a bandanna around it. The rest of their hair hangs down on their shoulders. They look like members of a Turkish harem. One of them wore a midriff top, so that she really looks like an odalisque. There are long, shiny, black Asian heads of hair; blonde page boys; brown curly pony tails. Nancy wears corn-rows; one of the boys has dreadlocks. Top-knots are very big with the African-American girls. Several of the boys have wedge cuts. The best "do" is on a Latina. She's got a silver-filigreed snood decorated with colored gemstones over her chignon. There's a huge silver hair pin skewering the chignon. Then she's draped a silver chain several times around the chignon, bringing the remaining chain over her head. She pins it to her scalp with bobby pins. How long did it take her to put it together?

Stratas begins his day with the Pledge of Allegiance. The principal leads the recitation over a scratchy loudspeaker system. All the students stand, turn to the flag, and place their hands over their hearts; most follow along. They do not listen to the rest of the barely audible messages.

Stratas's cavernous, 25 ft by 30 ft room is filled with brightly colored, graffiti-free plastic and wood laminate desks in carefully ordered rows. In the spring there were 30 desks; now, in the fall, there are about 25. (Required to take nine credits in Teaching English as a Second Language over the summer, Stratas returned to his classroom to find that all the ESL students had been pulled out of his heterogeneously grouped classes. As he relates the incident to me, he shrugs at the irony.) The walls are decorated with posters: "Famous African-Americans"; "George Washington"; "Lincoln and the Gettysburg Address"; and "Famous Explorers" (including Sally Ride). A border of explorers crosses a side wall; a frieze of presidents commands attention at the front of the room. Stratas's desk is in the center front. Two large bookcases contain items from his personal collection: a number of volumes on the Civil War, *Global Black Biographies*, picture books (including one on Windsor Castle), magazines, and newspapers.

In September 1993, a pile of textbooks is left in a corner. There aren't enough for each of Stratas's four classes. Even if there were, he tells me he would use the book sparingly. (I saw him use it only once in the course of my seven visits to his classroom.) The text, *Civics for Americans* (Patrick & Remy, 1991), is new and shiny; it has attractive pictures and is attentive to pluralistic concerns. Significant space is given to civil rights; names such as Sanchez, Wong, and Schwartz appear in the homework problems and classroom exercises. Stratas has no quarrel with the text; he objects to the subject. He had been assured that he would teach a second year of American history, not civics. He has decided to weave the two subjects into a combined American history–American government curriculum.

All of the available blackboard space is filled with notes in Stratas's neat handwriting. He expects his students to copy this text, consisting of vocabulary and concepts, into their notebooks. The vocabulary list includes terms and proper nouns pertaining to the topic under consideration. When Stratas reviews the meaning of the vocabulary items, he routinely teaches the etymology of the words, pointing out with ethnic pride the Greek roots of words such as *democracy*, *aristocracy*, and *oligarchy*. He plans his lesson from the notes on the blackboard. Occasionally a student forgets his or her notebook, but that is a rare occurrence. Nearly all of the students dutifully copy the notes from the blackboard into their notebooks.

Class begins with a review of the homework, generally worksheets based on the lesson. On Tuesdays and Thursdays students bring in current events issues, which they must write up and present in class. More often than not, Stratas can use current history to find analogies to what the students are learning in his class. The extent of his pedagogical content knowledge (Shulman, 1987) is apparent even to the most casual visitor. A suggestion to tax weapons and ammunition as a solution to urban violence conjures up the Whiskey Rebellion. Reform in the former Soviet Union recalls the previous week's discussion of the political spectrum. Stratas contrasts the leadership of cult leader David Koresh with that of George Washington. Most of the period is devoted to Stratas's lecture, based on the blackboard notes. He punctuates his remarks with gems of stories and personal examples, strung on what Gudmundsdottir (1991) calls a vertical axis, as he moves up and down the rows.

Stratas is 38 years old, with a boyish face. His preppy clothing—button-down broadcloth shirts and chinos—cannot disguise a bulging midsection. He wears a small gold cross on a chain around his neck. The fact that he is short (about 5'4") and left-handed engenders much good-natured bantering between him and his students. He proclaims James Madison brilliant because that president was both short *and* left-handed.

A history major in college, Stratas had always wanted to teach. When he graduated, he entered the Marines. (Echoes of the former Marine can be heard in his voice on the few occasions when he loses his temper at some student's breach of behavior.) Stratas returned to Springfield after his discharge, hoping that the tight job market would yield up a job in the Springfield public schools. No job materialized, so he joined some of his Greek friends, who were opening a pizza parlor. He worked in the restaurant for five years, saving his money.

Predicting that the large chains would soon threaten his livelihood, Stratas sold his share to his partners and used the proceeds to return to school to earn a master's degree in history. He took education courses in the late afternoons and evenings as he substituted in the Springfield schools. In 1990, when early retirement options freed up a position at Franklin Pierce, Stratas signed on as a teacher and as chair of the social studies department.

Stratas's Definition of Moral Education

Stratas speaks eloquently about what moral education means to him. His definition includes five strands: setting boundaries, practicing the "conscience of craft," encouraging his students to demonstrate the courage of their convictions, exhibiting good citizenship, and transmitting what he calls "core American values."

Setting Boundaries. Stratas is troubled by what he sees as a blurring of moral boundaries. He traces it to the Vietnam era and a breakdown of norms of propriety.

> In the early '60s, when I was in elementary school, right and wrong had clear definitions, both at home and in school. Then when I got to be

around 13 or 14, and even though I was just a kid, I could sense what was happening. I saw a turn towards moral relativism, where all of a sudden things were no longer clearly defined. Right and wrong no longer had the same meaning. What was acceptable became unacceptable and so on. And I saw things like teachers coming to school for the first time with clothes on that I didn't think were appropriate, that I had never seen a teacher wear in the school.

For Stratas, moral propriety has clear demarcations. Without them, young people lose their way. "The whole concept of boundaries, right and wrong, what's acceptable behavior, what's unacceptable behavior—they're kids, they have to be directed."

Conscience of Craft. Closely related to the issue of boundaries is the domain of standards. Standards play a large part in Stratas's views on instruction and moral education; he is uncompromising about what he believes is appropriate. His rich vocabulary and literary references are undiluted, even for a seventh- or eighth-grade audience. During my visits he explains deism, Calvinism, the "cult of personality," charisma, and Machiavellian to his students. He tosses off quotations from the diaries and letters of the Founding Fathers and from *Das Kapital*. He teases out definitions of phrases such as "divide and conquer" and "laissez-faire." Stratas's goal is to send as many of his students as possible to the academic magnet high school, equipped to handle whatever their history teachers might demand of them. For this reason he assigns a research paper that requires footnotes and a bibliography. Several times he repeats his credo: "I send you to the ninth grade prepared or not at all."

Stratas expects his students to work hard and to assume responsibility for the caliber of their schoolwork. He urges them to set high standards for themselves: "You know what responsibility means. You're 13, 14 years old. I was 14 once. I had to do homework. You set low standards for yourself, you get low results." He sneers at what he calls the "self-esteem movement." In his view, there can be no self-esteem without standards: "Now esteem comes from accomplishment. Right? Working hard, getting that A, and then sitting back for that one moment and saying, 'I did it. I did this. I'm proud of myself.' "

Demonstrating the Courage of Convictions. The importance of moral courage plays a large part in Stratas's definition of moral education. He wants his students to know that sometimes they have to do what's right, no matter what the personal cost. He garnishes his classroom discourse with examples of people who have or have not taken a moral stand. In discussing the Founding Fathers, who ducked the issue of slavery at the Constitutional Convention, Stratas comments:

You can't say one thing and do another. That's hypocrisy. They were hypocrites. Thomas Jefferson owned slaves. He lacked the courage of conviction.

Good Citizenship. A fourth element in Stratas's definition is the goal of citizenship in Durkheim's sense. This is the rationale for his attention to current events. He tells all four of his social studies classes about the abysmally ignorant adults who were interviewed about NAFTA by a television news reporter, and he commends them for knowing significantly more than the man or woman in the street:

> I stress citizenship all the time. I say even if you don't like listening to this in terms of theory, you're going to be taxed some day. You're going to get a paycheck and you're going to flip it over, and you're going to see what Uncle Sam takes out of you. It's in your interest to be aware of what the issues are and what the government wants to raise money for and what they want to spend money on. There's no magic box in Washington, DC, that contains cash that they can continually dip their hands into and take out. *Of course, you have to be an informed, responsible citizen* [emphasis added]. You have rights and responsibilities and duties that go along with them. You know, democracy's not easy. You could always have somebody tell you what to do, but when you reach adulthood you're expected to be a participatory citizen, and I stress that all the time.

Stratas worries about the decline of a country that ignores civic education. He believes that moral education is in part a cognitive process whereby people can be taught to know the good.

> There's no civic education involved with people anymore, whether it's on juries, or to be an informed citizen to make decisions that have to do with taxation, budgets, or anything like that. They just go on whatever instinct or whatever propaganda is first spilled out at them. There's no thoughtful analysis of anything that takes place, and that's a real shame because that lack of civic education is going to hurt this nation severely in the future.

Core American Values. Moral education means the transmission of a set of values that undergird American society. To George Stratas, being an American means accepting the central values of a democracy:

> What I do think Americans share or should share is a common set of values that make us Americans: belief in political liberty; democratic decision making based on majority rule; most importantly, the concept of equal opportunity which doesn't exist anywhere else in the world to any

great degree—respect for minority rights; the rule of law. You know, this may sound like a recitation from a civics book, but I really think that those are the core values that unite us as a people.

Stratas is outraged at the reporting of Ted Kennedy Jr.'s wedding, one of the current events chosen by the students to discuss: "I'm bothered by that expression, 'America's royalty.' I don't like hearing that applied to American society." Stratas emphasizes the fluidity of American society and lauds the openness of a meritocracy; both militate against a monarchic form of government.

Some of the core values to which Stratas returns repeatedly in his teaching are belief in process, patriotism, opportunity, perseverance, and pluralism. Regarding process, he jokes, "We solve problems with money; other societies solve them with pain." He shares with his students his amazement at the brilliance of the Constitution and its ability to create a workable system of government.

Stratas is an unabashed patriot and shares his pride with his students, most of whom were born elsewhere.

If you come from somewhere else in this world and you've seen the problems and the human degradation and everything else that we associate with other parts of the world. . . . What we have here in America is by far and away the greatest nation in the history of the world. Period.

Interviewer: You're still a believer in the American dream.

Stratas: Completely.

America is a great country because it is still the land of opportunity. Stratas tells his classes about Bill Clinton, a poor boy from a tiny town in Arkansas. How did he get to Georgetown, Yale, and Oxford? ("Good schools. Some of the best in the world.") He writes a formula on the blackboard. "See if you agree. I was taught this when I was young." The students listen as they watch the chalk move on the board: Success = preparation + opportunity. Stratas looks at what he has written and nods. "I really think that this is a good formula."

Stratas preaches the message that hard work pays off. The day before the deficiency reports are due to be given out, he exhorts his students:

I'm seeing a lot of things I don't like. Tell me if this isn't the truth: I see lazy summer habits. You don't do the work so you get a deficiency. You get into trouble at home, so you run to get good grades in November. Then you go into a two-quarter swoon; you fall down in the second and third quarters. You run in the fourth quarter to pass. Don't get trapped in it. At the end of the year, I become an accountant. I add up the zeroes.

Stratas has made the criteria for success clear in his class. Students need to keep their notebooks up to date, review them nightly, and do their homework. Perseverance will produce rewards.

The grandson of Greek immigrants, Stratas grew up in the Greek Orthodox Church, where he served as an altar boy. He has not forgotten his roots.

> I heard all the stories from my mother growing up in Boston. She was the daughter of two very poor immigrants growing up in the West End. After my grandfather died, my grandmother said about having Social Security, "God bless the United States of America."

Immigration and pluralism are threads that run through the fabric of his teaching: "Every one of us comes from somewhere else." He tells his students about Irving Berlin:

> When people asked him, "Do you remember anything of the old country?" he said, "I remember being outdoors in the woods, hiding while the Russians burned our house down." He wrote "God Bless America" and said, "I believe every word of it." He was still hated because of his religion. Being a nation of immigrants doesn't make us immune.

I ask Stratas how teaching in a multicultural school has shaped his notion of moral education, particularly his concern for the core American value of pluralism. He responds:

> I think it plays a big role. You have to show sensitivity to the diversity that you have around you. You may see kids grouped almost by their neighborhood associations, but I say all the time to kids, "I can't make you friends with each other—people from different races or backgrounds or whatever, I can't do that. You pick your own friends. . . . But what I can insist upon in the classroom is that everyone respects everyone else, that everyone is cooperative with everyone else, and at least on the surface, everyone is friendly with everyone else."

The notion that there is a conflict between the celebration of pluralism and the transmission of core American values is foreign to Stratas. In his mind, respect for ethnic diversity is in itself a core American value:

> The fact that somebody's Italian-American or Irish-American, African-American, Latino, whatever. . . . We all have our home culture that

revolves around things at home, whether it has to do with the ethnic festivals that we attend, the ethnic foods that we eat, the church associations, all of those things. That's part of the tapestry that makes America, what makes us strong. . . . They in no way contradict the civic values, with what it takes to be an American.

Stratas is aware that multiculturalism can be abused. He worries about balkanization:

If I were just going to teach ethnic studies and "What did my group do?" history, then I run into a real problem with it. I don't want to have Italian-Americans say, "Well what did my people do?" and then have African-Americans come and tell me, "Well what about us?" and Hispanic-Americans, "What about us?" and Irish-Americans, and so on. I don't really want it to be broken down to that. There's enough of Yugoslavia around.

In his study of a multicultural high school, Peshkin (1991) ponders the tension between ethnic maintenance and "the historic Americanizing mission of our schools" (pp. 6–7). Stratas's approach, emphasizing nationalism and celebrating pluralism (both of which are core values), eliminates this tension.

The diversity of the Franklin Pierce student population finds its analogue in Stratas's many-faceted definition of moral education. It is strikingly more textured than the definition of Rebbe Tuvia Kaplan, who teaches in a far more homogeneous school. Kaplan relies on Jewish texts to provide a foundation for the moral education he hopes to convey in his classroom. Stratas's texts are fewer, less comprehensive, and less authoritative. Although the Constitution can be used to support his views of citizenship and core values, and the Declaration of Independence as an example of standing up for one's beliefs, these texts cannot possibly engender the same reverence or obligation created by the Bible and Talmud in Kaplan's community.

Who Is a Hero?

For Stratas, as for Kaplan, the hero serves an important structural role for a given culture. Stratas defines the hero in functional, Durkheimian terms: "At best a hero shows us in some very tangible ways the principles that we all claim to believe in." The notions of moral courage, standards, and boundaries, which play a significant part in Stratas's definition of moral education, also inform his understanding of the hero.

A hero is a person who could be very ordinary in many circumstances and in a moment's notice, whether a crisis or something out of the ordinary where everyone else cowers, *that person steps forward, steps out of the anonymous crowd, and says, "No more, enough," and puts his life or his reputation or her reputation on the line to stand up for principles that transcend us all.* Someone like Martin Luther King, because I think he may be, with Franklin Delano Roosevelt, the greatest man of the 20th century. The idea of adopting the principles of nonviolence of Gandhi and shaming American society into doing what was right, the risks he took in the south were absolutely enormous. . . . *These are the people who step outside the bonds of normal society, where it's nice and cozy, and do things that change the world* [emphasis added].

Heroes represent ideals, but because heroes are human beings they are invariably flawed. Stratas's classes hear about the homogeneity of the white, conservative, landholding men who met to reform the Articles of Confederation. In discussing the secrecy rule passed during the Constitutional Convention, Stratas engages in a guided inquiry with his students as to why it was necessary:

These guys were away from their wives and families. They stayed in hotels. At night they went to taverns. They might be a jerk, have too much to drink with the press around. They might say something they shouldn't have. Also, this gave them the freedom to change their minds without looking like a fool.

In some sections of this class, Stratas says, "They're away from their wives, kids. They're in the largest, most cosmopolitan city in the United States. What are they going to do?" The students respond animatedly, shouting out answers. "Party." "Drink." "Womanize."

This is a rich unit for my analysis. Stratas uses the Founding Fathers to remind his students that when people drink, they can become indiscreet, and that's stupid. But he's also saying that the Founding Fathers, American heroes, were capable of doing stupid things. They had flaws. By pointing out the flaws, Stratas titillates the students, playing up to their interest in the indiscreet, hoping to engage them in American history.

Stratas is unequivocal on the issue of slavery. On numerous occasions he points out that the Founding Fathers were slaveholders. In discussing the "three-fifths compromise," he accuses the Constitutional Convention of copping out: Slavery was a "hot potato," so they avoided dealing with it, thus making the Civil War inevitable. Stratus said, "What did they do, these giants of American history? They decided, 'Let's not use the word *slaves*. We'll call them persons.' They wanted to look good for posterity."

The central fact of slavery becomes the prism through which Stratas views American history. The narrative of slavery and the extension of civil rights to African-Americans serve as the curriculum structure, the horizontal axis (Gudmundsdottir, 1991) for his course. It is his way of crafting a story that will engage those students who are most at risk.

If Stratas is harsh toward the Founding Fathers, he is no less forgiving of the Abolitionists' hypocrisy. He tells his classes that many of the leading spokespersons for abolition of slavery never believed that African-Americans would be absorbed into the United States. Turning to a student from Liberia for confirmation, Stratas tells the class that some abolitionists collected money to transport freed slaves to Africa. He informs them that at one time even Lincoln favored expatriation.

When I ask Stratas whether he thinks showing American heroes with all their warts will weaken his students' attachments to the core values these men embody, he answers:

> No, I don't, because at the same time I'm talking about the genius of the Founding Fathers with the document that they developed. The Constitution is clearly the greatest plan of government that was ever developed. It's the oldest written constitution in the world and it's served the country very well for over 200 years. What they did in Philadelphia was sheer genius by anyone's estimation. Because there were serious flaws in it doesn't make the document any less great—or the Founding Fathers, for that matter. Too often we carve these men out of stone and put them up there like they're monuments. They're great people, but they have real flesh and blood and were moved by political, economic issues just like anyone else.

Like Kaplan, Stratas wrestles with the issue of the icon and the human being. He too is looking for his version of "the *emes*," the truth. He muses about revisionism and relativism, whether it is fair to hold heroes up to absolute standards or to view them as products of their time.

> Sometimes I don't know quite how to approach it. I've read historians that'll turn around and say well, you can't judge people who lived 200 years ago by our standards. But at the same time you have to say those were people with the same emotional responses and intelligence levels that we have today, and in some sense, maybe we're making excuses for them.

Stratas has no difficulty in enumerating his personal heroes. He votes for Christopher Columbus, acknowledging that such a choice is "almost politically incorrect nowadays." His list is multicultural:

I'm impressed with Thomas Jefferson. I'm impressed with Andrew Jackson; Frederick Douglass. I'm impressed with Abraham Lincoln. I'm impressed with even some of the things I hear in black separatist movements. I'm impressed with some of the things Marcus Garvey said. I'm impressed with Woodrow Wilson, and most importantly, above and beyond, I'm impressed with Franklin Delano Roosevelt.

On at least two of my visits, he refers to George Washington's giving up the opportunity to become president for life: "He was a hero. What made him great? He could have been emperor for life. He walked away from the presidency." Another hero held up by Stratas in his teaching is Paul Cuffe, an African-American shipbuilder who refused to pay his taxes when he discovered that he was being taxed at a higher rate than his white neighbors. Stratas mentions Nelson Mandela as well.

Stratas's contemporary hero is Pope John Paul II. His reasons for this choice are consistent with his definitions of moral education. His analysis touches on moral courage, principles, and unwavering standards:

I think in a world that's battered by moral relativism that he's very uncompromising. The news media portrays it in a very negative light. If you're really the principal person standing for your religious faith, a faith that's timeless, a faith that sees itself in absolutes where *standards* cannot be bent under any circumstance, and it's not a question of what the latest trend is or what the latest social revolution is taking place. The news media calls him narrow-minded and traditionalist, old-fashioned. *I think he's principled, and I think he probably stands for something.* He sees his office, the papacy, as something much higher than any social trend going on in the world or in any particular nation [emphasis added].

Who Is a Role Model?

Stratas's definition, like Kaplan's, is shaped by the ethos of his school. Kaplan looks to role models as exemplars of *halakhah*, Jewish law (literally, *the way*). Stratas too singles out those individuals who represent the proper path:

A role model is just a good representative for young people to look at. Now, not everybody's going to be rich and famous, which is what I always tell the kids when they use sports figures as role models. Take a look at the world around you. We've got people, we've got parents who I think are really good role models. Some of the parents that I've met, getting up every day, doing what you have to do in life, going to work, providing for your family, taking responsibility for the things in life that are important to you. . . . There was once a time in the United States of America where questions like this would have been self-evident to people, but not anymore.

Stratas describes role models using themes that resonate throughout his discourse, both with me and with his students: opportunities, achievement, perseverance, and responsibility. His father was such a role model. A railroad worker, he offered the example of doing one's best. Stratas attributes the value he places on integrity, what I have referred to above as the "conscience of craft," to lessons he learned from his father:

My father's a very hard-working guy . . . a very serious guy when it comes to work. You get up early, you do your best, you turn an honest spade, and nobody can criticize you. . . . When you go home, you collect your check, you don't feel that you cheated anyone out of anything.

According to Stratas, role models serve a function other than making values concrete. They also allow the observer glimpses of other worlds,

to show young people that here's someone like you, who started off like you in life, didn't have the advantages that you have. They've stretched beyond their neighborhood, beyond what the narrow confines of their world [were] when they were younger. . . . They've broadened their horizons —that they can see the world in far different ways. . . . [Role models] are right up there showing you that you can reach out and obtain these things, that you're not limited to where you are right now.

Stratas had several such role models who interested him in the life of the mind and in teaching. One was a high school teacher whom he calls "a really good guy"—he was not a great teacher, but somehow he captured Stratas's imagination: "I remember him covering the American Revolution, and almost to this day it's why I spend a lot of time on the American Revolution 'cause I remember what he did. He just made it fascinating for me."

Another teacher, a college professor, opened up the world of historical thinking for Stratas. Like Kaplan's *rebbe* who served as a window to another world, this professor helped Stratas discover historiography and the process of history:

I had another guy in college who I thought trained my mind in a historical way. Up until then I was recording facts—names and dates and stuff—and I didn't really stop to do anything that was interpretive in history. This guy focused me and really started to give me the ability to reason critically.

Stratas tries consciously to present role models to his students, and he selects stories to make his point. African-American role models who achieve in arenas other than sports and entertainment are prominent in these efforts. Stratas chats with his classes: "Who is someone you admire?" he inquires. The students toss out responses: their parents, Martin Luther King, Malcolm X, relatives, movie and television stars, teachers. He tells one class that when he asked the question of a group the day before, a number of students named Shaquille O'Neal and Michael Jordan. Writing their names on the blackboard, Stratas adds LeVar Burton. "Anybody know who he is?" There is muttering in the back. One student suggests *Reading Rainbow*; another, *Star Trek: The Next Generation*; a third, *Roots*. Stratas acknowledges their responses; my field notes capture his remarks:

> He was a big star, an overnight sensation. He could have screwed up, done drugs, "gone Hollywood." He was just a freshman at UCLA when he got the part of Kunta Kinte in *Roots*. He could have spent all his money, [but] he went back to UCLA to finish up. Why does he do *Reading Rainbow*? He studied education and the media. He never forgot about it. He's not like a basketball star who shows up at a community center, dribbles a ball, and walks away. Shaquille O'Neal and Michael Jordan are college dropouts. You see them everywhere, selling sneakers. Not LeVar Burton. His face isn't on a Wheaties box. What message is being sent? We value athletes. Jordan has a reputation for gambling, for being connected to the Mafia, but his picture is on a Wheaties box.

I ask Stratas about this exchange. He worries that the students have unrealistic expectations. Many of the boys who have even a modicum of athletic ability expect to become professional athletes; school is unimportant to them. Stratas tells them that these hopes are foolish and reminds them that the competition will be keener as they get to high school and college. Warning them that even becoming an All-American in college is no guarantee of a successful professional career, he drops names of once-famous athletes who are now using drugs or have been convicted of breaking and entering. Stratas urges them to remember that educational achievement, not athletic ability, is the ladder to success.

A look at the eighth-grade yearbook seems to confirm Stratas's fears. The yearbook, *Triton*, includes pictures of the students and their career choices. At least one-third of the boys want to be athletes—to play soccer, basketball, baseball, or football. Many of the girls want to be singers or actresses. A number of them mix their celebrity fantasies with aspirations for careers that require schooling, and come up with bizarre combinations such as pediatrician and actress; nurse or model or lawyer; atomic physicist or pianist. At Pierce, many students aspire to lives of glamor and celebrity, as the "ideal person" studies suggest (Duck, 1990; Havighurst & Taba, 1949; Wechter, 1981). Unlike the respondents to the Balswick and Ingoldsby (1982) study, however, these girls envision themselves as celebrities, not as celebrities' girlfriends. Perhaps the passage of more than a decade has changed the fantasies of teenage girls.

The week when Michael Jordan retired and Toni Morrison won the Nobel Prize provided Stratas with a "teachable moment" for current events time. My field notes record the following:

Stratas writes "Toni Morrison" on the blackboard. He asks if anyone knows the name. A student muses, "Did he do something wrong?" Stratas: "No. *She* did something right." He tells them Morrison won the Nobel Prize for Literature. "Some of you people were bothered last week by Michael Jordan's retirement, bothered and pained to no end. Eleven Americans have won the Nobel Prize. She was the first African-American. This is a great achievement for Americans, and African-Americans in particular. The same week as Michael Jordan's retirement and you haven't paid attention to it. There isn't enough attention to academics. There's too much attention paid to sports, to entertainment. Too much attention paid to nonsense. Not enough to what is really important."

Michael Jordan figures in any number of exchanges I had with Stratas. One of his former students was chosen as a scholar-athlete and went to Washington with the other winners.

This kid had the opportunity to jog on the south lawn with the President, had the opportunity to go into the Oval Office. I saw him. I said, "Wasn't that a thrill to have done that?" "Ah, it was okay," he says to me. "I would have rather met Michael Jordan."

Stratas is enraged.

Another class gets the Toni Morrison lecture. He addresses Mark, a tall, athletic African-American who is bright but lazy:

Mark, you were upset about Michael Jordan retiring. If I were to say, "Who was the most important person in the news last week, what would you say?" "Michael Jordan." Well, I beg to differ with you. I'd say, "Toni Morrison." The kids are quiet. She got knocked off the front page by

Michael Jordan. We have plenty of athletes, singers, dancers, people who tell jokes. It's not every day that we get a Nobel Prize winner. It tells you about society's priorities. Just 'cause a guy can dunk is he more important than a Nobel Prize winner? There are all kinds of ways to achieve in this life. It's too bad when someone of the caliber of Toni Morrison gets pushed off the front page. Knocked off by someone who sells Nikes.

In her essay, "Wide-Awakeness and the Moral Life," Greene (1978) limns a portrait of moral reform that begins with engagement. Stratas, the moral educator, functions as an alarm clock, awakening his students to the existence of healthier role models. He exhorts them more than the religious educator, Tuvia Kaplan.

Stratas self-consciously and selectively models for his students. In discussing his views on standards, he reflects, "If you set that example, then you can expect them to show that example." When I ask him about his being a role model, he replies,

They know I won't steer them wrong. They know I won't tell them something that isn't for their own good, and that may sound like a parental lecture , but I think they do sense that. I had one of the kids the other day and she said I'm always in her business. She writes on the pad up here, "You think you're everybody's father or something." I said, "When your parents aren't around, and you're with me, you are my business." And I said, "That doesn't just go for the classroom. If I were to see you outside somewhere and there was no adult supervision around, and you were doing something that you shouldn't be doing or with people that you shouldn't be with, or any kind of environment that I didn't think was good for you, you are my business."

Stratas makes a point of letting students see him with a wad of currency with which he buys raffle tickets and tickets for school dances, ostentatiously peeling bills from what students call his "nut." Several students comment to me and to each other about how much money Stratas has. I ask him about this little drama. He tells me it is a way for street kids to respect teachers, to learn that money can be made honestly.

David Stewart, Stratas's former principal, corroborates that Stratas is a powerful role model for his students. Stewart mentions a strange outbreak of bow ties on Stratas's students. "They see him coming to school—he'll wear a certain outfit. They love his bow tie. When he wears a bow tie, they kid him to death. They think he's a wonderful person."

Students hang around his desk before school and before classes. One girl signs her name—in Greek letters—next to Stratas's ubiquitous notes. She is not Greek; she has learned the Greek alphabet to please him. The African-American and Hispanic girls hover around him whenever they get the opportunity. They tease him about the gold cross he wears. "Did your girlfriend get it for you?"

In our focus group interview, Lucy, a Hispanic student and one of the hangers-on, calls Stratas a role model.

> *Lucy:* I always talk to him. I could tell him anything and he won't tell nobody. I wouldn't tell him real personal stuff, but I tell him other things. I just admire him a lot.

> *Interviewer:* Why do you admire him? Because he can maintain a confidence?

> *Lucy:* He understands you, and he's not like other teachers who try to teach, and they just can't because the students are being too loud. . . . He can control the students and be nice at the same time. He don't have to yell and stuff.

I ask Stratas about the theory that people learn best from someone like themselves, that role models should resemble the learners in gender, ethnicity, and race. Stratas is incensed; unlike Kaplan, he thinks he can be a role model for all of his students:

> Emphatically no. I don't buy into that at all. I can be white and a male and be sensitive to the needs of students of various backgrounds. To imply that I can't be is to say something awful about us all in the final analysis. Role models can come in any shape and size.

Stratas then tells of his own high school experience, when "a young, fresh-out-of-college" African-American teacher who filled in for his white teacher helped him fathom the mysteries of geometry. "He'd go down to the gym and play ball with us, and you couldn't ask for a better role model at the time."

Cultural Context

When Tuvia Kaplan refers to "the system," he means the religious, cultural, and moral expectations of the yeshivah. When Stratas refers to "the system," he means the Springfield School Department—what the cognoscenti call "downtown." Except for a rare visit from a supervisor, the system leaves him alone. "I can't imagine anyone coming in here or commenting to me, or making any kind of statement of any kind of encouragement or anything. It's a thankless job."

Unlike the Torah Institute, an independent institution with only voluntary ties to a wider network of Orthodox schools, Pierce is a piece in a bureaucratic puzzle. The bureaucracy often complicates and confounds, as when it first insisted on ESL certification and then removed Stratas's opportunity to implement what he had learned. The best one can expect from a bureaucracy is to be left alone. At Franklin Pierce, as at the other public schools in Springfield, the teacher, no matter how talented, receives little support from the system. If he or she is fortunate, that support will come from administrators and other teachers.

The Administration. David Stewart used to compliment Stratas on the good things he heard from his students' parents. Stewart's views on moral education include many of the themes articulated by Stratas. He too believes in the transmission of what Stratas calls "core values": "When I hear it, what it calls to mind is traditions, a moral tradition that might be carried on from generation to generation within a country."

Stewart convened a group of teachers to draft a mission statement for the school. It includes many of the elements of Stratas's definition of moral education: "a core academic program with multicultural emphasis," "internal motivation," and "thinking skills." It also professes a concern for self-esteem (a term that triggers Stratas's disdain) and "social responsibility and community service." Although Stratas never mentions these aspects of moral education, I notice that his students collect for UNICEF and jump rope for the Heart Fund.

Like Dean Cahn at the Torah Institute, Stewart points out that the appearance of the building communicates these values. I tell him how impressed I am by the neatness of the building. (During my six weeks in the school, I see only one example of graffiti. The salmon-colored cinderblock walls of the girls' restroom announce that Sabrina and Little B have preceded me.) Stewart observes:

> People comment about how nice this school is, how beautiful it is, what wonderful children, what a wonderful school this middle school is. You keep sending this message out to the children. It's not saying we don't like graffiti, but by eliminating the graffiti and finding out how beautiful everything is, we're sending that message. It's an indirect message, and it's the message we send about discipline.

As Dean Cahn says, "The walls are *rebbeyim*" (Yiddish: mentors).

Stratas is reserving judgment on Stewart's successor. He worked with Stewart in other schools while serving as an itinerant substitute, but he barely knows the new man. He has yet to be visited by him.

I ask what Studs Terkel calls "the impertinent question": If the administration offers no support for his endeavors, aren't they part of the problem? Stratas sighs audibly.

I don't know how far I'd be willing to push it. When Dave Stewart was here, for instance, he had an open door policy with me. If I wanted to go down there and talk to him about anything, I could. Very friendly, very cooperative. The assistant principal's around. . . . Their hands are tied by a lot of things. They can't send too many people down to student relations because then it looks bad that he doesn't have control over the building. What if the number of kids for suspension has too many kids of minority groups as opposed to white? What kind of perception is that going to send? There are so many factors that filter into what they're doing, that I understand their viewpoint. They're looking for a promotion too.

No principal at Pierce can screen prospective faculty members as does Dean Cahn. They are hired "downtown" by the system and are placed in schools where there are openings.

Other Teachers. I ask Stratas if his commitment to moral education makes him an oddity on the faculty. He denies it, yet often he alludes to differences between himself and some of his colleagues, between his expectations and theirs. Although he and Stewart had planned on these students being under his tutelage for two years, Stratas has inherited students who were taught seventh-grade American history by other teachers. He admits, "They've got to get used to a higher standard. Some of them aren't used to me." His students are well-behaved; others are not. Stratas comments on school discipline:

I think when a lot of teachers complain about problems in their classrooms, some of it is due to their own lack of standards and the kids feed off of that and become lazy, become disruptive, and it leads to all kinds of problems that snowball one on top of the other.

Stratas is one of a team of four teachers situated in one corner of the third floor. He and the science teacher have the reputation of being among the most demanding in the school. Without maligning his other colleagues directly, Stratas separates himself and his team from them.

They know that up here at least, in this corner of the building, that there is a watchful eye—teaming and breaking the school down into smaller units. I fully agree with that idea. It's a more manageable community, and that's what we're trying to achieve. As a result, the kids behave much better here than I think they do in other parts of the building. In fact, I'm sure of that 'cause I've caught their act in other places.

His words sound like Kaplan's "we" and "they," but Stratas, unlike Kaplan, is not referring to the community outside the brick walls of his institution when he says "they."

Parents. Parents are pleased by Stratas's efforts. All three of the parents I speak to mention him by name as a teacher who makes a difference in their children's lives. Ms. Dekoe, an émigrée from Ghana, names Stratas as a role model for her daughter, Hannah: "He plays with them. He teaches them. The kids aren't scared of him like I was of my teachers." Paul Goldberg, Renée's father, agrees. "Renée is looking for someone to emulate." Stratas, along with two women teachers, is that someone. Arlene Short, Arletta's mother, appreciates Stratas's efforts to add achieving African-Americans to the American history curriculum: "Being African-American, she needs to see heroes and role models of her kind. She needs to look at where they've come from and where they've gone."

All three parents discuss moral prototypes in their children's schooling in subjective terms: how these exemplars will help their children "grow in the right direction," in Ms. Dekoe's words. Of the three parents, only Ms. Short uses the term *hero*.

Popular Culture. George Stratas, his students, and the members of the Franklin Pierce community live in popular culture. Unlike Rebbe Kaplan's classroom or school, from which television, rock music, and movies are shut out, or where they are certainly unwelcome guests, this urban school is suffused with popular culture. T-shirts proclaim allegiance to athletic teams, rock bands, and television celebrities. One student, bored, occasionally beats his fingers on the desk to the rhythm of a rap song. Referring to Malcolm X, Stratas asks his students how many of them saw the movie about his life. He urges them to see *Gettysburg* and reminds them that they will see *Glory* before the end of the year.

References to television are everywhere. A cluster of students discuss what happened on *I'll Fly Away* the night before. In describing the Constitutional Convention's secrecy rule, Stratas compares it to the oath taken by a group of aliens on *Star Trek*. He depends on television news to prepare for his classes on current events.

I watch a lot of television, but I watch a lot of documentaries. I watch a lot of government access like C-SPAN, so I watch a lot of government debates. I watch what goes on in the House and the Senate, and because I watch it so much, it's almost like *Inside Baseball*. I try to integrate that into issues when we talk about current events.

For Stratas, television is a teaching tool. He expects his students to watch television to keep posted on current events as well. "Anyone see what happened in Somalia? In Russia?"

When I ask him to comment on the negative aspects of television, he answers,

> What they watch at home, what their parents allow them to watch at home. They go home; what's on television? Soap operas, which [are] nothing but sex; talk shows like *Oprah*, *Phil Donahue*, and all of that, which focuses on sex and all sorts of deviations; and MTV. That's what they go home [to] and they're tuned to: gossip, soap operas, and bad role models on a music video show. I know I sound like an old fogey, but I look at these videos and I look at these messages that are coming out of [them], whether it's heavy metal from white kids or that gangsta rap that a lot of kids listen to. There's nothing redeeming about it.

The sexuality on television worries Stratas. So does the violence. He fears that his students have become desensitized to violence because of the massive doses they see on their television sets and in the movies. Referring to a recent killing in a school 20 miles away, Stratas broods. He addresses his students:

> Our values are mixed up. Bush brings in Arnold Schwarzenegger on the campaign trail. You have to stay in shape. Fitness. You're supposed to admire him, but the next time you see him, he's killing everybody in sight in the movies. He's the Terminator. . . . And people ask why kids in Danfield shot their friends. The violence in our schools is because people can't tell the difference between real and make-believe.

The students are very quiet.

At the Springfield Torah Institute, movies, television, and rock music are kept separate from the life of the school. Not so at Franklin Pierce. Stratas's relationship with popular culture is far more complex than Kaplan's. Homeopathic doses can help to cure classroom ills; television, for example, can bring world news to the homes of both teacher and students. But the very medium that can educate can also poison.

The violence on television has seeped into the walls of the Franklin Pierce School.[1] Arletta expects mothers to watch over their children. "You ignore children and let them do what they want and get into drugs and guns. Then you're going to a funeral two years

---

[1] I interviewed the students at Pierce in October 1993. In February 1994 Mark's brother was killed in a shootout with the police that resulted in two deaths.

after they turn fourteen because they got shot over something stupid." The school handbook lists felonies that can result in expulsion: physical assault on a teacher or staff member; possession of weapons; extortion; possession of drugs; possession of alcohol; arson; inciting to riot.

The atmosphere in the school cafeteria resembles the prison culture described by Foucault (1977): enclosed, hierarchic, anonymous. It is a grim hall on the basement level, with teachers (guards) patroling the rows of identical tables. At a signal from one of the teachers, students are allowed to approach the line of steam tables, where they can take a tray and receive uniform portions of uniformly beige food (hamburgers, applesauce, overcooked green beans). Some show identity cards that exempt them from paying; 61% of the students receive free lunches, having met the federal and state guidelines for such assistance. "We" and "they"—The tamers and those who must be tamed, or (in Foucault's idiom) disciplined and punished.

Discipline and punishment do not extend to infractions of language. Violence shapes the vocabulary at many of the tables in the cafeteria. A tiny special education student watches a group approach the steam tables for seconds. "Greedy bastards," he comments to me. The boys swagger behind a language of violence and misogyny: "Go fuck your mother, the fucking bitch." "Give me my fucking bag, you fucking bitch." I notice the student in Stratas's class who had rapped through the current events discussion. He randomly repeats a mantra of the streets: "Your mother's on crack; fuck your mother; fuck your sister." No one seems terribly surprised. No teacher intervenes.

I revisit Stratas's classroom after lunch. One of the students grumbles about an assignment, saying it was "a hell of a lot of work." Seeing me, he quickly apologizes and changes his phrase to "heck of a lot of work." I acknowledge his apology and tell him I've heard worse, having just returned from the cafeteria. Overhearing our exchange, another student says, "I bet you heard a lot of f-words."

Noddings (1992) describes the school cafeteria as a moral desert:

> Looking seriously at the school day from the perspective of caring, we see that lunchtime is usually an educational dead spot. Teachers (except those on lunchroom duty) take a break from students, and students all too often take a break from everything civilized. (p. 65)

The Pierce cafeteria represents a departure from the oasis of Stratas's classroom, with its Greek roots, literary allusions, and college preparatory notes.

Who are the Students' Heroes and Role Models?

Eight of Stratas's students participate in a focus group interview about moral prototypes. They are two boys and six girls: three whites, three African-Americans, and two Hispanic students. Besides differing in race and ethnicity, they differ in socioeconomic class, academic achievement, and parents' involvement in the life of the school.

Some of the students are uncomfortable with the idea of the hero and define the hero in the most concrete terms. Mark snorts, "A hero is a cartoon. I can't respect a cartoon." For Donald, the son of a university professor, a hero is fictional, the main character in a work of literature, "like Moby Dick." Lucy agrees: "Heroes are make-believe."

Some students, slightly more abstract in their thinking, believe that a hero must possess physical courage. Hannah claims that a hero is "a person who saved a life." Martina agrees: "A person who saves you from some worse fate."

Sounding like their teacher, Anna and Arletta are the most sophisticated members of the group. They require that a hero demonstrate moral courage, and they repeat the story of George Washington's ability to walk away from power. Their definitions revolve around phrases such as "make a change in the country" or "stand up for the country when needed." Arletta produces the most elevated definition: "A hero is someone who does great things which help others, has special abilities, and is a special person."

At the beginning of the interview, not one student claims to have a hero. By the end, however, Renée has reconsidered. She decides that a classmate whose mother recently died of cancer is a hero: "Loretta was so strong all through school. She went to school all the time and she really dealt with it well, I think. It was amazing how well she handled it." Unlike the students of the Torah Institute, seven of whom have heroes, only one of the students at Pierce has a hero. The classical hero, the distant, nearly immortal personification of virtue, has no place in these students' lives.

Like the students at the Torah Institute, the Pierce students overwhelmingly admire parents and parent surrogates. Because four of these students come from single-parent households headed by women, mothers are named far more often than fathers. An aunt who has earned a law degree and has received many offers from prestigious firms ranks high on Arletta's list. Arletta, an African-American honor roll student, wants to be a lawyer like her relative.

People who show determination and optimism in the face of adversity are admirable to this group of students. Anna includes a multiple category, women athletes, on her list. She chooses them because "they struggle against the odds, really earning what they get." Her choice adds credence to a recent press release distributed by the National Coalition of Girls' Schools on the importance of female athletes as role models for young women. This choice is significant for another reason. Anna is beginning to select qualities from several individuals to create her vision of an admirable person. Havighurst and Taba (1949) and Wechter (1981) note that the creation of composite moral models is the most sophisticated level of adolescent thinking regarding ego ideals.

Anna's women athletes and the mention of so many admirable mothers add a female cast to the Pierce list, in striking contrast to the male-dominated list at the Torah Institute. Glamorous figures from the world of entertainment, absent from the Torah Institute list, appear as role models at Pierce. African-American students choose African-American entertainers such as Martin Lawrence and Janet Jackson. Athletes appear on both schools' lists, with the significant addition of Anna's women athletes. The Pierce students' choices are shown in Table 4.

The Pierce students' moral prototypes reflect their surroundings. Unlike the Torah Institute, this is a world in which women play an important part as parents and celebrities. It is most assuredly a world colored by race; many of the persons selected as exemplars are African-American. Arletta, whose identity as an African-American is confident and secure, cites Thurgood Marshall, Malcolm X, and Martin Luther King as role models. One of her African-American classmates wears a T-shirt with "Great Heroes" emblazoned across the front and back. The "Great Heroes" include Martin Luther King, Bob Marley, Malcolm X, Marcus Garvey, and Nelson Mandela. (None of these men is a hero for Arletta; her definition is too stringent, and

Table 4.
Franklin Pierce: Students' Exemplars

	Parents	Parent surrogates (including teachers)	Religious figures	God	Athletes	Peers	Political figures	Glamorous celebrities (authors, entertainers)
Girls (6)	6 (5F; 1 both)	5 (4M; 1F)	1 (F)	0	1 (F)	1 (F)	1 (M)	3 (1M; 2F)
Boys (2)	2 (1 both; 1F)	1 (M)	0	0	1 (M)	0	1 (M)	0
Total (8)	8 (2M; 6F)	6 (5M; 1F)	1(F)	0	2 (1M; 1F)	1 (F)	2 (M)	3 (1M; 2F)

M = Male; F = Female

they are too human.) Two of the three glamorous celebrities named by the girls are African-American as well.

Stratas's view that role models can cut across gender and race seems to be borne out by his students. Two young women, one white and one black, have named him as a role model. The white students include another member of Stratas's team, the much-lauded science teacher mentioned earlier. The African-American and Hispanic students refer to a popular African-American guidance counselor as a role model. Although the students usually select role models whose race is the same as theirs, many make an exception for Stratas. Race has a vote, but not a veto.

Popular culture shapes these students' moral prototypes. Religion plays a limited part in their lives. Only Renée admires religious figures, the women counselors at her Episcopalian summer camp. Five of the eight students at Pierce, thoroughly immersed in popular culture, select exemplars from athletics and entertainment. Their mean score on my popular culture litmus test is 8.25, in contrast to the 5.25 figure registered by their peers at the Torah Institute. It is easy to forget that these two schools are separated by only two city blocks.

Competent Women,
Not "Good Little Girls"

AMY MEDEIROS, SHAW SCHOOL

Amy Medeiros's Classroom

To enter Medeiros's classroom, a visitor approaches a complex of architecturally eclectic buildings standing in a parklike setting surrounded by oak and maple trees. A cheerful receptionist in the main building directs the newcomer to the middle school next door. Girls of various sizes dash about. About half of them wear short green-and-blue plaid kilts, and half wear long pants in solid colors. The rule about the school uniform is quite flexible: a kilt or pants (no jeans) and a top, either a blouse or a sweater, in approved solid colors.

I pass a lounge with soft, comfortable furniture where the girls can chat and study between classes and where middle school meetings are held. The walls are hung with quilts made by each of the classes. The reception area between the lounge and the middle school office is decorated with framed photographs of girls in white and flowered dresses. In the portraits of the classes of 1994, 1995, and 1996, two or three Asians or African-Americans grin happily in each photo, along with 20 or so white, equally smiling, generally blond classmates. The walls of the reception area are studded with announcements about tryouts for plays, ski trips, lost and found articles, and a tag and yard sale to raise $600 for the middle school yearbook.

Amy Medeiros's classroom is located in the basement. It holds 18 chairs which fill up rapidly with the largest mathematics class in the school, the seventh-grade prealgebra group. The room has small windows at the top of the back wall; in pleasant weather the sounds of the Lower School students playing in the schoolyard filter in. Brightly colored geometrical shapes are suspended like mobiles from the ceiling.

Student-made posters illustrating a penny project decorate the walls. When a representative from UNICEF visited the school as part of a statewide effort to collect 35 million pennies, Medeiros responded with an exercise in problem solving. Creating cooperative learning groups, she asked each group to brainstorm about what 35 million pennies would look like, how much they would weigh, and the size of the vehicle that would be needed to transport them.

The students' posters are interspersed among the artwork Medeiros has hung. This includes architectural drawings, paintings by Escher, reproductions of French Impressionist art, and tessellations. The furniture is shabby but unmarked. Medeiros's desk, which occupies one corner, is surrounded by bookcases filled with mathematics and reference books. An overhead projector stands ready for use in the front of the room. A blackboard fills the wall facing the students' desks.

Medeiros's prealgebra class looks far more homogeneous than George Stratas's social studies class. Seventeen of the 18 girls are white; Mei-Li, whose parents still speak English with difficulty, is the sole contributor to racial diversity. Mary Carparo, the head of the middle school, tells me that approximately one quarter of the students receive some form of financial aid, but there is no way to tell who they are simply by looking at the girls. The uniform requirement creates an appearance of homogeneity; every student is wearing brown shoes, either oxfords or boat shoes. I see none of the huge, shiny hoop earrings so popular with the African-American and Hispanic girls at Pierce; no neon colors; no T-shirts with the names of singers, athletes, or other celebrities. Like the girls at Springfield Torah Institute, these young women wear conservative jewelry and long-sleeved sweaters or blouses in solid colors. They are animated, bouncy, and prepared for class. Each girl has a notebook and writing implements; these are carried in huge book bags that seem to overpower the smallest members of the class. (Only once in my six visits to the class did I see a girl who failed to complete her homework. She came to Medeiros before class to explain the situation and was given permission to complete her work for the following day's class.) The girls chat with each other and their teacher until a buzzer sounds to announce the beginning of the 45-minute period.

Amy Medeiros is in her mid-40s; her dark, closely cropped hair is beginning to show flecks of gray. About 5'8", she appears even taller because of her long neck and her swanlike way of moving about her classroom. She dresses smartly and professionally, favoring dark colors and tailored dresses, pants, and blazers; occasionally she wears short pleated skirts and matching colored hose. Her deep, musical voice hints at her favorite leisure activity, choral singing.

Medeiros has been teaching for approximately 20 years in both private and public schools, in high schools and in middle schools. It never occurred to her to do anything but teach. A mathematics major in college, she and her two roommates entered master's degree programs to prepare them to teach mathematics. She has been at Shaw for seven years, having taught previously at an independent school for boys. She entered the independent school circuit when she moved to this city from Vermont and found that only the independent schools offered part-time employment. Because her children were young, she and her minister husband agreed that it would be best for the family if Amy worked part-time. Now that her children are 19 and 13, Medeiros teaches full-time and is head of the middle school mathematics department at Shaw.

One member of her department has just left to take a better-paying position in the public schools, but Medeiros would not consider that option. She jokes that her husband thinks about it all the time. But she refuses, saying: "The faculty here is what makes it really worthwhile. Really fine, fine people who are well-educated, who communicate well, who travel, who have interesting things to talk about."

Medeiros is most comfortable when talking about her subject; she loves mathematics. When I play back the tapes of our interviews, I can hear her voice speed up as she recounts the latest trends in mathematics education—for example, the need to appeal to a diversity of learning styles. She is confident and excited. When I ask her to reflect about herself, however, she is ill at ease and punctuates her remarks with nervous laughter. She clips her speech, leaving off the subjects of her sentences. "Never occurred to me"; "Not my style." Medeiros agreed to work with me after Mary Carparo, the head of the middle school, thinking her a perfect example of someone who takes moral education for girls seriously, asked her to read over the abstract of my project.

Medeiros opens her class by reviewing the previous night's homework. She walks around the room, looking at the girls' results, and asks each one to recreate problems on the blackboard or to share her answers. She introduces new material, demonstrates how to solve one or two problems, and invites the students to model the problem solving in preparation for the next homework assignment.

Occasionally the girls gather in small groups to produce definitions of terms they have agreed upon mutually or to work on problems together. The Penny Power project was an example of such a collaborative endeavor. Medeiros employs hands-on materials, commercially available or of her own making, like strands of spaghetti to illustrate length or volume. She uses the overhead projector with multicolored acrylic chips to demonstrate the algebraic properties of addition and subtraction.

Medeiros shows me a textbook series for the algebra course that she teaches to the eighth grade. I am grateful that she owns four editions, which date back more than 20 years, because the series captures the changes in mathematics education over that generation. In the 1970 edition, a 500-page volume, the word problems that refer to women are about filling trading stamp books, losing weight, or spending money. Professors and wage earners are male. If Jim goes blueberry picking, it is because he is with Sally. Gender roles are clearly defined, and the authors make no attempt to introduce racial or ethnic diversity.

By 1990 the same text has ballooned to more than 800 pages; it now includes biographies of men and women of all nationalities and races who have contributed to mathematics and science. They include Albert Einstein, Maria Mitchell, Hypatia, Hsien Wa, Juan de la Cierva, Emily Warren Roebling, Daniel Hale Williams, and Srinivas Ramanugan. This edition contains fewer word problems involving people, and more about items such as boats, cubes, gold, and stamps. The 1990 edition also includes a section on careers with photos of an astronomer, a statistician, and a pharmacist, all female; a white male electrical engineer; an African-American draftsman; and white and Asian male operations researchers. In addition, it contains some suggestions to the teacher about using cooperative learning in teaching mathematics.

The book that Medeiros uses for the seventh-grade prealgebra class is similarly multicultural. *Mathematical Connections: A Bridge to Algebra and Geometry* (Gardella, Fraze, Meldon, Weingarden, & Campbell, 1992) prides itself on including "the contributions of various ethnic groups to history, music, science and language" (p. 122). Timelines memorialize the Seneca Falls Convention, the Iroquois Confederacy, and the completion of the railroads by Chinese laborers. Included are biographies of Florence Nightingale, who used statistical graphs to highlight the poor conditions of the British military hospitals; Fannie Merritt Farmer, a pioneer in nutrition who had to use accurate measurements in her work as a dietitian; and Hilda Geiringer, a mathematician who paved the way for Mendelian genetics. Photos capture girls participating in sports. Word problems feature Juana, who tosses a paper cup; Kiko, who runs; Margaret, who commutes. The problems pose questions about "a baseball player" and "an engineer"; they avoid using pronouns.

The burning questions in women's moral development center on the early adolescent years and the concomitant loss of self-esteem

(Belenky, Clinchy, Goldberger, & Tarule, 1986; Brown & Gilligan, 1992). This issue is particularly acute in mathematics and science (National Coalition of Girls' Schools, 1992; O'Brien & Tracy, 1991). The changes in Medeiros's textbooks represent one strand of curriculum reform. The goal is to place a female reflection in Adrienne Rich's (Bruner, 1990) mirror, which previously had reflected only male faces. In her article on curriculum reform, Countryman (1992) describes a phase theory that includes replacing "womenless, white male mathematics" with "women injected into the curriculum" (p. 74).

Another approach to reshaping mathematics for women is to teach it through methods that approximate the way women learn—through cooperative learning, for example, an approach that Medeiros uses frequently (*A.A.U.W. Report*, 1992; Hopp, 1992). Medeiros explains why she favors this approach:

> The idea is that in our modern world people don't do math independently. If you're working in industry or business, you're part of a team. You have to learn to talk about it with other people, how to listen to other people, how to share in the problem-solving process. Everyone has something to give to the process and can teach each other and can benefit from each other, and so it really is a big push right now. The books are full of it. Every workshop emphasizes it. So we're all learning to do it.

Advocates of multicultural education recommend cooperative learning as particularly effective with African-American students as well (C.A.M. Banks, 1993); George Stratas, however, unlike Amy Medeiros, prefers to lecture or lead discussions with the entire class.

Medeiros's Definition of Moral Education

Until she was approached by Mary Carparo, her supervisor, Medeiros associated moral education with something she does as a teacher in her church Sunday school, not in her mathematics class at Shaw. Initially, she thought the term *moral education* meant direct instruction or indoctrination. She didn't do moral education, she said, because "no one is forcing, preaching, anything like that." Unlike the other teachers in my study, Medeiros did not originally define herself as a moral educator. Carparo, however, is thoroughly committed to moral education, particularly in girls' schools and in mathematics and science; she used my appearance as an opportunity to encourage Medeiros to think about her philosophy of education.

Interviewer: When you heard that I was interested in moral education, or what some people call character education or values education, what came to mind?

Medeiros: What came to mind was a question. Why would you want to do that in a math class? (laughs) Though I see that in everything that I do, whether it's teaching or whatever. . . . Why would somebody want to research that in a math class particularly? What could you possibly be looking for?

Medeiros reevaluated her definition and then offered her second thoughts:

What kinds of values are we setting forth in front of these kids? What do they see daily—which probably has a bigger effect on them than what we say directly—what do they see day after day after day? Those values definitely affect them. How do I present myself? How do I present math? What does the book have to say about people in society?

Her definition of moral education contains a number of themes: integrity, fairness, respect, a conscience of craft, and building independence.

Integrity. During our first interview, Medeiros uses the word *integrity* five times to refer to herself. By integrity she means a consistency of personality. Loving mathematics, having standards, caring for students' well-being are not aspects of a persona that she affects only during school hours:

I think it's important, and I try to get that across to the kids, that the person they see teaching the class is the person they see outside the class. I'm not two separate people. I try to bring my own self into what I'm doing—so that what I believe, what I do, who I am, what I teach, should all be one. That's where I come from.

Fairness. Being fair is central to Medeiros's definition of moral education:

I try to be fair, and try to let them know that I'm being fair, and even though they might not interpret it that way, I point out why I do that. I try to value each of them equally. No discrimination. I hope that comes across.

Morality for Amy Medeiros is a code of beliefs that hinges on abiding by the rules. She teaches under an unwritten agreement to treat each of her students equally. In a time when the language of moral education is reconstructed in two voices, the voice of justice and the voice of care (Gilligan, 1982), Medeiros's resonant soprano reverberates with the sounds of the voice of justice (Rawls, 1971).

Conscience of Craft. Medeiros views herself as a person with "pretty high standards academically." Her students corroborate this view. When she tells one of her classes they will be getting a surprise quiz, they grouse good-naturedly: "You're too domineering"; "You're a tyrant." She does little to change their image of her as a demanding teacher. When the students try to persuade her not to give homework, Medeiros does not budge. "Come on. This won't take you long." The students look over their grades. "Do you ever give a check plus?" one asks. "Once every 10 years," Medeiros quips. When she announces a chapter test, the girls mutter, "This is hard work." Medeiros replies, "Why don't I give less? Because then you'll be sitting in front of the TV, rotting away." (This is the only reference to popular culture I hear from an adult in 10 visits to the school.)

Being a tough grader is one aspect of having standards. Another is expecting certain work habits and techniques. Medeiros demands both of her students. Like George Stratas, she works hard and expects her students to measure up. Like Stratas, she is the product of immigrant grandparents who scrimped so that their children and their children's children could succeed. Industriousness is important to her. As she struggles over her definition of moral education, she isolates another component: "The work ethic. I mean you really have to work for what you want. You really have to be consistent. You have to be responsible."

Being responsible means using the appropriate methodologies for deriving knowledge. "A sturdy format," as Medeiros calls it, is one of her stringent requirements: "We're trying to learn good techniques. Make sure your format is good." The girls correct their own papers. Medeiros asks them to form the habit of checking their work when they finish—not only homework, but tests and quizzes as well. "Not for my sake, but for yours," she explains. A conscientious student checks her work; Medeiros expects this of her pupils. She also expects that they may not get their work right at the first attempt. Part of her code of ethics is perseverance: "Your first try may not be perfect. You may have to do it several times before you get it right."

Getting it wrong may even be a learning experience: "It's okay to try those dead-end things. It's even better to leave them on the page to leave a trail to see where you've been. Then you won't make the same mistake twice."

Medeiros's conscience of craft greatly resembles what the authors of *Women's Ways of Knowing* (Belenky et al., 1986) call "procedural knowledge." Procedural knowledge is "the voice of reason" (p. 87); it requires "conscious, deliberate, systematic analysis" (p. 93): "Truth lies hidden beneath the surface, and you must ferret it out. Knowing requires careful observation and analysis" (p. 94). Mastering techniques—"sturdy formats," "tools," and "procedures"—enables girls to succeed. It gives them choices, or, as Medeiros claims, "the flexibility to choose a course of action."

Medeiros teaches her techniques in a no-nonsense, efficient, matter-of-fact way: "This can be done in one step instead of two. . . . It's your choice. It amounts to exactly the same thing." The world is a rational place; mathematics is logical; there is no need to be afraid. The mathematics teacher reassures her students: "It's a simple concept. This way you don't have to be scared in the 11th grade. You're at an advantage." No one needs to memorize rules. Mathematics has an intelligibility, which Medeiros demonstrates constantly by teaching prealgebra inductively: "Why do division and multiplication have the same rules? These rules weren't just dropped out of the sky. They make sense."

Several times during the class, the students come up with theories and then test them. "Let's do another so we'll believe this," says Medeiros. The message is that mathematics is accessible. "Let's do a whole collection of these and come up with a rule." Medeiros wants her students to streamline their theories to make them more efficient: "Margaret came up with two rules which work, but it's complicated. Charlotte came up with one rule; it's the same, but less process." Learning mathematics is learning process; Medeiros's attitude is that process demands attention to detail, perseverance, a willingness to experiment, and a belief in order and rationality.

According to Belenky et al. (1986), procedural knowledge requires formal instruction or tutelage (p. 93). Medeiros models the rationality and competence she expects of her students. She asks them what they thought of the word problems about automobile engines that they had to solve for homework. Predictably, the girls groan. She responds, "I think it's kind of fun. My father made me learn all about a car before I could drive. I used to jump-start big guys' cars' batteries when they thought the engine was dead."

Respect for the Individual. According to Medeiros, an obligation to the individual student distinguishes Shaw and other independent schools from public schools:

> In the independent school setting as I see it—again this isn't necessarily in writing (laughs)—as I see it, the student is far more important than the system. The success of the student is the ultimate goal. And sometimes we bend over backwards and kill ourselves and avoid our own families so that that student can succeed. I see that as the differ-

ence; in the public school typically that particular student would be lost.

One senses Medeiros's respect for her students in her dissemination of teacher lore: the way she passes on tips, shortcuts, and mnemonic devices. She assumes the role of a mentor. "My experience is greater than yours, I grant you. I'm trying to share it with you." Or she says, "My advice is always write out the original problem so you won't get messed up. Don't touch the first numbers."

No student is ever made to feel unimportant or inadequate. Medeiros calls on everyone. If a girl does a problem wrong, Medeiros turns to the class to ask how many agree or disagree with the answer. She then addresses the student, saying something benign like, "Want to look at it again?" or, "Let's talk that through." The end product is a class of young women who know, in Jackson's (1986) felicitous phrase, "that it is safe *not* to know" (p. 59). Some girls also have come to believe in the power of "talking it through," in sharing their thought processes with each other. Their learning is connected, not separate, a hallmark of feminist pedagogy (Belenky et al., 1986).

Medeiros aims at making her learners competent and self-assured. She hopes to develop independent, self-reliant students:

> You have to be willing to ask for help; honesty, forthrightness, a willingness to speak about what you're doing. That's one thing that Shaw really encourages. To be able to ask the appropriate questions at the appropriate time and learn how to do that with guts.

Medeiros hopes to encourage her students to find their "voices." The diffident, self-effacing "good little girls" are to be supplanted by competent risk takers. She dismisses the "teacher-pleasing" behaviors of "good little girls":

> I have one girl in the eighth grade now who's come from a public school system where she wasn't in a challenging environment at all. She can produce a lovely paper that's very pretty and decorates everything with art, but misses the content of everything. Yet where she was, she was getting good grades because she had figured out how to do that. (laughs)

According to Medeiros, Shaw intends to graduate girls who will please themselves, find their own paths, and speak their minds. Medeiros constantly urges the girls to do this. Her refrain forms a theme and variations:

Talk to me. Some of you saw it in miles, [others in] feet. It doesn't matter. It depends on your point of view.

I start on the right side, probably because I'm right-handed. You can do it either way.

You all arrived at the same place, but you traveled differently.

Medeiros never uses the term *self-esteem*, but the literature does. By waiting longer after asking questions, by instituting small-group dialogues, and by reiterating the message that she expects everyone to succeed, Medeiros builds the confidence that researchers have found ebbs in young teenage girls, particularly in regard to the study of mathematics and science (Gilligan, Lyons, & Hanmer, 1990; Gross, 1993; Moulton & Ransome, 1993).

Feminist literature on girls' attitudes toward mathematics and science suggests that young women need to see mathematics as accessible and useful (Henrion, 1992). It was a feminist outcry that forced Mattel to remove from toy stores a Barbie doll that said, "Math is hard"(Davis, 1994). Throughout her prealgebra course, Medeiros repeats the message that math is neither hard nor irrelevant. She does so by giving her students what she calls "a context." She tells them that she had to convert ounces into metric equivalents when she bought the food for the middle school camping trip. She cautions the girls not to be fooled by soda specials in restaurants; the thickness of the container will determine whether their drink is a bargain. Medeiros brings ingredients from her kitchen to demonstrate the measurement of solids and liquids. Mathematics is no longer abstract and removed from life. It is contextualized—as real as restaurant menus and cooking procedures.

For Medeiros's students, as for Kaplan's, the subject matter has utility. One student, Alyssa, explains:

> Not only do we learn math skills and stuff, we learn critical thinking and thinking application—those kinds of skills which don't only help with math. It helps you to think about problems, and that just goes for everyday life. . . . So it's more than just math. You really can get a good feeling about how to go about solving a problem.

Alyssa says that Medeiros's approach to mathematics makes her feel competent. That attitude is derived from her teacher's views toward her subject and her students. Medeiros's definition of moral education adopts a concern for academic excellence and the work ethic from the objectivist school of moral education and takes the message of self-esteem and transformation from the subjectivist school.

Who Is a Hero?

Amy Medeiros speaks tersely on the subject of heroes. Her definition implies a loss of one's independence to an outside force, a surrender that clearly makes her uncomfortable. She claims that she never had a hero:

> *Medeiros:* I've never been the one to be a hero-worshiper kind of thing. So no.
>
> *Interviewer:* You didn't have heroes as a kid growing up?
>
> *Medeiros:* I don't think so. No. Nothing that stands out.
>
> *Interviewer:* And not now? Not today?
>
> *Medeiros:* I don't think so, no. Bits and pieces, a piece of this person, a piece of that. I guess I would see a hero more as . . . an all-encompassing kind of thing. That's kind of a level for me. Anyway a hero is—like some kids get all involved with a rock star or something—that's their hero; everything revolves around that. I don't see myself doing that. Never have. Not my thing.

Some researchers recommend infusing the formal mathematics curriculum with achieving women, augmenting the patterns in Medeiros's textbooks (Countryman, 1992), but Medeiros does not:

> I'm not saying "Well, here's so and so, and she did such and such. You know you can be one of these." Or, "Here's somebody, be like her." I think if you were to investigate what goes on in our English and history classes you would see more of the direct—where they study great women in history; women authors, that kind of thing. But in the math class? In the book, now and then it will mention something, but no, I don't do that directly.

Who Is a Role Model?

Although some educators call for an infusion of heroes into the formal curricula (Brodbelt & Wall, 1985; Tomin & Burgoa, 1986), feminist pedagogy more commonly calls for role models (Brown & Gilligan, 1992; Maher & Rathbone, 1986; Moulton & Ransome, 1993; National Coalition of Girls' Schools, 1992; Tinajero, Gonzalez, & Dick, 1991). Gilligan (1977) argues that if girls develop their identities through attachment—as opposed to boys who develop through individuation (Erikson, 1985)—then role models play a significant part in early adolescent girls' moral development. Amy Medeiros's voice picks up tempo as she speaks of role models. She becomes more expansive than when we discussed heroes:

> Role model, I guess for me, is probably someone from whom I take little bits and pieces of things. (She names a choral conductor.) Like I just mentioned, when he's directing, I find things in what he does that for me are useful and adaptable. In that sense he is a role model for a little piece of something.

A hero is more global than a role model. Medeiros, always concrete and rational, sounds like one of the respondents quoted in *Women's Way of Knowing* (Belenky et al., 1986):

> It's not a battle between the gods that concerns women. Women are concerned with how you get through life from minute to minute . . . each little teeny tiny incident—how it can affect everything else you do. Women see things close at hand and are more concerned with minutiae. (p. 199)

Medeiros describes a role model as a mirror: "Kids mimic what they like, whether it's a hand motion or a bigger behavior."

Like Gilligan (1977), Medeiros is convinced that girls need role models more than boys. She agrees that talented young women do not achieve in proportion to their numbers. Reflecting on her teaching at an independent boys' school, she compares the needs of her male students with those of the girls at Shaw:

> At Greeley Country Day there was never the approach that we try to raise up great men in front of them and show them that yes, they too could be like that. That's not needed for boys. And yet girls in our society need that. We're realizing that they need more the role models which we as female teachers for the most part are for them. I think that is very important. We're trying to give them the advantages that boys have had for years and years.

Medeiros maintains that role models exert their power implicitly rather than explicitly. It is the cumulative process of exposure to an exemplar that sends a moral message to girls: "what they see daily, which probably has a bigger effect on them than what we say directly."

Like Stratas and Kaplan, Medeiros regards teachers and parents as her role models. Her contention that she takes "bits and pieces" from role models emerges clearly in her description of her high school mathematics teacher.

> *Medeiros:* As far as my approach to teaching math—at least when I was beginning, it definitely went back to my high school math teacher and

the way he did things. But he was a funny-looking little old man. Nothing like me (laughs). But I could see how his techniques worked, and how effective they were. So you pick up something from lots and lots of different places, I would hope.

Interviewer: So this funny little old man, would you say he was one of your role models?

Medeiros: As far as that goes, yes. As far as personality, no (laughs). Lifestyle, no (laughs).

Medeiros is very proud of her parents. Are they role models? "Big time. Right up there." Once again, she speaks quickly with more assurance. Her parents, like Stratas's, were first-generation immigrants; Medeiros's parents were Portuguese. Her father, a trade school student, had become a mechanic, working his way up to the position of service manager of a large automobile dealership. Hating his job, he went back to school and earned a high school equivalency degree as well as a degree from a local teacher training college. He made that decision when he was in his mid-30s, while Amy was in junior high school. Working two jobs while attending school, and assisted by Amy's mother who went back to work to help her husband achieve his goal, her father eventually became a teacher and administrator in a state vocational school. Medeiros comments, "A teacher. Get that one? So that probably has something to do with who and what I am." At the end of our first interview, I ask Medeiros if there is anything she wishes to add. She proudly volunteers more information about her parents.

As with Stratas and Kaplan, religion played a formative role in Medeiros's early life. Her church gave her two more role models:

Our church was very, very musical and so, looking for more role models, I would say that the pastor and his wife at the church where I grew up in Glenview were really high on that list. They were there for over 30 years. Mrs. Vieira was an excellent musician.... She was the director of the first junior choir I ever sang in and, as you can see, I'm still in music (laughs). So that was very important to me. That whole combination. Those were my first role models (laughs).

Stratas reacted with annoyance when I ask him what he thought about the literature suggesting that students need role models who resemble them. Kaplan agreed, however. Medeiros, who had no female mathematics or science teachers until college, responds quickly: "I think you need some role models, but I can't imagine why they would all have to be the same type. That's a little restrictive isn't it?" Her remarks recall Stratas's: To require a close match between mentor and mentee confines each of the partners and implies an inability in each to bridge their differences.

Cultural Context

Agreement on Values. Like Tuvia Kaplan and unlike George Stratas, Amy Medeiros is surrounded by a school culture that reinforces her moral messages. She spends a good deal of time discussing individual students' progress with her colleagues: "It's what we talk about when we get together." She senses that she is a valued member of an institution that respects her growth as an individual as well. Each faculty member receives a $500 grant which can be used for professional development. Medeiros has used hers to attend summer workshops in teaching mathematics.

The school portrays itself in its literature in much the same way as does Amy Medeiros. The program booklet of the local symphony orchestra contains an advertisement for the Shaw School. It features a photograph of a smiling girl with tousled hair, dressed in the Shaw kilt, juggling schoolbooks, sneakers, and a lacrosse stick. She is quoted as saying:

> What I like best about Shaw is that you're always treated with respect no matter how old you are. My opinion counts. The classes are hard, but they're fun, too, and the teachers are always there when you need help. Shaw is more than just a school—it is a place to grow, take risks, and mostly to learn more about yourself.

Medeiros's concern for academic standards, her respect for the individual, her dedication to her students, her commitment to students' growth are echoed by the smiling girl who is too busy pushing herself academically and athletically to comb her hair. She is too engaged, too ambitious to bother about looking like "a good little girl."

The prospectus, *Introducing Shaw,* is an important recruitment tool for the school. With demanding teachers and through small classes, it emphasizes both an "inside-out" approach—the boosting of self-esteem—and "outside-in" expectations of success. The latest edition of *Introducing Shaw* welcomes the findings on girls' development:

> Current research on girls' schools reconfirms what we at Shaw have known for more than a century: that an all girls education does make a positive difference in each girl's life. At Shaw, girls have a healthy respect for their own intelligence. They learn to trust in their ability to

achieve and to make a difference. They are challenged to stretch intellectually and experiment creatively by teachers who themselves demonstrate high standards of competence and a love of learning.

The student handbook includes a similar message. The 1993–1994
edition, which specifically mentions mathematics and science, was created under the leadership of Barbara Burns, the new head of school.
Burns, a former teacher of mathematics who has herself written
widely about the specific issue of girls and mathematics, cites the findings on gender equity:

> Recent research highlights the ways in which schools often shortchange
> girls. When there are fewer chances to participate, lower expectations
> for achievement, discouragements in science and mathematics, and lim-
> ited opportunities for leadership, girls must struggle for attention in ed-
> ucational settings that do not focus on their needs. For generations of
> Shaw students, however, school has been the place where confidence,
> self-reliance, and ambition are nurtured and celebrated.

In 1984, the Shaw School published a centennial book. It was designed and executed by Mary Giddings, a retired faculty member and
former head of the science department, who first came to Shaw in
1924. Those who knew her told me that Miss Giddings, who died recently, was the embodiment of the Shaw School. The centennial book
quotes from the 1982 investiture speech of Katherine Williams, the
(then) newly installed headmistress:

> A school should be a place of high expectations—of each other—of per-
> formance—of character—of ourselves—of ourselves within the frame-
> work of community—and finally—of ourselves in providing service to
> that community.

That message, delivered 15 years ago, is similar in tone to Barbara
Burns's message: Both emphasize expectations. But differences exist
as well. The two women's titles—headmistress and head of school—
represent the two traditions of the school which have been joined in
a sometimes tenuous bond: Junior League and Nancy Drew. The older
alumnae of Shaw were and are expected to serve in their communities
and on the tennis court. (An annual tennis fund-raiser for the school
is held at a country club that reputedly discriminates against Jews.)
The younger alumnae, who do not attend such events, are expected to
be ambitious, to take risks, and to speak out. They are heirs to the
fictional girl-detective, interest in whom has skyrocketed in feminist
academic circles (Brown, 1993).

Clothing school messages in both historical and contemporary garb was noted by Johnson (1990) in her description of independent school culture. Shaw, like other girls' independent schools, rewrites its history in light of the new feminism. Although Johnson comments that grounding the school mission in historical terms makes it impervious to "shifting values in society" (p. 226), the corollary is also true: Conveying an image of a school that is responsive and timely gives that school a marketing edge. Even so, the alliance between the debutante and the detective is often strained.

Laura, the middle school music teacher, prepares Shaw students for their parts as choristers in the annual Vespers and Hanukkah pageants. These two performances are among the traditions that build the Shaw School culture. The 1992–1993 school prospectus describes these (and other) events as providing "rites of passage and heartfelt memories." The Vespers program, featuring a Nativity pageant, has always been mandatory for the upper school. This year, however, an observant Jewish student has asked for and received permission to be excused. The Hanukkah pageant, which is not mandatory, is performed by the fourth grade with musical accompaniment by the middle school. It was added to the school's December traditions in the late 1970s.

Margaret Samir, a Muslim born in Egypt, came to Laura to discuss her discomfort and that of her parents about her singing the Christmas carols in the Vespers ceremony. (The Hanukkah songs presented no problems for the Samir family.) Ultimately, they agreed that Margaret could sing whatever she felt comfortable with. Laura asked her to explain the Muslim religion to the group, but Margaret, who had just joined the school in September, was too shy. Laura adds that there are at least two Buddhist girls in the middle school, but they too are unwilling to speak about their religion.

As a music teacher, Laura recognizes that she has many opportunities to convey moral messages in her classroom. She defines moral education as multiculturalism. She observes that the school could be doing much more to promote religious and cultural diversity, such as introducing the students to Passover and Ramadan, but acknowledges that the school has made great strides over the past years. She concludes her discussion with me by noting that the faculty at Shaw is far more liberal than the students.

The Administration. Mary Carparo, Amy Medeiros's immediate supervisor, is responsible for the Shaw School Math/Science Day. This event, established in 1990, is designed to bring middle school girls from across the state to Shaw. There they participate in a Saturday morning of presentations by women who use mathematics and science in their careers. Each girl can select two one-hour workshops introducing them to robotics, conservation, zookeeping, landscape architecture, forensic toxicology, medicine, archaeology, and other disciplines. Between the presentations, the participants gather in the spacious Shaw cafeteria, decorated with students' artwork and posters that suggest opportunities for community service, for snacks and the opportunity to socialize. Each girl who registers for the program receives a red T-shirt imprinted with mathematical formulas as well as a packet of materials about girls' schools, which includes a recruitment brochure for Shaw.

This year the school received funding for scholarships enabling two groups, each consisting of 30 inner-city girls, to attend the program. One group was extremely well-behaved; the other, less carefully chaperoned, was not. Carparo, who hosted the program, curtailed the activities to admonish the noisy girls, saying, "We do not behave that way here." Interrupting a speaker or treating someone rudely is unacceptable at Shaw.

Carparo blames the girls' teachers for the misbehavior: "They want to know what the limits are. If we just leave it wide open, they're just going to go and go and go until something drastic happens." For Carparo, moral education takes place in a secure environment, one that establishes limits. The 1992–1993 student handbook reiterates that view: to encourage individualism and risk taking, there has to be "an environment that is structured yet flexible." Carparo would agree with Stratas that students need safety and security.

Like Rabbi Liebowitz, Tuvia Kaplan's supervisor, Carparo encourages her teachers to find the teachable moment, the opportunity to do moral education. A science teacher herself, she claims that no subject is immune to an infusion of moral education:

> We have wonderful conversations, and they do happen quickly, and then you have to get back. They happen sometimes more in a class such as mine than in history, with a teacher who has a syllabus in front of her and has to get through so many pages. But very often the history teacher or an English teacher will bring in something deliberately to bring it up. They're reading *To Kill a Mockingbird*. Now, there are a million things you can bring up there, and they're all coming up—in the eighth grade.

The themes of academic excellence, standards, and respect for the individual that Amy Medeiros cites in her definition of moral education provide the basis for Mary Carparo's definition as well:

> I think the Shaw School's mission clearly states that we value the whole person. We value her for who she is and not for where she comes from,

what she wears, what she does. I think we emphasize that a lot. We have high expectations for our girls, and they know that, and they are mostly motivated toward stretching themselves and reaching the goals and reaching the expectations that we set for them.

Reaching and stretching do not fit the self-image of the "good little girl." Carparo agrees with her colleague, Amy Medeiros, that the Shaw School is not about the creation of "good little girls":

I think we're not just working on the good old-fashioned values system that I had going to an all-girls' school, which was, "Now be a good girl and be good to everybody and reach out and help." We talk that way, but it is different. I think that it is different in that we are saying, "Reach in every direction. You can be whatever you want to be. You can walk into a room and feel confident. You can have a good feeling about yourself to go forward in your history project or your science fair or whatever you call it. Reach, stretch, push yourself. You can do it." I think that's what makes the difference.

Pushing, reaching, and stretching are institutionalized in an elaborate after-school sports program. (Shaw celebrates National Girls and Women in Sports Day. This year's events included a one-woman show on the history of women's athletics, titled "Nice Girls Don't Sweat.")

Like Medeiros, Carparo is concerned that "good little girls" translates into passive, unquestioning girls. She says, "We encourage children to think, and certainly encourage them to think aloud in a class." If girls are to reach and stretch, they must discover their voices. The silence of "good little girls" is often deafening in mathematics and science classes.

These are the years when the girls become silent; the years when girls step back and let the boys handle the science equipment; the years when the girls take the notes and don't do anything physical; the years when we are told, as females, that math is for boys, girls don't have mathematical minds, female brains can't do math. If you do do math, you're going to land up looking like something you don't want to look like, locked in a closet.

Carparo repeats the themes raised by feminist researchers such as Gross (1993):

A wealth of research shows that girls are largely shortchanged in traditional classrooms, particularly in math and science, where boys tend to dominate discussion, receive more of their teachers' time, and wring the

self-confidence from girls who enter school equal in achievement and attitude but leave with lower test scores and diminished dreams. (p. 1)

Carparo uses the term *self-esteem*, which Medeiros implies but does
not employ, the term so prevalent in feminist literature about early
adolescence: "I think we emphasize the self-confidence and self-esteem
that we want our young women to achieve before they leave the Shaw
School" [emphasis added].

Self-confident girls are tough-minded, willing to make the difficult
but appropriate choices. The 1992–1993 recruitment brochure suggests that one of the goals for the students of the middle school is "to
learn basic decision-making skills." Carparo agrees:

> We talk about decision making. We talk about choices all the time here
> at Shaw. I particularly want them to be ready to be able to make a wise
> decision in a flash. So we talk about things such as when you go to a
> party and there's alcohol. . . . Or what are you going to do when all the
> kids are having a cigarette and you don't want to have one? Are you
> going to be strong enough to say at that moment, "No, I don't do cig-
> arettes"? "No, I'm not into alcohol. Leave me out of it. I think I better
> go home now." You have to be ready to make that decision then, so
> make up your mind now.

Carparo is well aware of the difficulties of balancing individualism
and community. Individuals resist conformity. The flexibility regarding
the school uniform—the choice between plaid kilt and plain pants—
symbolizes the compromise the school has had to make between tradition and tough-mindedness. "They do test us on a daily basis. 'How
far can we stretch this uniform, folks?' " Carparo mentions community more than Medeiros does. She notes proudly that two newly hired
staff members, the sixth-grade mathematics teacher and the middle
school secretary, have told her how caring the girls seem to be.

I have seen this aspect of community myself. When Mei-Li mis-
places a silver ring, the entire prealgebra class mobilizes on her be-
half. "Where did you see it last?" "Did you check the bathroom? Your
locker?" When one girl sneezes, a flurry of "God bless you"s ensues.
Another girl coughs. A classmate turns to her: "You okay?" she asks
solicitously. When Emma leaves her jacket in the previous class,
Nancy brings it to her: "Here. You forgot it again."

The operative pronoun in the prealgebra class is "we." When
Medeiros's seventh-grade students ooh and ah over the geometric
shapes made by the tenth grade, they tell their teacher that "we
should make them too." Medeiros reminds them that they have run
out of origami paper. Mei-Li responds, "Why don't we all chip in?"

Medeiros models the ethic of community. She asks the girls to share the graphs they have made with the group. "Learn from each other—what each of you has done." She holds up a chart she has made on exponents, and she notices that some of the students in the back are squinting. "Can you read this?" she asks. "Some can, some can't—so we'll help each other."

Carparo defines a hero as someone "you don't necessarily want to be like," but someone who inspires respect and wonder. Her definition implies distance. When she was young, her hero was Roy Rogers: "I liked the adventure of it. I liked to pretend I was riding a horse, running through the bushes and shooting at bad guys. I had a girlfriend who did the same thing. She married my brother, and we're best friends."

Like Medeiros, Carparo has some difficulty with the notion of the hero. For several days after our interview, she apologizes for what she perceives as a paltry list:

> Who are my heroes now? Oh, my goodness gracious, I can't say that I ever really stopped and thought about it. I really don't know. I admire a lot of women in my life now, who I see as achievers. I don't mean in the Hillary Clinton way. She does not excite me as a hero. I can't even think of names right now. I'm sorry. Somebody who is more involved in—well, like Mother Teresa is a hero. I like what she's doing.

She tells me proudly that when the time came to name the 12 computers in the computer lab, the students decided to name them after famous women. Now the girls compose or play games on Elizabeth Blackwell, Rosa Parks, Sally Ride, Marie Curie, Harriet Tubman, and others.

Carparo's role models are some of the nuns from her parochial school days and her spunky mother, who decided to forgo a Radcliffe education for a career in vaudeville. Carparo, like Medeiros, is conscious of the need for role models for the development of self-assured young women. She expects her teachers to be exemplars for their charges: "You are a certain way yourself. Isn't that what we have to go out and teach them?" She shows me the latest issue of *Science*, which features a picture of men playing football on the cover, and says with annoyance, "There's never a woman on the cover."

Carparo differentiates between mentors and role models:

> I think a mentor is somebody who inspires you to a greater depth than a role model. A role model is someone you might begin to look towards and follow, but a mentor is someone who really helps you along. You

may not even realize it at the time, and you may look back and say, "Yes, she was the one."

Interviewer: So the role model relationship may be a more passive one [than the mentor relationship] on the part of the young person?

Carparo: Yes.

Barbara Burns, the new head of the school, reinforces the values messages of her middle school principal. Lists of independent schools' goals generally begin with academic excellence (Johnson, 1990); Burns's list starts with academic achievement, but moves quickly into the moral domain:

We can celebrate how strong we are academically, but we also have so-cial, ethical, individual concerns. There's a concern that, whether the schools are religious or secular, that we are responsible for helping kids make decisions about what people would call ethical issues: concerns about their own bodies, concerns about their relationships with other people, concerns about the wider world, and ways to live responsibly in the world, too. This is what most of us in independent schools say is the glue that holds the thing together. It really is the reason for existence—not SAT scores.

Like Carparo, Burns speaks of decisions, individualism, and com-munity. Her speech at her installation is a tribute to the strong women in her life. She begins with her forbears, including a former slave, and highlights her grandmother, who asked her questions and respected her answers: "She taught me at a very young age that I had every right to my own ways of doing and being." Burns tells me that Eleanor Roosevelt, one of her grandmother's heroes, became her own:

My grandmother spoke of Eleanor Roosevelt. She called her "Mrs. Roosevelt." It was as though she were her best friend. She was some-body that she admired so much that she wanted me to know as a lit-tle kid everything that she could possibly tell me about Mrs. Roosevelt. Doris Goodwin's new biography explains some of the reasons: some of the things that she did for black women and some of her relationships with the black community. Obviously my grandmother just tuned right into them.

Other heroes include Hillary Clinton and Marian Wright Edelman. Burns attributes the loss of heroes to a loss of distance:

We've got this odd thing out there because of technology and television and all that. In a way we know more about those figures than we would like to know or need to know. There's a lot of skepticism about what these people represent. I think that's part of what goes on with kids: They know more about these exemplars; they know too much, so that they can no longer admire them. What's complicated in our society right now is that we spend a lot of time shooting down people who might be heroes. It's partly because we have the illusion of closeness to them. The president is your buddy 'cause he's on TV all the time.

Role models, on the other hand, "are people that you are very close to and can watch all the time." This category includes her African-American parents, who sacrificed to send two daughters to some of the most prestigious schools in the country, and teachers who encouraged the girls' efforts. Burns traces the evolution of a hero to a role model:

Martin Luther King was a hero, but I knew him. Actually I worked with him a little; it started out that he was a hero and then he was reachable, approachable, and so I . . . I certainly shared, understand the problem of a hero as a human being. I see him not as a saint, but as a wonderful man who had some positive qualities and some negative qualities. In that sense he's much closer to what I would say is a role model than a hero.

Carparo asked Burns to address the participants on Math/Science Day. Reiterating the message of expectations, Burns tells the girls, "You are all going to go on and study lots and lots of mathematics." She then profiles four women "who made significant contributions to mathematics or the understanding of mathematics. They serve as wonderful models for us": Olga Taussky Todd (matrix theory), Mina Rees (cryptology), Maria Agnesi (mathematical analysis), and Constance Reid (perfect numbers). "Be like them," urges Burns, "even if you probably haven't heard of any of them."

The Quaker Dimension. Burns is a Quaker, the first to head the Quaker-affiliated Shaw School in recent memory. She uses Quaker philosophy to underscore her concern for the respect for individuals:

. . . this very elusive idea about the individual worth, respect for the dignity of every individual, which I think is expressed in Quaker schools in the way you treat a kindergartner—the kind of expectations you have for kids to relate to each other. And I think for me that is the groove that makes it worthwhile to struggle with all the things we struggle with.

Burns compares the Quaker emphasis on consensus to the caring that seems to characterize Shaw. Quaker philosophy is well suited to a school for girls:

What also strikes me here, and I see this in other girls' schools, is that there is a kind of ethic of caring that you feel in the halls. I mean even when the kids are having an argument, there's a sense of concern for each other that I think has to do with being female.

The blending of individualism with community is best exemplified in the Quaker Silent Meeting, a Shaw School tradition. Every Friday, the middle and upper schools, both students and faculty, meet in the auditorium for 20 minutes of silence. The day I attended, one ninth-grader got up and spoke after almost 10 minutes of silence. She shared her nervousness about the opening of the freshman class play, the illness of one of the leads, and how she hoped everyone would support their efforts. Barbara Burns then spoke to the group about the meaning of silence: the platform on which respect for the dignity of each individual is built, a silence that creates connectedness.

In our interview, Burns expands on this subject:

One of the things I like about Quaker education is a notion of exemplars: That is, we should be exemplars for each other. My relationships with the faculty, with the other administrators, with the staff, should all represent the best of what I hope the students would learn. One of the places the kids get that message, I think, is in Silent Meeting, because in a Silent Meeting everybody's on the same level. Anyone can stand up and speak and be heard. I think over time the message that it conveys to children, and actually to everybody, is that we do, in fact, value your concerns. We value you. We respect you as an individual and want to hear and share with you the things that you think are significant for us to think about. So, for me, that's where it starts.

Parents. Burns has been meeting with parents to discuss the goals of the school. She tells me about one of these exchanges: "One of the mothers said that the ethic here is not putting yourself first, not being mean, especially since little girls can be mean. Cruelty to other children is not acceptable here." My conversations with parents elicit a discussion of moral exemplars. Ms. Nardolillo, Barbara's mother, sends her daughter to Shaw because of the teachers. She explains that the teachers exemplify the values she and her husband believe in: Everybody's views are important; everybody is special; academic success is important; girls need to be strong; and they can be anything they want to be. Kate Weiss's mother is pleased that "many of the teachers set good examples of how to conduct themselves." Emma Bennett's mother deals more philosophically with the question of moral exemplars. Like Doniel's father at the Torah Institute, she speculates that moral exemplars make the abstract concrete: "A person who is alive makes a lesson about values much more real."

All of the parents, like Medeiros, are skeptical about heroes. Kate's and Barbara's mothers wonder if there are any heroes today. Mrs. Weiss is unequivocal: "I don't think there are any heroes in today's world." Mrs. Nardolillo refers to the change from the transcendent hero to the more immanent role model: "In today's society, kids don't have heroes. In my day it was Superman. Today it's the person who does the right thing, treats people the right way."

None of these parents mention their daughters' teachers with as much appreciation and gratitude as do Pierce parents. They are paying substantially for their daughters' education; they expect that the faculty will be first-rate.

Who Are the Students' Heroes and Role Models?

The students sound like the Shaw administrators and like their teacher, Amy Medeiros, when they discuss the general goals of the school. Their thoughts are captured in the Memory Books that the middle schoolers traditionally create in the sixth, seventh, and eighth grades. In answer to the question "What have I learned this year?" the sixth-grade students discuss meeting challenges, gaining independence, and self-esteem. Their Memory Book responses include "Be yourself"; "That everyone is different"; "You can become friends with anyone if you just work at it"; "That middle school is hard, but I can handle it"; "If I keep trying I'll succeed"; "That I don't need to be just like everyone else to make friends."

Seventh-grade students had to complete the phrase, "The most important thing I discovered about myself this year was . . ." Among their responses were "That I am my own person and I can make my own choices and decisions"; "That by braking [sic] things up from step to step, I can get anything done"; "That I can do a lot more than I thought I could if I put my mind to it"; "To act like myself"; "That I can do a lot of things if I put my mind to it."

I interview eight girls from Medeiros's class. They comment volubly on the goals of Shaw and single-sex education.

Emma: I used to want to be like a hairdresser, and a lot of women are hairdressers. Now I want to be like a brain surgeon or an architect. I think it's because Shaw has made you think you can do anything if you want to. A man doesn't have to do a big job like that; a woman can.

Alyssa: At Shaw you can really talk to people, and you can express your feelings and opinions strongly without having to be shy about it. They encourage that you talk about what you think.

Mei-Li: The sports we play—like basketball and soccer and stuff—they make you think that it's not just for boys. Girls can play just as well as boys in sports.

Emma: In math class we learn how to work in groups. In a way—it kind of seems weird—but it kind of makes you independent because you're not always going to be working with the same person. You're going to have to figure out how to get along with other people.

Melissa: We even saw a video on this last year. Boys are mostly picked in co-ed schools more than girls, and girls just end up not raising their hands, or they're not independent. They're just silent, and I don't think that's right. I think that boys and girls are equal. I think that it should be [that] either one could get it, but usually it's more . . . the boy than the girl. So the girl's just going to stop raising her hand if she never gets picked, 'cause she's gonna figure it's not worth it. So I think this school has made all of us more independent than any other school would.

The students echo the prevailing sentiments of their parents, their teacher, and their school culture regarding heroes and role models. Only Barbara Burns, the African-American head of the school, is comfortable with the Durkheimian idea of the hero. The Shaw students struggle with the term, much like their counterparts at Franklin Pierce. No one has a hero. Their definitions begin with the concrete: someone who saves a life, "like Superman." In this category the girls include the cardiac surgeon who operated on Melissa; Barbara, who prevented Mei-Li from falling out of a classroom window; a school administrator who used the Heimlich maneuver on a choking Alyssa; and a former classmate of Margaret's who saved his sister from a burning building. The girls can, and do, list people who save lives; they know that others might consider them heroes. They appreciate their heroic behavior, but do not appropriate them as heroes for themselves. No one mentions moral courage, political or military leaders, or the women for whom the computers are named.

As the girls continue their discussion, Barbara observes that someone can save a life and become lionized by the press. The resulting attention blurs the line between a hero and a celebrity. Barbara does not discuss the reverse situation: a celebrity becomes a hero, not by virtue of what he does, but because of his fame. Emma makes a case for the new hero, the quiet hero. Referring to her father, she explains, "You can just be a good person, not necessarily some Superman guy." She implies that there is a spectrum of heroic behavior from the cosmic to the everyday. Margaret also discusses the heroic in terms of degrees. She writes that heroes have achieved their goals; role models have not.

Seven of the eight girls use the expression "someone you look up to" in describing role models. They demand observability. Only Barbara writes that a role model must be a "leader, kind, nice, and respects other people." The Shaw students generate the most nuanced discussion of role models I have heard to date. In addition to being observable, their role models must be accessible; for many of the girls, the ability to communicate with their role models is essential. They do not name celebrities or glamorous figures, despite the literature to the contrary (Duck, 1990; Havighurst & Taba, 1949; Wechter, 1981). Melissa is incredulous that teenaged girls might choose celebrities as role models. "Someone like Cindy Crawford? You could never *talk* to her."

Feminist literature (Belenky et al., 1986; Gilligan, 1982) characterizes the feminine voice of morality as one of connectedness. Melissa and her classmates dismiss celebrities as role models because they cannot engage distant movie stars and models in dialogue. They have learned the lesson taught by their school: The young woman who raises questions in class and who expresses her opinions is far preferable to the quiet "good little girl." Gilligan's (1982) rejoinder to Kohlberg is titled *In a Different Voice*; these Shaw girls have not only found their voices, but have made dialogue a criterion for choosing a moral exemplar.

Only Margaret mentions that she admires a movie or television star. She makes it clear that what is appealing is neither her beauty nor her fame. In fact, Margaret does not know the celebrity's name. The girls and I determine that she is describing Marlee Matlin, the deaf actress. Margaret respects Matlin's ability to overcome the challenge of being hearing-impaired. Shaw students' reluctance to include celebrities or glamorous figures is clearly not the result of immunity to popular culture; pictures of movie stars and pop singers decorate the insides of their lockers. The Shaw students score 8.25 on my popular culture index, the same mean score registered by the Pierce students, but they apply a different set of criteria than their counterparts in choosing role models.

The students expect their role models to maintain a confidence. Five of the girls use the word *trust* in their discussion. This criterion makes some of them dubious about their teachers; only Kate names teachers as role models. Emma explains her hesitation:

Well, I think a teacher can be a role model, but I don't think it would be for me unless I knew them really, really well. Because you can't tell them everything. It's just like maybe you won't be able to trust them; maybe they would tell, like, their husbands or boyfriends or something, and then maybe you'd be afraid or something. Maybe they won't even do that, but you'll just think that they will, and so you're afraid to tell them everything.

Alyssa agrees. Teachers could be role models, but "you really don't know what they're like outside of school." She needs more information. "I would want to know what they are like in all situations." For this reason Alyssa rejects fictional role models as well.

In a pilot study I conducted in another independent girls' school, I noted a similar reluctance to commit to heroes. There, as at Shaw, the girls were more comfortable talking about role models than about heroes. The teacher and the administrator I spoke to were equally uneasy; they perceived *hero* as a masculine term suggesting physical prowess. It had no place, they believed, in a girls' school. It was also normative. Neither respondent said so directly, but I sensed that they felt the term was more at home in the chapel than in the schoolroom. Both educators were much more comfortable with the less prescriptive, more do-it-yourself term *role model*. (In fact, they asked me to remove the word *hero* from my student questionnaire.)

The interview with students at Shaw is striking in that the Shaw students' requirements for becoming a role model are almost as stringent as those for becoming a hero. The need for corroborative detail, for connectedness, and for three-dimensionality looms large in their discourse. A generation ago the new technology, particularly television, was able to provide these elements in regard to the hero. The process of providing them, however, reduced the hero's scale, thereby destroying the very icon that the technology was supposed to enhance. The Shaw students' need to know applies now to potential role models. As their definitions become more multidimensional, their options shrink. It is remarkable that their parents still qualify; all eight named their mothers, their fathers, or both.

Table 5 records the people whom Shaw students admire. It includes no religious figures, no political or military heroes, no athletes, and only one celebrity, Marlee Matlin. This list is overwhelmingly female; grandmothers, family friends, classmates, school administrators appear as choices. The only males to appear on the list are the girls' fathers.

I ask the girls about the predominance of women as their choices. The roster includes Matlin, mothers, grandmothers, female friends of their families, a woman doctor, fellow students at Shaw, and Shaw educators. Alyssa, who has been at Shaw since nursery school and whose mother is a state legislator rumored to be considering a run for governor, answers my question matter-of-factly:

Table 5.
Shaw School: Students' Exemplars

	Parents	Parent surrogates	Religious figures	God	Athletes	Peers	Political figures	Glamorous celebrities (authors, entertainers)
Girls (8)	8 (1F; 7 both)	5 (F)	0	0	0	3 (F)	0	1 (F)
Total (8)	8 (7M; 8F)	5 (F)	0	0	0	3 (F)	0	1 (F)

M = Male; F = Female.

It's not good or bad or anything. I think it's kind of more natural that girls would admire more female role models and heroes, and that it's just as natural that boys would admire, like, male role models and heroes. It's not like putting them into a category or anything. I just think that that's how it is.

The abundance of female role models in the lives of the girls at the Shaw School contrasts sharply with the absence of women, other than mothers, on the list generated by the students at the Torah Institute. The culture of the Shaw School has made the acquaintance of admirable women a commonplace; at the Torah Institute it is a rarity.

7

"Quiet Heroes"

JOHN MACDONALD,
ROGER WOLCOTT SMITH SCHOOL

John MacDonald's Classroom

The two-story Smith School straddles a rise on a wooded tract of land at the end of a cul-de-sac in suburban Midvale. This community of 90,000 is nine miles from a major northeastern city of 800,000. As I cross from the parking lot into the circular driveway, I approach a two-story beige brick building decorated with blue, green, orange, and yellow panels positioned under each bank of classroom windows. Through the windows I can see well-appointed classrooms: globes, plants, stacks of books and magazines, decorated bulletin boards, and coffee supplies. Midvale's per-pupil expenditure is $6,508, one of the highest in the state.

A sign invites visitors to check in at the office. At the Pierce School, teachers immediately direct a stranger not wearing a visitor's badge to the office; nobody stops an adult who walks through the halls at Smith. Teachers smile and say hello as I move through the hallways to announce my presence to the office staff.

The display cases in the front hall are filled with papier-maché sculptures of oversized toy airplanes, eyeglasses, and toy cars. A Japanese student has used her materials to make a geisha. Another case contains watercolor still lifes, silver wash landscapes on gold paper, and Mexican Day of the Dead sculptures: papier-maché skeletons who dance, picnic, or ride bicycles. Posters invite sixth grade students to join clubs, like the environmental or karate club; to take trips, such as the ski trip to Mount Simmons; or to participate in the school's production of *Bye, Bye Birdie*.

At Smith School, each student is assigned to a House, a homeroom in which he or she stays for three years. The Houses vie with each other to create interest in their social action projects. House-made posters announce drives for mittens and hats for a battered women's shelter and canned food for a shelter for the homeless. Four Houses are celebrating Valentine's Day by selling flowers; the proceeds will go to help children with AIDS. Two more Houses have banded together to organize a poster contest on diversity as part of Black History Month. Commercially prepared posters feature African-American heroes including the singer Bessie Smith; Garrett Morgan, the inventor of the traffic signal; Crispus Attucks, who died in the Battle of Bunker Hill; and the astronaut, Ronald McNair. I am reminded of Dean Cahn's dictum: "The walls are *rebbeyim*" (Yiddish: mentors). They deliver a message of inclusivity and social concern.

Separate wings house a music department, a well-stocked art room, a home economics area, and a library. The corridor to the art room displays the work of women artists such as Mary Cassatt and Frida Kahló. The walls of the library wing are decorated with posters of multiethnic and multiracial celebrities asking students to visit their libraries and to read; Oprah Winfrey, Ruben Blades, Glenn Close, Michael Chang, and William Hurt are among those issuing the invitation.

The library is large, airy, and welcoming. It is covered with rust carpeting on which movable tables and chairs are positioned. Record collections, plants, and globes fill the cabinets. One of the posters reads, "What's the worst ethnic joke you've ever heard? Prejudice." A framed chalk drawing of Martin Luther King decorates one of the walls. A poster featuring Mary McLeod Bethune livens up another. Quotations from the works of author Katherine Paterson are posted on oak tag. (She has recently visited the school.) One poster reads "Before the gates of excellence, the high gods have placed sweat." A timeline of Jewish history rests against the windows. Foot-high signs indicate the location of reference, fiction, and nonfiction collections. Students are using CD-ROMs to create bibliographies. Only the school cafeteria looks shabby; dingy olive-green drapes droop listlessly, with several pleats detached from their rods.

Graffiti are kept to a minimum. The girls' restroom has been scrubbed of telltale hearts and protestations of undying love. Although a one- or two-day suspension is the punishment for defacing school property, the words *ubba dubba* are painted on the front door of the school. In the art room, the tables are covered with names of students, past and present.

The carpeted hallways delineate the corridors of a classic "egg-crate school." Bright signs carrying the teachers' names and the numbers of their classrooms relieve the monotony of the decor. Teachers decorate their rooms very differently: A math teacher's room is quite spare, adorned only with a few drawings of geometric shapes. A young social studies teacher who coteaches a course titled Black-Jewish Relationships decorates his room with posters of peace concerts, portraits of Native Americans, and pictures of Maya Angelou. He is the Jewish partner on the team. Each room is equipped with an American flag, although no one recites the Pledge of Allegiance, as in the Pierce School.

John MacDonald's room is a riot of color and printed messages. It is a comfortable 25-by-25 foot square, almost as large as Stratas's room. Unlike Stratas, however, who teaches five periods a day and is chairman of his department (and who has brought a grievance to his union because of his schedule), MacDonald teaches only three periods, all electives: Art and Architecture; School and Society, which he team teaches with a respected colleague; and Heroes and Sheroes. He also has a House assignment.

Rather than occupying one-piece desk/chair combinations, MacDonald's students sit at tables with freestanding chairs. The students' seats form a rectangle around his desk. Behind the desk is a mural, painted by one of his Houses, of MacDonald in 1970s garb: a flowered shirt, bellbottoms, and sandals. Over the teacher's head is a sign: "This dope can't hurt you." Another sign on the mural reads "MacDonald House is numero uno." The two chalkboards are surrounded by bulletin boards covered with items from the world of art and culture: memorials to Mozart and opera; examples of folk art; a photograph of John Lennon; paintings by Botticelli, Norman Rockwell, Renoir, and Sargent; an illustration of *Mad* magazine's Alfred E. Neuman; travel posters from Prague and Charleston; movie posters for Dracula, A Day at the Races, The Wizard of Oz, and The Return of the Living Dead. One poster shows the backview of a man holding open his trench coat in front of a nude female statue, and the inscription "Expose yourself to art"; another proclaims, "Poverty sucks." A picture of a hearse carries the caption "Last night Jimmy Dennehy traded in his Chevy for a Cadillac. Don't drive drunk." A plaque inscribed "Love one another" hangs in a corner. The room contains a VCR and a portable slide projector. A small refrigerator sits in a corner. A Native American village made of straw and craft supplies rests on the floor in front of MacDonald's desk. A sickly plant with yellowing leaves is propped against the wall.

Aside from the plant, the message is overwhelmingly life-affirming, an exuberant collage that trumpets the power of the humanities. All sort of moral messages are offered here: exhortations to avoid harm, the timelessness of art and beauty, the appeal of the life of the mind, and the importance of not taking oneself too seriously.

Twenty-four students are enrolled in the class, the largest I have visited in my study. Although the students I pass in the hallways seem diverse ethnically, this particular class is as homogeneous as Amy Medeiros's. Almost all the students are white, except for an Indian boy and a Chinese girl. Most of the students dress like models for a J. Crew catalog: They have the woodsy look created by jeans, long-sleeved T-shirts, and flannel shirts, bottomed off with Doc Martens or work boots. I see none of the Day-Glo oranges, turquoises, or lime greens favored by many students at Pierce. Several of the girls soften the androgynous costume by wearing scrunchees on their wrists. All of the boys and girls are slim. Several boys wear baseball hats, visor forward or backward, emblazoned with the names of athletic teams. College sweatshirts are very popular, particularly with the boys.

The students chat about ski trips and winter vacations in the sun. Some are considering joining MacDonald's school-sponsored summer trip to Prague. When I asked them if there is any provision for students who cannot pay for lunch, one girl says she thinks there is, but she doesn't know for sure. She adds that most students bring or pay for lunch. The contrast between Smith and Pierce is unavoidable; at Pierce, 61% of the students receive free lunches. Everyone at Pierce knows what the lunchroom policy is; identification cards are distributed daily during homeroom period.

Although the students seem homogeneous in socioeconomic status, they differ markedly in size. A mixture of seventh- and eighth-grade students, the Heroes and Sheroes class includes Elena, nearly six-foot tall, and Phyllis, well under five-feet tall. The students seem to sit in clusters, by grades. Most have taken other courses with this teacher, whom they refer to affectionately as Mr. M., Mr. Mac, or Big Mac.

Mr. MacDonald *is* big, over six-feet tall, and looks taller because of his barrel chest and large head. He dresses casually in open-necked striped sport shirts, with the sleeves often rolled up, chinos, and work boots or sneakers. He tells me he is 58, but his face is unlined. After several visits I detect the slightest tremor in his head and right hand. MacDonald's square face is adorned with tortoise-shell glasses and topped by a shock of pure white hair that falls over his forehead.

MacDonald was born in Midvale to middle-class parents, but grew up in a rural community about 20 miles away. Although raised in the Unitarian church, he does not consider himself religious. He describes himself as a humanist: "I believe in the goodness that exists, can exist in any one of us." Unlike the other teachers in my study, MacDonald does not describe his parents with admiration; he mentions them only when I ask. He does not remember his early schooling fondly. He is an outspoken fan of the House system because it encourages young people to seek the advice and guidance he feels he missed while growing up. He and his brother were the first in their family to attend college; in fact, they were the first students from their high school to go to college.

Launching his career in a boys' independent school, MacDonald began to teach; he had received a bachelor's degree in English and history, as well as a master's degree in immigration history. He had started a doctoral program in history and literature at Columbia.

When MacDonald had completed all but the dissertation, he was invited to teach in an exchange program in England. It was the early 1970s; he discovered and subsequently embraced the open school movement. He and a few friends decided to open an alternative school in the English countryside, 20 miles from London. MacDonald was elected headmaster and served in that capacity for about four years.

Worn down by the financial struggle and the tension of trying to raise three children in a foreign country, MacDonald elected to return to the United States; he and joined the Smith faculty in 1974. He was attracted to the school by

> kids choosing their own courses, a very strong House system, and a lot of humanistic elements that I very much liked. I absolutely fell in love with the curriculum, with the people I worked with, with the students, and have continued to feel very, very positively about it, even though it's become a more centrist establishment than it was then.

MacDonald's principal, Janet Howell, describes him as follows: "In many ways John is the school. He keeps reminding us about . . . what were the philosophical bases of the school. I think that he is a very special person himself."

MacDonald's Definition of Moral Education

John MacDonald becomes animated as he answers my questions about his views on moral education. This subject makes him effusive. He is more comfortable sharing ideology than divulging details of his personal life. (I learn from other faculty members that MacDonald has had to miss a few days of school to take his wife to a radiologist for chemotherapy to treat a recurring cancer.)

> Well, I think it's got a lot to do with *decision making* and *risk taking*— and being faithful to whatever *principles* one has, and *being very deeply concerned about other people* and everyone's quality of life, not just one's

own; of knowing when to make the *necessary sacrifice for someone else*, of *being very civil*. I think civility is really important. Yeah, it's all of those elements, I guess [emphasis added].

Decision Making. MacDonald has organized his course so that students pace themselves in completing assignments. He alerts them to a major paper that will be due eight weeks into the course. With each book the students read, they receive a packet of projects to complete. Each assignment includes vocabulary words, which the students are to define in context, as well as questions about plot and character. MacDonald gives his class a due date for completing the packet; each student decides for himself or herself how much or how little to do as daily homework.

In describing his goals for Heroes and Sheroes, MacDonald explains the place of decision making in his course:

I'd like them to think about why people do some of the things they do. Why, not necessarily heroic things, but why, given a certain situation, might you do one thing and I another. Risk taking. Saying no when everyone expects you to say yes.

MacDonald shares his own decision making process with his class. Having returned to Heroes and Sheroes after taking a personal day, he comments on the good report he received from the substitute teacher about the class. The students besiege him with questions. Why was he absent? Was he sick? MacDonald explains that he took a personal day to go Christmas shopping with his daughter, who is visiting from California. The students pretend their feelings are hurt. Does he really prefer her to them? MacDonald ducks the question: "My daughter came all the way from California to go shopping with me. What would you do?" He raises a moral dilemma: a long-standing family tradition versus a professional commitment. The students change the subject.

Risk Taking and Sacrifice. For MacDonald, the moral individual is one who will take risks, ones which may even lead to the loss of life. The movie *Schindler's List* is mentioned frequently during class discussions. MacDonald tells his class about seeing the film with a friend whose great-aunt died in the Holocaust. From her place in a line of prisoners waiting to learn whether they would be sent to a labor camp or a concentration camp, the great-aunt saw that one of her two daughters had been selected for a work detail; the second, younger and frailer, had been herded into the group that was destined for Auschwitz. Without waiting for the armed guards to decide, the woman left her place in line to stand with the younger daughter in the group marked for death. Perhaps she could comfort her daughter; perhaps they might be spared what seemed inevitable. She risked instant death at the hands of the guards to accompany her daughter. MacDonald shares with his students his admiration of her commitment.

Principles. MacDonald assigns his class to read Arnold Bennett's *The Grand Babylon Hotel*. One of the reasons for its appeal is an unabashedly brave, spunky heroine, Nella Racksole; she is a *shero*. (MacDonald tells his class that Maya Angelou introduced him to the word shero.) Although he loves the book, he is troubled by its anti-Semitism, which he describes as "abhorrent." He comments to his students: "A lot of the language of writers at that time reflected those sentiments. That's a real flaw in the book."

In the school community, MacDonald is known as a man of principle. He cares passionately about the threat to homogenize middle school education in Midvale, which would make Smith just another middle school. It is he who urges the faculty to withstand the attacks on student choice and governance by consensus. He enjoys his reputation as a gadfly, and jokingly refers to himself as a dinosaur.[1]

Concern for Other People. MacDonald defines a teacher's role as "a caring advocate" or "an adult advocate," phrases he sprinkles throughout our interviews. He speaks the same language as Nel Noddings (1984, 1988, 1992) . Before class he chats with his students; he moves around the rectangle of desks inquiring about dance classes, the camps they attend, their progress in other courses, the well-being of friends and siblings, their health. My notes capture an exchange with Sally:

> You've been absent a lot. Anything special? Is it a winter-related thing? Come to think of it, you were absent a fair amount in my other courses. Are you taking care of yourself? Eating right? Getting enough sleep?

During a free period he wanders down to the library to see which of his present and former students are there and to talk with them about their research, their hobbies, and their progress in school. My field notes read: "He is a kid junkie."

MacDonald is solicitous toward me as well; he volunteers to rearrange his lessons to accommodate my schedule, concerned that I

---

[1] MacDonald left Smith after the school year was over to teach in one of Midvale's two high schools.

might be traveling a long way for only a modest harvest of data. When I ask him for information or literature, I usually receive it before the end of the day. Concerned that I will not receive material I requested until after the winter recess, he gives it to his colleague, my friend, on the assurance that she will visit her mother, who lives in my community.

Being a caring advocate means being accessible. MacDonald explains:

> I tell the kids that I am here, and this is true. I am here every day at seven in the morning and if they want to come in, I will be here to help them. Every day by seven-thirty I probably have six to ten kids in my room. This is an hour and fifteen minutes before they have to be here. Now, when they see adults willing to do that and they know that the adult is not being directly compensated for that—I don't have to be here until eight-twenty-five I think, legally—but I'm here, and I'm here for them, I think that's a powerful values lesson.

Students not only drop by before school; they pop in between classes. MacDonald has his "groupies," students who sign up for all of his courses and who visit when they are no longer on his rollbook. Smith yearbooks regularly name him as "Favorite Teacher."

Another aspect of showing concern is being responsible. MacDonald models responsibility by returning students' work promptly. He gives a test on *The Grand Babylon Hotel* on Thursday and returns it on Friday. The test includes about 30 vocabulary words, five character identifications, and 10 questions on plot and setting. (During the course of my interview with his students, they comment on how much they admire the promptness and seriousness with which MacDonald grades their papers.) He says, "If I give a test, it's always back the next day. If I give a paper and it's not back [to them] within a week, they get an automatic A on the assignment, and they know that." The *quid pro quo* is that MacDonald expects responsibility from his students as well.

MacDonald revels in his assignment as a House master, which he describes as a "cradle-to-grave sort of thing." It is an ideal forum in which to demonstrate the concern for others that is so much a part of his teaching persona. He contacts his students over the summer, helps them choose their courses, and fusses over them during their three-year stay under his care. A researcher eager to learn more about the House system interviewed his students, wanting to discover what the students liked best about MacDonald House. MacDonald tells me,

> They said "He trusts us, and he listens to us." I was ripped. I said to them, 'Why are you saying that when I take you to [baseball] games and

I do your schedule, buy doughnuts, and all this sort of thing?' But then, as I was thinking about it, I think that is the key to kids this age. It's not the overt activity-type stuff that all of us do in one degree or another, but it's the listening and the trusting.

Civility. Listening and trusting are manifestations of concern. They are also manifestations of civility. *Civility* and *civilization* come from the same root; a social order cannot be built without respect for the other. MacDonald's classroom is built on respect, that which he gives and that which he commands in return. Janet Howell, his principal, expresses a perception that his students corroborate:

Mr. MacDonald has very high expectations for all students, and he gives them difficult work to do. I think that they see his work as not just difficult but also meaningful, and I think that when students see work as being meaningful, they're really willing to put more effort into what they do.

The 1993–1994 course booklet includes the following description of Heroes and Sheroes:

Throughout history and literature there runs a rich vein that is called the heroic tradition. People have needed heroes and sheroes and, when there were no legitimate ones around, they have been created. This English course will focus on four heroic personalities: the Greek warrior and traveler Odysseus as seen in excerpts from Homer's classic *The Odyssey*; the woman-warrior Harimad-sol in Robin McKinley's novel *The Blue Sword*; Mary, Peter, and an Australian aborigine in James Vance Marshall's adventure *Walkabout*; the improbable duo of Theodore and Nella Racksole in Arnold Bennett's melodramatic novel *The Grand Babylon Hotel*.

In addition to literature the course will be very much involved with real-life heroism, both past and present. Each student will conduct research and write a long biography/analysis of a personally selected hero or shero. Specific heroic events (e.g., the art produced by the children of Terezin, the defense of the Alamo, the resistance to McCarthyism) will be the subject of shorter papers. The phenomenon of the recent decline of the role of the hero/shero will be examined in depth. Attention will also be given to the ways heroes and sheroes are presented in films, television programs, comic books, sculptures, and paintings.

Among the skills to be developed in this course are close textual reading, expository writing, interviewing techniques, and clear oral expression.

The reputation of the course, and MacDonald's steadfast refusal to "dumb it down," keep out the poorer readers or the students with learning disabilities.

MacDonald prepares his latest Heroes and Sheroes class for what lies ahead. He sets forth his expectations clearly. The students will need a notebook every day; a notebook with a pocket would be helpful, he says, for holding the heaps of materials he plans to distribute. Students must bring their notebooks, writing implements, reading books, and worksheets to class every day.

> Make a commitment to be highly focused and organized. You'll love the course, but if you're not organized, you'll be in big difficulty. I won't let you fail, but you have to do your part. We have a contract. I'll assume at this point that everyone has an A.

MacDonald defers to their superior knowledge in certain domains. Discussing the Richter scale, he turns to Jacob, an amateur meteorologist, and says, "Correct me if I'm wrong. Every tenth of a point is 10 times more powerful?" He is aware of their sensibilities. As he arranges them in groups to discuss "heroic quotations," (remarks about heroism from folklore, Carlyle, Emerson, Hawthorne, Hutchins, and others), he asks, "Can you work with this group?" "Is this group okay for you?"

Although gentle and soft-spoken, MacDonald demands respect from his students. He often opens his class by playing what he calls "heroic music" or "heroic videos." Before he plays one of his heroic videos, MacDonald walks over to where Mark is sitting. He quietly tells Mark that he noticed, during the last class, that he was punching a boy who was sitting next to him instead of listening to the music. MacDonald points out that he was being disrespectful; that he, MacDonald, expects a different attitude in class. When MacDonald subsequently shows ABC's *Persons of the Week*, a video clip about heroes of the Los Angeles earthquake, Mark is very attentive. During my many visits to his class, I notice that MacDonald quietly reprimands several students for not meeting his expectations.

When I ask MacDonald to define moral education, he does not initially mention the needs of African-Americans, which figure so prominently in George Stratas's teaching, or those of young women, which dominate Amy Medeiros's pedagogy. These subjects come up later:

> I've been acutely aware of both of those subjects since I've been here and since I've been on the—ever since Day One it seems—Black Achievement group. We've done all sorts of things on that subject, not with universal success. But I've become increasingly sensitive to what happens to girls starting at about now. It really saddens me when junior and senior girls come back from the high school and so much of their soul has been eroded, and their self-confidence, and their wit, and their

sense of independence and so forth. I certainly agree that those are big issues.

Although MacDonald begins his discussion of moral education by describing it as a cognitive process—that is, making informed decisions—he ends on an affective note. In passing he touches on one of the central themes of the Shaw School, self-esteem: "I think the key thing for kids this age is issues of the heart rather than issues of the head. I want them to feel better and better and better about themselves. So I think I succeed."

Who Is a Hero?

John MacDonald's thinking about Heroes and Sheroes reflects his own experience with the heroic. When he was a boy, his heroes were larger-than-life baseball players: Rudy York, who played first base for the Red Sox, and Ted Williams, the "Splendid Splinter." Later his heroes were professors. The last hero he recalls was Adlai Stevenson, "because he had a lot of impact on my social sense and political sense." He has no heroes today. "There are people I respect a great deal, and I really love the work that people like Ralph Nader have done, and some of the environmental protection people and so forth. But I wouldn't say that I have a hero."

For nearly 20 years MacDonald has been thinking about how to teach the heroic; he has taught Heroes and Sheroes, off and on, for 10 years. In the orientation he gives to the students enrolled in the course, he spells out some of his assumptions about the nature of the hero. One of his premises is that the hero is mortal and therefore flawed. James asks if he can do his required research paper, an analysis of a hero, on a god. MacDonald denies his request, explaining that by becoming a god figure, the hero loses his human qualities: "They become immortal. We're studying mortals. Your hero or shero has to have been alive at one time, human beings. Human beings can't be perfect." The directions for the paper include a warning that the students are expected to write not a biography, but an analysis. They are required to include a discussion of the hero's tragic flaw or flaws, his Achilles' heel.

One can experience the hero or shero intellectually by reading about his or her exploits and by discussing them. For MacDonald, however, the heroic is often expressed through music and art. As mentioned earlier, he routinely begins his classes by playing "heroic music," excerpts from popular and classical music. Students are expected to listen, to reflect on how the music communicates the heroic ideal, and to jot down their thoughts in a journal that they periodically submit to MacDonald for his comments. On the day when MacDonald plays "God Save the Queen," the tape is muffled. Several students complain that they can't hear the words. MacDonald tells them it doesn't matter and asks, "What feeling is evoked by the music?"

MacDonald used to teach Heroes and Sheroes by beginning with the *Odyssey*, with what he calls "Heroes with a capital H":

> When I first started teaching Heroes and Sheroes, I remember I started with the *Odyssey*, but then I found myself trying to humanize Odysseus and make him more of a person. I think now what I do is I tend to start with the quiet heroes and people that I hope they can identify with. *I guess I want them to think that their English teacher can be their hero* [emphasis added].

In describing his course, MacDonald touches on the paradox that troubles Tuvia Kaplan. Classical heroes are not ordinary folk. If a teacher wants his students to identify with them, he invariably adds detail, and in doing so, transforms them from "Heroes with a capital H," metaphors, into human beings, "heroes with a small h." MacDonald is dubious about the power of Heroes, such as Odysseus, to effect change in his students. In fact, he is unsure of the social role of classical heroes.

> Well, there's some sort of connection, I suppose, to belief in some sort of higher order, or God-worship and things of that nature, because it has come up in virtually every society I can think of. But I don't think that if people look at those heroes [they] are necessarily looking for connectors. Maybe just a form of voyeurism, or I don't know what it is. I really can't explain it.

During our second interview, MacDonald imparts a theory about the function of classical heroes:

> I started thinking back to when in my life I had heroes. I think it relieves pain when you have heroes. They are not us; we are not going to be them, but it's a little bit of the fascination that sports have or movies or television has. It allows us to live temporarily in another world. It suspends some of the pain of our here-and-now stuff. And so I think it's—it's medicinal. That's the word.

He uses the same rationale as Kaplan when he describes the function that the broken King David can serve: to model a way of coping.

But unlike Kaplan (or Durkheim), MacDonald does not believe that "Heroes with a capital H" help shape behavior:

> There are some studies that indicate that people, particularly young people, are less inclined to have heroes now than maybe in an earlier generation. . . . I don't see the necessary connection between that, if that's a reality, and any decline in morals. I'm not so sure that we need the large-scale hero in order to have morals.

With all of his reservations about the mythical hero ("The word *hero* is hard to deal with; we tend to apply it to forces outside ourselves") and his predilection for presenting human beings at their best, it is fitting that John MacDonald's course consists largely of "quiet heroes," ordinary people who do extraordinary things because of circumstances. His course is the literary equivalent of The Giraffe Project (1991) and highlights moral exemplars like those profiled by Colby and Damon (1992) in *Some Do Care*.

One of MacDonald's examples of heroic music is the Mariah Carey song "Hero." It contains these stanzas:

> But then a hero comes along
> With the strength to carry on
> And you cast your fears aside,
> And you know you can survive.
>
> But when you feel that hope is gone,
> Look inside you and be strong,
> And you'll finally see the truth
> That a hero lies in you.

During the class discussion of the song, animated by the students' familiarity with the lyrics, both the teacher and the students choose to discuss the idea in the second stanza, the potential for heroism in everyone. They do not comment on the message in the first stanza: the hero's power to inspire and transform.

Anyone can be a hero; anyone can live a life of moral commitment. In a winter marked by a heavy accumulation of snow, MacDonald tells his class about a former student who plows walks and driveways. When MacDonald asked the student how many walks he clears and how much money he has made, the student told him that he gets paid for some walks, not for all. He won't take money from his elderly neighbors. "I think that's heroic behavior," MacDonald says to his class. "What about you?" The students agree.

MacDonald shows his students a clip from an ABC news segment on the Los Angeles earthquake of 1994. It profiles as "Persons of the Week" a pair of newlyweds who risked their lives to save others in their collapsed apartment building. The interviewer calls them heroes. When the students discuss what they have seen, they mine nuggets from the video to create a definition of heroism: concern for others rather than for oneself; lack of premeditation (the conscious wish to become a hero); fame after the event rather than before; and humility, the denial of their extraordinariness and discomfort with celebrity.

These themes reemerge in a discussion based on a second video, *Heroic Adventures*, produced by a Canadian publisher of curricular materials. This video, designed for seventh-, eighth-, and ninth-grade students, features interviews with heroes, all of whom are rescuers, and commentary by a psychologist who believes that the rescue is the paradigm for the heroic act.

MacDonald turns the discussion to a time when he was a rescuer and was considered a hero: "I'm going to tell you an anecdote, but don't consider it boastful or self-serving. I was teaching in England. A thousand people credited me with being a hero. I was unable to accept it." A student had gone into convulsions; he was beginning to bleed from banging his head repeatedly against a radiator. MacDonald's first thought was to run for help, but he stopped himself and managed to dislodge the boy's tongue. In the process the student bit MacDonald's finger and vomited all over him. At an assembly the following day, the headmaster of the school credited "our brave American friend" for saving the student's life.

After the predictable groaning at the mention of the word *vomit*, the students are impressed. MacDonald downplays the heroism. He emphasizes that long after the event, he remembered his initial response to flee and felt like a coward, not like a hero. He reiterates the observation of the researcher in the Canadian video: There is no way of predicting how one will respond until the flashpoint—the moment of crisis.

In fact, there is a growing body of literature on bystander or altruistic behavior that offers some predictors: parents who were models of caring, previous experiences in helping others, and being able to empathize with the plight of the other (Oliner & Oliner, 1988). MacDonald reminds his students that Midvale is organizing an earthquake relief effort through the mayor's office: "It's one thing to help out on a one-shot deal; it's another to continue after the immediate crisis is over."

Once again, MacDonald rephrases his message: Anybody can be a hero, a moral exemplar. He tells his class about a book on self-love that influenced him profoundly. Its theme was negative thinking. Before reading the book, MacDonald used to think that if you loved yourself it meant you were egotistical. Now he believes that love is understanding and feeling good about yourself: "How can you expect to be loved if you don't love yourself? You can't attract love without loving yourself." Insights on self-esteem, a thoroughly subjectivist view, inform MacDonald's perspectives on heroism. "How can you express heroic behavior if you don't think you have a heroic quality within you?"

In this exchange, MacDonald captures the essence of the "ordinary hero," which shapes his course as it does the Giraffe Project (1991) and much of the contemporary writing on the hero (Berkowitz, 1987; Dunn, 1991; Gerzon, 1982). Being heroic is being involved in the other. Quiet heroes inspire others by their example. They are role models, maps directing travelers to the good life. In doing so, these ordinary folk not only make their community more livable but also help their neighbors achieve their potential for goodness. Quiet heroes are not larger than life; only their commitment makes them extraordinary. It is as if the monumental figures on Mount Rushmore were replaced by a billboard with faces of one's friends and neighbors.

Who Is a Role Model?

I ask MacDonald to clarify for me the difference between a classical hero and a quiet hero. He explains:

> I think the difference is we don't have the connector to the big, heavy-duty hero. I mean, that person has done such special things that we can admire and respect [the person], but we can't really say, "I'm going to apply what that person did to my own life." Now if you look at any great hero, either in literature or in real life, *I think there's a distance there*; whereas I find with the quiet hero or the private hero, there's more intimacy and more lessons to be learned [emphasis added].

Like Tuvia Kaplan, MacDonald understands the classical hero as a denizen of a higher order, too remote to effect change. If a person is to exert influence, connectedness must exist. That connectedness is found in the fellowship of ordinary mortals. When MacDonald differentiates between "heavy-duty" and quiet heroes, he echoes Kaplan, who refers to *gedolim* (Hebrew: great ones) on a higher *madreigah* (Hebrew: level) and to role models to show the way. I ask MacDonald whether quiet heroes are synonymous with role models; he agrees that they are.

MacDonald's role models, or quiet heroes, like those of all the teachers in my study, include a former teacher. For Kaplan, it was a teacher whose erudition astounded him, who "opened windows." For Stratas and Medeiros, the impressive quality was the teacher's mastery of technique. For MacDonald, it was a the demands made by a teacher-coach. A lackluster student and a wise guy to boot, the young MacDonald met a teacher-coach in junior high school who would accept neither shortcoming. He remembers the incident well:

> He was in his car; he stopped his car, got out of his car, came right up to me, and said, "If you ever want to be a success in my class or if you ever want to play on the baseball team, you'd better get your act together." He, more than anyone else, is why I ended up doing what I presently do.

Another role model was his college chaplain:

> He was one of the first Blacks I had ever met. My mother was raised in the South, and one thing she did give me was an awareness of other groups, but it had always been sort of an intellectual process. He sort of introduced me to a whole world: his family, his friends, his parishioners, and so forth. He was definitely a role model.

MacDonald is the only teacher in my study who mentions that former role models can lose their allure. He refers to an older brother who served as a quiet hero when MacDonald was young: "But he's a good example of a role model that goes sour because he got all sucked into materialism and making zillions of dollars, and has lost his humanism." For MacDonald, moral prototypes are not static. Role models, unlike classical heroes, are time-bound. The gallery of moral prototypes can and does change.

Each of the teachers in my study sought out and found exemplars who modeled values they admired. MacDonald learned from the chaplain that "individuals can make a difference." His brother's influence paled because his materialism repelled the idealistic MacDonald. Kaplan's teacher served to initiate him into "really big stuff," the world of Jewish learning. Medeiros, the most technically oriented of the teachers in this study, chose as a model a teacher whose pedagogy matched hers.

MacDonald's role models are not limited by gender or age. He mentions a colleague, a younger woman who coteaches Schools and Society with him, and whom he views as a role model: "I really have not only a great love, but enormous respect for her, and it's sort of a mutual thing. So we have become better educators because of each other." He also includes former students in this category:

> Then there have been some kids I have taught who have been role models for me. I think it can go generationally that way. I was talking to a girl who is presently a senior at the high school who called and said she'd been accepted to Williams on early admission. We were talking, and she's a kid who every couple of months since she left this school comes by, and we go out and have ice cream together.

What MacDonald admires in this young woman and tries to emulate is her zest and optimism. His role models serve as moral exemplars: signposts to self-realization and self-fulfillment.

Not surprisingly, given the range of his role models, MacDonald rejects the idea that one's role models must be similar to oneself in race, ethnicity, gender, or age. Like George Stratas, MacDonald feels he can be a role model for all of his students. Like Stratas, he engenders the trust of the girls he teaches: "Oh definitely. I bet of all the teachers in this building, I have counseled more girls about having their period than anyone else. I'm very serious about that. People don't understand it, but it is true." MacDonald revels in being a role model. It is what he likes best about House and is one of his most important objectives in teaching Heroes and Sheroes. "I guess I want them to think that their English teacher can be their hero."

Cultural Context

My base of operations is the guidance office, where the school houses a large staff of support services: English as a second language teachers, learning disabilities specialists, social workers, psychologists, and guidance counselors. The bulletin board is covered with announcements of workshops on children at risk, gender issues, support groups for boys with little impulse control. The room bustles with authority and expertise, as does the central office. Teachers bring in food, from bagels to birthday cakes, to share with their colleagues. Flyers announce that members of the PTA have baked snacks for a "pre-holiday treat in honor of the administrators and teachers."

A common topic of conversation among the teachers is the crowding. A school that was built for 800 students now holds almost 1,000. The sixth grade has not been integrated into the program because of a budget shortfall. For 1993–1994 they function as a school within a school.

The teachers complain about the lack of space. Rooms are scarce; some double rooms, separated by sliding screens, have been divided into three rooms. Consequently, the room in the middle has no windows. Lunch periods have been cut from 25 to 20 minutes. The guidance staff has no place for private conferences. The increased number of students and faculty results in crowded hallways, heightened noise levels, and more irritability.

The school's moral concerns are reflected in the Smith School parent manual. These include developing individual potential, fostering social skills, celebrating diversity, nurturing academic and decision-making skills, and balancing individual needs with those of the group. Whatever friction exists between MacDonald and Janet Howell can generally be traced to the weight given by each to these various elements. MacDonald, the subjectivist, concerned about his students' self-esteem, always comes down on the side of the individual. Howell, more traditional, committed to building a school community, opts for conformity over individualism.

The tension between the individual's needs and those of the community exists in any school. At Shaw the Quaker tradition, particularly the Silent Meeting, eases that tension through religious doctrine. At Smith, however, there is no easy solution to implementing the mandates of the middle school reform literature (Carnegie Council, 1989; Stevenson, 1992). Breaking down the students' world into manageable units, such as Houses, militates against a common school culture. Encouraging individualism may result in self-centeredness at the expense of community.

I ask John MacDonald whether the school is a supportive environment for him. He replies:

> Well, I think everyone is entitled to their own view of that. I think that Janet's okay, and she's never said no to me or anything, but it's just that I don't think she's really on my wavelength. I don't think she sees kids the same way I see kids.

He describes their differences as related to the nature of middle school education. According to MacDonald, Howell views the school "as a stepchild of the high school." A former high school teacher herself, Howell is concerned about getting the students "ready for what is ahead." MacDonald is present-oriented. He states, "My theory is that you go with the kid, wherever the kid is. You maximize that kid's sense of self-worth, and then the kid flies and doesn't look back." According to the classic dichotomy, Howell is more subject-centered; MacDonald is more student-centered. His concern about the students' self-worth is characteristic of the subjectivist, "inside-out" orientation of moral education.

Another area of disagreement is MacDonald's firmly held view about the student-teacher relationship. MacDonald uses the word *advocate* six times during our interviews and considers the House system as an incubator for caring relationships, but he fears that Howell will try to institutionalize the informal guidance and counseling, thereby changing MacDonald's relationships with his students. The House system was central to MacDonald's decision to come to Smith, and he resists any attempt to change it. "I think every kid has to have an adult they can intimately attach to."

Only the public school teachers in my study express concerns about their administrators. The two private school teachers are thoroughly complimentary about their principals. Amy Medeiros and Mary Carparo are friends as well as colleagues; Tuvia Kaplan admires and emulates Dean Cahn. John MacDonald acknowledges Janet Howell as a competent professional, but he feels that his views on the teacher's role and on the *raison d'etre* of the school differ from hers.

The Principal. Janet Howell's notions of moral education certainly differ from John MacDonald's. One reason she speaks more of community than MacDonald does is that she was strongly influenced by a course on the Just Community which she took with Lawrence Kohlberg. She alternates between referring to Smith as a school and as a community. Her attempts to build community include her encouragement of cooperative learning and her concerted efforts to integrate minority and immigrant children into the school. The daughter of immigrants herself, she speaks empathically of an eighth-grade student who got into trouble at school and had been pilfering cash from his mother's purse. The mother, a Japanese widow who worked long hours in a bakery to support her family, had expected the boy to be the primary caregiver for his younger siblings. In counseling the mother, Howell referred to her grandmother, an Italian widow, who raised her children on her earnings as a tailor.

Howell's views on the hero, like her philosophy of middle schools, are more traditionalist than MacDonald's. Like Bennett (1993), Kilpatrick (1992), and Vitz (1990), Howell finds the hero in literature. The hero is didactic, instructing through his or her struggle. Howell, a short, attractive woman in her late 40s, recalls that her first heroes or heroines were characters from the classics like those by Hardy, Dickens, and the Brontë sisters, as well as Nancy Drew. She laughs when she remembers how she loved the girl-detective: "I would always identify with the hero who was the problem solver. Look where I am now! Look at the problems I have to deal with day in and day out!"

Howell understands that the difference between the hero and the role model lies in the obstacles faced by each. Her role models were competent women: her grandmother and Ann, a next-door neighbor:

> She just was an amazing woman—off a farm. She could do anything. She could fix anything. Car broke down? She'd fix it. She was just such a role model; an independent woman who didn't have children of her own who taught me a lot, and she was a great companion. I just loved her.

Howell expects her teachers to be role models, and she explains why in developmental terms. As young people separate from their parents, they need other adults to turn to. Middle school teachers are the most likely candidates:

> I enticed Jerome Kagan out of Harvard two years ago to come and talk to us about developmental issues of this age, based on his research. What he said to us was you can have the best curriculum in the world. You can work really hard on it. It can work or it cannot work; it doesn't matter. The thing that's most important to middle school students is the relationships they develop with their teachers.

I tell Howell that my teacher, the late theologian Abraham Joshua Heschel, used to say that education needed not more textbooks but more textpersons. Howell agrees; the teacher, by virtue of her being, teaches. As Rebbe Kaplan says, "I am a little *Avraham avinu*."

Popular Culture. For John MacDonald, as for George Stratas, popular culture is ever-present in the classroom. MacDonald uses popular music and movies to augment his teaching. He, like Stratas, knows the latest hits. One day, to his students' delight, he sings a song by Meatloaf as he distributes papers. I ask him whether he views popular culture as an ally or as an enemy. Having observed him discussing movies with his students, and hearing him play songs performed by Bette Midler and Mariah Carey, I know what the answer will be, but I ask anyway. MacDonald responds with his usual animation and candor:

> I can't stand our librarian at this school for a lot of reasons. One of the things is she discourages kids from reading adolescent literature. Well, when are you ever going to read adolescent literature other than when you're an adolescent? And I think the same thing is true of popular culture. If we aren't aware of it, it means that their stuff is going on, and our stuff is going on. They'll do our stuff because they have to do our stuff, but then we're not sharing. *We're not going back and forth* [emphasis added].

Going back and forth means making connections, building bridges. This is part of MacDonald's philosophy of meeting students where they are. "Where they are" is immersed in the world of popular music, movies, television, and sports. Smith yearbooks are filled with lists of favorites: favorite singers, actors, actresses, rock groups, music videos, radio stations, and television channels. The names of athletic teams decorate the hats, T-shirts, and jackets of the boys in the class. I overhear Janie, one of MacDonald's students, discussing her vacation reading with friends; all three are reading novels by John Grisham. They eagerly await the opening of the movie *The Pelican Brief* and wonder how faithful it will be to the book. Many of Janie's classmates choose heroes from popular culture as the subjects of their research papers. Among them are Larry Byrd, Elvis Presley, Jim Henson, Arthur Ashe, and Yoko Ono. Having seen the movie *Schindler's List*, Stacey selects Oskar Schindler as her hero. While choosing the subjects for their papers, several mention that they recognize one person or another because they have seen that person on a television talk show. They turn to each other for validation: "Did anyone see that on *Donahue*?" Elena confides to MacDonald, "That's where we get our facts." She rejects several of her teacher's suggestions for subjects. Shaking her head, Elena insists, "I want someone famous." Her candidates must be legitimated by Oprah, Maury, or Phil to be considered heroes. The Smith students score highest on my cultural index, with a mean of 8.63. Jacob, a classical violinist, makes the lowest score of the group, answering only four of 10 items correctly.

Parents. The parents of the Smith students are the only parents I interview who explicitly state their concern that popular culture presents inappropriate role models for their children. In discussing Stacey's heroes and role models, Evelyn Hane says, "She never talks about movie stars and sports people. I'm thrilled." Louise Trustman is pleased that her son Edward is taking a course such as Heroes and Sheroes:

> It's good for him to know about heroes and role models. There are a lot of things on television that kids could consider to be heroes and role models. To be frank, it's rubbish. They have to know the difference between TV and what's real. Although Edward is good; he knows the difference. He says to me, "I know. It's for TV. It's not real."

The first question I ask all the parents in my study is, "Who are your child's heroes and role models?" The Smith parents respond with a disclaimer, some variation on, "Oh, my goodness. Who knows?" They seem the least knowledgeable of any of the parents I interview.

As they continue to reflect on my question, the three mothers eventually produce some names. Rebecca Chambers, Alan's mother, thinks her son may consider sports figures as heroes. Louise Trustman agrees as she mulls over the question and comes up with some names: "Well, maybe Edward would think that his mother and father were role models. And maybe his grandfather for a hero, because he fought in World War II." Evelyn Hane, Stacey's mother, suggests that she and her husband might serve as role models. She does not think Stacey has any heroes. Mrs. Hane and the other mothers I contact are more at ease when discussing people their children admire than in speaking about their heroes or role models.

When I ask Torah Institute parents, "What part do heroes and role models play in your child's schooling?" I hear about the importance of learning about the *gedolim*. Parents at Pierce express gratitude for the opportunity to study African-American heroes. Not so at Smith; when I ask about the place of moral prototypes in their children's education, the responses to my question are, "I don't think they [have a place]"; "Minimal"; and "I have no idea." Louise Trustman describes Edward as "self-motivated. He does what he wants to do. He doesn't care what others do." For Trustman, as for the girls at Shaw, having role models is a weakness, a sign of conformity.

None of the three parents mentions teachers as role models. Teachers do not appear to have the same status in this middle- to upper-middle-class community as at Pierce. Two of three parents, however, add that their children admire some of their teachers, including John MacDonald. Evelyn Hane notes: "We talk about various teachers; who's a good one, who's a bad one. He's a good one." Louise Trustman elaborates on what makes MacDonald a good teacher: "He's interesting. He enjoys teaching and teaches well. He goes over the papers and doesn't let things slip by. He's difficult but fair." Like the parents at Shaw, who resemble them most closely in socioeconomic terms, the parents at Smith differentiate between objects of admiration and role models.

The parents differ in their assessment of a course such as Heroes and Sheroes. All three admit to being unsure what the course is about. Louise Trustman confesses, "We're just happy that he (Edward) has a good teacher." MacDonald's reputation is such that many parents don't seem to care what he teaches. Parents such as Mrs. Trustman are simply relieved that their child got one of the much-coveted places in MacDonald's classes. Evelyn Hane tells me that she thinks it's useful to think about the subject of heroes: "It helps define who you are and what you value." Rebecca Chambers is the most negative: "To be frank, it's not that important. Learning the basics of English and history are more important. I'd rather he take a course in grammar. Something concrete. He needs to learn basic skills, like how to write a sentence."

In fact, that morning Alan had turned in a three-page paper in which he wrote an ending to *The Grand Babylon Hotel*. (MacDonald doles out the reading in packets; students have no way of knowing how the novel ends until they receive the last packet.) During class the students had reviewed a list of 25 vocabulary words in preparation for a major test on the novel. The list included words such as *pluck, wizened, laconically, contused,* and *discursive.*

Among the four groups of parents, the Smith parents' discourse seems to have the flattest affect. The parents at Pierce and at the Torah Institute express enthusiasm about their children's opportunity to meet mythic heroes. They are unanimously grateful to teachers who model appropriate behavior and values for their sons and daughters. The Shaw parents, although reticent on the subject of heroes, are eloquent about the moral messages the school conveys to their daughters; two out of the three Shaw parents mention the importance of the faculty as embodiments of the values they espouse. The parents of the Smith students, however, know little about the course their children have elected and attach only modest importance to moral prototypes in their lives or those of their children. MacDonald and the faculty members I consult suggest that in this community, children and parents lead very separate lives. Their lives are so heavily programmed that they do not spend much time talking together. The Smith parents are reluctant to use either of the terms *hero* or *role model*. Although all three mention how much their children like MacDonald, none confirms his hope that "their English teacher can be their hero."

Who Are the Students' Heroes and Role Models?

At Pierce the students do not share their teacher's belief in the importance of heroes. At the Torah Institute and the Shaw School, the students sound like their teachers when discussing the subject of moral prototypes. The students at the Smith School echo MacDonald's views. The subject of heroes is the essence of the 12-week course they have been taking with MacDonald. At the time of our interview, they have been struggling with the definition of *hero* for nearly eight weeks. Thus it is not surprising that their discussion of who is a hero is the most sophisticated and most nuanced of the four groups.

Like their peers in the other schools, the Smith students begin their definition of a hero with the notion of the rescuer who is willing to risk danger for another. Edward includes as a hero someone who would endanger himself in order to save an animal as well as a person. Jon and Caitlin disagree on the issue of bravery. Jon expresses the conventional view, that the hero is fearless. Caitlin points out that it may be more heroic to be fearful and to conquer one's fear. Students at Pierce and Shaw, who have not spent so much time discussing heroism, may not move beyond the idea of hero as rescuer; Smith students do so. Sydney and Jacob include the altruistic hero, who dedicates his or her life to helping other people. Elena repeats MacDonald's views on the quiet hero, saying, "I think also that a hero doesn't have to do anything known or special. Like, any of us could be a hero."

The students also raise the question of intention. Is a person who attempts something heroic and fails still a hero? Caitlin thinks so. Alan emphasizes selflessness and humility, "not looking for credit for it." Jacob insists that one aspect of heroism depends on the recipient's need for the hero's attention: "It's not like giving someone 50 cents or even $500 when they don't need it."

Alan, Elena, and Jon wonder about obligation. If someone is obliged by the nature of his or her occupation to save a life, such as a firefighter or a lifeguard, is that person still a hero? Alan and Elena apply this line of thought to parents, whose duty it is to protect their children:

Alan: If they, like, save their child, I wouldn't consider that heroic because you're not going to let your child die if they're in a situation like that. So I wouldn't consider it heroic if you saved them.

Emily: Like those mothers that get that burst of adrenaline and lift up those cars 'cause their adrenaline gets going. That's not really, like, heroic because . . .

Adam: It's their kid.

Emily: It's, like, something in their blood or something.

Elena admits that she had never considered "the flaw thing" before she took MacDonald's course. It is "the flaw thing" that appeals to Jacob, who remarks that true heroes evolve: "I think that when people are being heroic they need to become stronger inside themselves to really be considered a hero."

MacDonald's students accept the idea that heroes are social constructions. They note that the definition of the hero has become privatized. Stacey observes, "Everybody's idea is different. A hero to one person wouldn't be a hero to another person." Alan extends the notion to countries as well as individuals. He comments that Americans think that Oskar Schindler was a hero, but the Nazis would consider him a villain. Alan knows that when everyone creates his or her own definition of a hero, the term can lose its meaning: "A lot of people overuse *hero*. Just because someone does one thing good doesn't mean they're a hero."

The students differentiate heroic behavior from heroic character. For some, being a hero means living a lifetime devoted to prosocial activities. In discussing his goals for the course, MacDonald says that he wants the students "to think about why people do some of the things they do." These eight students certainly have done so, and they admit to being confused by the subject. As Stacey says, "Before, when I didn't think about it, I just didn't think about it. Now it's cluttered my idea completely. I mean it's just made it harder to think about what a hero is because there are so many different definitions."

MacDonald does not use the term *role model*. Therefore, it is not surprising that his students are uncomfortable with it. At last, however, they agree on a spectrum of moral prototypes. First there are people they admire, then role models, and finally heroes. Elena says, " 'Admire' is someone you look up to, while a role model is someone you want to be like, and a hero is someone that did something heroic." The students point out that role models are observable; they are personal rather than public, and closer rather than farther away. Sydney suggests,

> I think a role model could maybe sometimes be a hero that's sort of like closer to home; like easier for you to be like them. Like a hero seems impossible to me. Sometimes you see them on TV and think, "I could never do that." But a role model is somebody who's more similar to you.

Her remarks correspond to those of her counterparts at the other schools.

The Smith students raise the gender question. Alan claims that his father is more a role model for him than his mother: "I guess there's a lot of things my mom does that I wouldn't want to do." His classmates joke, "Learn how to put your makeup on." "Shop." Jon, however, isn't sure.

> "Yeah. I guess more my father, but for some reason, whenever I sort of need to talk, like I have a question, and my parents are in the car, I always happen to say, 'Mom. . . .' I never say, 'Mom and Dad. . . .' "

The students winnow out possible candidates for role models. One defining factor is gender, as captured in the exchange between Alan and Jon. Another is factor is socioeconomic class and the profession of the potential role model. These upper-middle-class youths, the sons and daughters of professionals, are reluctant to confer role model status on teachers. They are willing to admit that they admire them, and many do so, especially Mr. MacDonald, but teachers are not role models. Elena says matter-of-factly, "I don't want to be a teacher. I want to be a lawyer, so I don't see them as a role model."

Like the students at Shaw, these teenagers are very reluctant to claim role models. To them the term connotes a surrender of autonomy, as it seems to do to Mrs. Trustman and to the girls at Shaw. Stacey is most adamant. Characterizing herself as "independent," she writes: "I don't have people I think of as role models. I just try to be myself. I might unconsciously try to be like somebody, though I don't think so." Sydney offers the insight that she has no single role model. "Maybe some things I do are a combination of things that I subconsciously picked up from other people."

Fewer students from this group than from the others select parents or parent surrogates as role models. Every student in the other school groups mentions one or both parents; only three of the Smith students, two boys and a girl, do so. One explanation may lie in what MacDonald and his colleagues call the separateness of the parents' and the children's lives. Another may be found in the students' discussion of duty and exemplary behavior. They have argued that a parent is expected to behave in an extraordinary manner for his or her child.

Two of the girls admire peers: one a cousin and the other a friend "who has a lot of problems in her life." These students, more deeply immersed in popular culture than any other student group, are less likely to admire athletes and glamorous celebrities than are their counterparts at Franklin Pierce. Those named by the Smith students include Magic Johnson, David Letterman, Arthur Ashe, Larry Byrd, and Harry Houdini. These selections are multiracial, unlike the Pierce students' list, which is largely African-American. Jacob, the classical music lover, adds high culture to the Smith heroes and role models: composer-performer Peter Schickele and aspiring musicians who practice with the diligence that Jacob himself sometimes lacks. National heroes on the Smith list include Martin Luther King, John F. Kennedy, Eleanor Roosevelt, and Jackie Kennedy. First Ladies are included only at Smith. Although women are mentioned as heroes and as admirable personalities, the Smith School list is predominantly male. Yet this list is strikingly international. Inspired by the movies, Stacey selects Oskar Schindler; Jon, Mahatma Gandhi. In this sophisticated and politically liberal community, two new categories appear: animal rights activists and people dying of AIDS. No one mentions religious figures of any kind. Table 6 summarizes the students' choices.

Table 6.
Roger Wolcott Smith School: Students' Exemplars

	Parents	Parent surrogates (including teachers)	Peers	Political figures	Animal rights activists	AIDS victims	Athletes	Glamorous celebrities	Classical musicians
Girls (4)	1 (both)	2 (M)	2 (F)	2 (1F; 1M)	1 (F)	0	0	0	0
Boys (4)	2 (both)	2 (M)	0	2 (2M)	0	1 (both)	2 (M)	1 (M)	1 (both)
Total (8)	3 (both)	4 (M)	2 (F)	4 (3M; 1F)	1 (F)	1 (both)	2 (M)	1 (M)	1 (both)

M = Male; F = Female

In a school that celebrates the individual, the students' choices reflect their cultural context. Authority figures such as parents, relatives, and teachers loom less large here than in the schools in the study. The political liberalism of the school and the idiosyncratic interests of the students (which include wildlife rehabilitation and classical violin) create an array of unusual exemplars. In their study of the ideal self, Simmons and Wade (1983) report on the presence of a vocal group of 15-year-olds who "reject the concept of an ideal person to which they might aspire" (p. 21). The Smith students' reluctance to acknowledge role models may reflect a similar impulse. Having a role model may be tantamount to an admission of dependence, or at least being unfinished.

A Cross-Classroom Analysis
of the Students

IMMERSION IN POPULAR CULTURE

Figure 1 depicts the average scores of students from the four schools on the 10-point popular culture index I created: Torah Institute (5.25), Pierce School (8.25), Shaw School (8.25), and Smith School (8.63).

Because they inhabit a world that separates itself from popular culture and attend a school that reinforces such separation, it is no surprise that the students at Springfield Torah Institute score lowest of the four groups. The other independent school, Shaw, does not encourage the inclusion of popular culture in its curriculum. During my visits there, I observed only one reference to popular culture, when Amy Medeiros laughingly told her students that it was better for them to do homework than to "rot away" in front of a television set. She and her colleagues consciously distance themselves from popular culture. The Shaw boundaries, however, are not hermetically

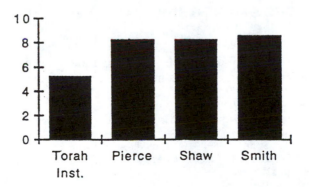

Figure 1.   Students' average scores on popular culture index

sealed. The students are certainly exposed to alternative messages. During my field visits, I noticed that the Shaw girls decorated their lockers with pictures of supermodels and movie stars. Even so, celebrity heroes are confined to the coatroom and are never welcome in the classroom.

It is also not surprising that the two public schools live in the world of popular culture. Both MacDonald and Stratas rely on movies, music, sports, and television as common ground on which they and the students meet. MacDonald embraces popular culture to get into what he calls "their stuff." In these settings, where the bonds of the school culture are looser, the teachers attempt to connect to their students by making curricular material meaningful to them.[1] The boundaries of the two public schools are far more permeable than those of Shaw, even though the Shaw girls' scores on my popular culture index indicate that they are as familiar as their public school counterparts with pop music, movies, television, and sports.

Springfield Torah Institute and Shaw School have a similar point of view regarding the perils of the wider society and its exemplars. The moral prototypes of the Torah Institute are not those celebrated by popular culture; thus one would expect that this school would be much more successful than the others at separating the world of Jacob from that of Esau. If the Torah Institute students' mean score on my popular culture instrument is any indication, they would appear to be far more strongly shielded from secular influences than their counterparts in other middle schools. (One student, however, received a score of 9 out of a possible 10.) Still, no boundaries are truly impermeable; despite the firmest resolve of a total institution such as the Torah Institute, some aspects of popular culture seep through.

THE STUDENTS' MORAL PROTOTYPES

In Tables 7, 8, and 9 I compare the choices of heroes and role models of students from the four schools. I also include answers given by the students when I asked them about people they admired.

---

[1] Popular culture, particularly television, is a significant component of young people's lives. According to *The Girl Scout Survey on the Beliefs and Moral Values of American Children* (Girl Scouts, 1989) 31% of middle school students watch fewer than two hours of television a day, 37% watch two to three hours, and 28% watch four to five hours or more (p. 112).

Table 7.
Girls' Heroes and Role Models

	Torah Inst. (3)	Pierce (6)	Shaw (8)	Smith (4)	Total (N=21)
Parents	3	6	8	1	18
Parent surrogates, including teachers	0	5	5	2	12
Religious figures	1	1	0	0	2
God	2	0	0	0	2
Political figures	0	1	0	2	3
Athletes	0	1	0	0	1
Glamorous celebrities	0	3	1	0	4
Animal rights activists	0	0	0	1	1
AIDS victims	0	0	0	0	0
Classical musicians	0	0	0	0	0
Peers	0	1	3	2	6

Several striking patterns emerge in the girls' choices (see Table 7). The girls in the independent schools, Springfield Torah Institute and Shaw, have far fewer categories of exemplars than those in the public schools. The number of categories (e.g., political figures, religious leaders, athletes, celebrities) is significant because it suggests the arenas of achievement that may be open to the students. The source of Rebbe Kaplan's concern—that the girls at his school have fewer role models than the boys—may explain the responses at the Torah Institute. It does not explain the responses at Shaw, however, where girls are surrounded by positive role models. It is striking that Shaw girls, who attend a school that celebrates National Girls and Women in Sports Day and for whom athletics is a major activity, do not single out women athletes as exemplars. Perhaps Laura, the music teacher, is correct in saying that the faculty is more liberal than the students.

I also found that the young women in the study are more likely to choose female exemplars than the research indicates.[2] The girls from Smith claim Jackie Kennedy, Eleanor Roosevelt, and animal rights activist Mary Jane Stretch as exemplars. Those from Pierce mention Janet Jackson and author Lois Lowry. Almost all of the Shaw girls' exemplars are female. (The exceptions are their fathers.) That six girls overall choose peers as exemplars adds credence to feminist observa-

Table 8.
Boys' Heroes and Role Models

	Torah Inst. (5)	Pierce (2)	Shaw (0)	Smith (4)	Total (N=11)
Parents	5	2	0	2	9
Parent surrogates, including teachers	1	1	0	2	4
Religious figures	4	0	0	0	4
God	1	0	0	0	1
Political figures	2	1	0	2	5
Athletes	2	1	0	2	5
Glamorous celebrities	0	0	0	1	1
Animal rights activists	0	0	0	0	0
AIDS victims	0	0	0	1	1
Classical musicians	0	0	0	1	1
Peers	1	0	0	0	1

tions about the importance to women of relationships and connectedness (Belenky et al., 1986). Friends are very important to adolescent girls, especially to the Shaw girls; many have had the same classmates since they were four years old. In my sample, only Margaret is a newcomer to the school. Five of the eight have attended Shaw since nursery school; two joined in the fourth grade.

The boys' exemplars seem to cover a much broader range. At the Torah Institute, the boys' heroes and role models include seven different categories of exemplars, as opposed to three for the girls. The Smith boys' exemplars fall into seven categories; those of their female counterparts belong to five.

Franklin Pierce School, the urban public school, is the exception. At Pierce the boys' range of exemplars is narrower than the girls', but any conclusions would be unwarranted because the sample contains only two boys. At Pierce the girls' choices cover seven categories, compared with four for the boys. Perhaps one explanation is that two of the four girls in the Pierce sample are African-American. The authors of *How Schools Shortchange Girls* (*A.A.U.W. Report*, 1992) suggest

---

[2] Balswick and Ingoldsby (1982) observe a singular absence of female public heroes and a tendency of young women to choose male heroes, even in fields such as popular entertainment. In 1985 Brodbelt and Wall (1985) noted little progress in the effort to add female faces to the pages of American history books. Perhaps the intervening dozen years have made a difference, however; the lists of heroes in the *World Almanac* have taken on a slightly female cast (*The World Almanac*, 1991, 1992).

Table 9.
All Students' Heroes and Role Models

	Torah Inst. (8)	Pierce (8)	Shaw (8)	Smith (8)	Total (N=32)
Parents	8	8	8	3	27
Parent surrogates, including teachers	1	6	5	4	16
Religious figures	5	1	0	0	6
God	3	0	0	0	3
Political figures	2	2	0	4	8
Athletes	2	2	0	2	6
Glamorous celebrities	0	3	1	1	5
Animal rights activists	0	0	0	1	1
AIDS victims	0	0	0	1	1
Classical musicians	0	0	0	1	1
Peers	1	1	3	2	7

that the gender gap in achievement that exists for white girls is not found among African-American girls; often they are much more confident than their white counterparts. These authors contend that lowered horizons are due to a failure of self-esteem.

One pattern that emerges from the boys' choices of exemplars (see Table 8) is their overwhelmingly secular character. Religious heroes inspire only the boys at the Torah Institute. Another pattern among the boys pertains to race: They admire athletes with no regard to skin color. A third is gender. The girls include male and female exemplars on their lists, but no boys include female exemplars in any category: athletes, celebrities, or political leaders (see Tables 3, 4, 5, and 6). Fourth, the boys are much less interested than the girls in glamorous celebrities, movie or television personalities, and musical performers.

Kaplan's students can transfer the larger-than-life from the religious to the secular domain. They are comfortable with the notion of the mythic hero, at ease with the hero as metaphor. In their lists of heroes, Springfield Torah Institute students include not only religious scholars but also American presidents and World War II personalities such as Claire Chenault. The Torah Institute students display different attitudes toward the *gedolim* (Hebrew: great ones), who are above reproach, than toward the secular heroes, who can be flawed. Many of the heroes selected by Kaplan's students look like those whose faces decorate George Stratas's classroom. The word *hero* is used in three classrooms: Kaplan's, Stratas's, and MacDonald's. There, students choose traditional political heroes: American presidents, military heroes, and international figures such as Gandhi and Schindler.

Students' exemplars are, generally, not the celebrities and glamorous personalities that dominate the media. In three of the four schools, students overwhelmingly choose their parents or parent surrogates—that is, other relatives, family friends, or teachers. My findings resemble those of Wechter (1981), who notes that younger children name parents and parent surrogates as "ideal persons." Unlike Duck (1990), I found very little hero-worship directed toward celebrities. In a study of more than 300 Australian teens, Duck observed that one half to three quarters chose media figures as heroes.

The teacher as exemplar presents a complex picture. Although the students comment on the importance of a personal relationship with their teachers, all of the Shaw girls but one are reluctant to include teachers as role models because they worry about whether they can trust them with their secrets. In contrast, one of the reasons that Lucy chooses her teacher George Stratas as a role model is that she can tell him "anything." The issue of the teacher as confidante is intriguing; I am inclined to believe that this issue is far more important for girls than for boys, and for students of lower socioeconomic class.

Wyman (1993) observes that teachers are more likely to be role models for students of lower socioeconomic status. Becoming a teacher means leaving behind the working class or the lower middle class. George Stratas's "nut," his wad of currency, symbolizes his success. The mystique of the teacher is certainly apparent at the urban Pierce School, where half of the students name teachers as role models. Of the 16 students overall who offer parent surrogates as exemplars, 11 name educators: teachers, a school administrator, and a volunteer coach in a community hockey league. These 11 include the students who refer both to "role models" and to "people they admire." Five students from the more affluent schools, Shaw and Smith, name teachers as people they admire, but not as role models. In both schools, students are reluctant to use the term *role model*. At Shaw, the girls are uncomfortable with both *hero* and *role model*.

At suburban Smith, four students speak at length about their admiration of John MacDonald, but do not refer to him as a role model. Their reluctance is based on a belief that possessing role models entails a loss of autonomy, an admission that they are not their own persons. One of the middle-class Pierce teenagers responds similarly: "I don't really feel I have any role models. I don't feel I want to be somebody else than who I am." This rejoinder resembles those heard by Simmons and Wade (1983) in their study of British young people's ideal persons: Nineteen percent of the respondents rejected models of any kind (p. 21). It is not surprising that students from Smith, a school that stresses individualism, would perceive having a role model as an admission of dependence. Both they and their peers at Shaw interpret the term narrowly in relation to one's occupation. The students don't want to become teachers; therefore, teachers cannot be role models for them. Because both of these schools attract students of higher socioeconomic status than either Pierce or the Springfield Torah Institute, that factor may be operating in their choice of role models. For these students, becoming a teacher is not "a step up."

Although the definition of *hero* varies from classroom to classroom, all the students understand that the difference between role models and heroes is a matter of distance. They can "look up to" role models, "ask them for advice," and "confide" in them. MacIntyre (1984) notes the "fragmentation" and "destruction" (p. 5) of the language of morality; my study shows that for the students as well as for their parents and teachers, the language of moral exemplars is equally fragmented and destroyed. *Hero* denotes a *godol* at the Torah Institute, an American cultural icon at Pierce, very little at Shaw, and a moral exemplar at Smith. I was not surprised to discover that *hero* conjures up very different meanings and associations in different settings, but I was surprised at the multiplicity of meanings attached to *role model*. Gender and class seem to offer some explanations for the many connotations of the latter term. The girls at Shaw expect a role model to be a confidante; the students at Smith read dependence into the relationship between role model and emulator. MacIntyre (1984) describes the fluid language of contemporary morality; the lack of consensus about who is a hero seems to pertain to the role model as well.

9

Conclusions and Implications

CONCLUSIONS

My intent was to explore how four middle school teachers in diverse settings, teaching different subjects, understood and used moral prototypes—that is, heroes and role models—in their teaching. I also wished to learn how students and students' parents interpreted and understood such prototypes. To answer the questions I posed, I had to contextualize them. I needed to learn more about the teachers' philosophies of moral education, their perceptions of the demands of their disciplines, and the ethos of their schools. I also had to compare the students' and parents' understanding of moral prototypes with those of the teachers and those reported in the psychological literature. Through field observation, interviews, artifact analysis, questionnaires, and survey instruments, I tried to capture the multiple meanings of moral education and the role of moral prototypes in shaping values.

The Teachers' Views of Moral Education

Society and Self. The literature describes two schools of moral educators: those whose primary obligations are to society and those whose primary obligations are to the self. Following Durkheim's functional example, character educators (Bennett, 1991; Kilpatrick, 1992; Wynne & Ryan, 1993) are more concerned with society; in contrast, those moral educators who advocate building self-esteem (Ascher, 1991; Brown & Gilligan, 1992) are more likely to be concerned with the individual. The character educators' usual choice of moral prototype is the hero; educators who stress self-esteem often opt for the role model. Benninga (1991) also identifies two strands of moral educators: those who employ a direct method of instruction and those who use an indirect method. Similarly, UCLA social scientist James Q. Wilson (1993) refers to a Janus-like moral education—one face turned to self-control and restraint, and a second face turned to liberation and self-improvement (p. 217).[1]

To learn more about how the teachers in my study use and understand moral prototypes, I began by eliciting their views on moral education. Theorists of moral education construct two neatly labeled drawers; instead, what I found were two untidy cubbyholes overflowing with ambiguities and contradictions.

All four of my teachers are concerned both with society and with self. The issue is not either-or; it is a matter of degree. Tuvia Kaplan, who teaches in a setting that seemingly would be the most traditional and therefore objectivist, "outside-in," and mimetic, nevertheless worries about the girls in his class and their lack of role models. Meeting young women's needs for self-definition is not the subjectivists' only concern: Amy Medeiros structures her mathematics course to build self-confidence and individualism in her students, but she also uses cooperative learning in order to build community. John MacDonald, the teacher most impassioned about self-esteem, regularly tweaks his more entitled students about their self-centeredness, reminding them of their obligations to society. George Stratas creates a niche for diversity by recasting the meaning of "core American values." By using as his narrative the evolution of civil rights in the United States, he tries to accommodate the pageant of American history to African-Americans' need to see themselves mirrored in that drama.

Theorists of moral education offer pairs of paradigms to describe the current state of the field: objectivist-subjectivist, "outside-in"–"inside-out," mimetic-transformative, society-self. Yet all of the teachers in my study espouse a view of moral education that is complementary rather than dichotomous. All, in varying degrees, concern themselves with both the community and the individual. On an objectivist-subjectivist continuum, Tuvia Kaplan is the most concerned with the traditionalist goal of enculturation: teaching the norms of group behavior and values to his seventh-grade Jewish studies class. He is a character educator who enacts the etymology of the word *character*: he attempts to incise a unique mark upon his students' minds and souls. Another character educator is George Stratas, whose goal is to teach

---

[1] This two-pronged depiction of moral education is one that dominates all the social sciences (Burrell & Morgan, 1979). Eisner (1985) describes educational philosophy as either "outside-in" or "inside-out." Others refer to subject-centered and student-centered learning (Dewey, 1974). Jackson's (1986) depiction of mimetic and transformative teaching is another such division. Mimetic teaching is concerned with society's need to transmit its skills and culture, whereas transformative teaching concerns itself with changing the individual without reference to the social order.

what he calls "core American values" to his multiethnic, multiracial eighth-grade social studies class. Amy Medeiros is closer to the subjectivist pole: By consciously increasing her prealgebra students' self-confidence, she appears to be following the tenets of transformative, reconceptualist, feminist pedagogy. By her own admission, however, she taught boys in an independent school and coeducational students in public schools in much the same way. John MacDonald is the most "inside-out," concerned as he is with the individual's needs. Although he bristles at administrative attempts to create community at the expense of students' autonomy, he persists in pointing out pathways to community involvement for his students.

Standards. Their fellow teachers agree that all four of these teachers are experts, thoroughly grounded in their disciplines. They are considered demanding by colleagues, students, and parents alike. In discussing their views of moral education, all of these teachers mention high standards, a concern that characterizes mimetic teaching. They teach traditional skills: to be able to analyze a Hebrew text; to describe the compromises that are reflected in the United States Constitution; to master the "sturdy formats" so necessary to mathematical problem solving; to write a research paper on a hero or, as John MacDonald likes to say, shero. Contrary to "either-or" theory, however, all four are resolutely transformative teachers. Each hopes to improve the life of the learners in his or her classroom. Kaplan and Stratas speak passionately about transfiguring them: Kaplan, by introducing newly arrived Russian émigrés to the beauties of traditional Jewish observance; Stratas, by convincing minority youths that their future lies in school, not in the streets.

Jackson (1986) states that some subjects are thought to be more amenable to a mimetic approach, and others to a transformative approach. He cautions that "exceptions are plentiful" (p. 131). My research corroborates that the exceptions in fact are the rule. Of all subjects, mathematics seems most intrinsically mimetic, especially as taught by a teacher who emphasizes "sturdy formats," procedures, and techniques. Yet the purpose behind Amy Medeiros's teaching is to build self-confidence, a thoroughly "inside-out" objective. Tuvia Kaplan teaches the story of David not only to fulfill his community's mandate to teach its "master stories" (Fowler, 1981), but also to prepare individuals for their inevitable life crises.

Teaching as a Craft. Even if subject matter does not necessarily determine the objectivist or subjectivist slant of moral education, it colors its presentation. From observing and listening to the teachers who collaborated with me, it became clear that there was no one form for moral education. Each content area has a moral character of its own. Bible, history, and literature build a moral education based on imagination. Mathematics constructs a moral education from control and precision. I began to imagine these teachers as craftspersons working with diverse materials. Like fine artisans, they respect their disciplines and what the disciplines can do. Writing about crafts, Needleman (1979) states, "It is as if the honorable craftsman in his journey of exploration of the material asks, 'What can this wood, this clay, this glass, do?' instead of 'What can I do with it?' " (p. 92).

They are master teachers, these skilled craftspersons, juggling the needs of their students, the curriculum, the school, and society. To watch them in action is to observe what Shulman (1987) calls "portraits in expertise" (p. 1). They know subject matter (Stratas, Medeiros, and MacDonald have master's degrees in a content area); they know how students think (Kaplan has a degree in psychology); and they have a wide array of pedagogical content knowledge (Shulman, 1987) as shown by the stories that each tells to connect the subject matter with the learner. Each teacher has a reputation for being "tough." Each speaks about what I have called "the conscience of craft." Their concern for high academic achievement shapes their notions of moral education. Needleman (1979) writes, "Crafts are about one thing: the secret of how to work." In demanding proofs, research papers, and mastery of texts, these "honorable craftspersons," like so many other committed teachers, introduce their students to the world of work.

Teaching as a Calling. The appeal of crafts to the craftsperson is a rejection of the shoddy and the mass-produced. A handmade article possesses the power to touch the inner life of both the maker and the user. All of the teachers in my study are dedicated to tapping into their students' inner life, often at a cost to their own private lives. Three of the teachers describe themselves as religious. MacDonald, although not a churchgoer, is a deeply spiritual person. All four treat teaching as a calling that absorbs much of their time as well as their physical and psychic energy. George Stratas attends nearly every extracurricular event at his school: dances, spaghetti suppers, and athletic competitions. Tuvia Kaplan spends his Sundays playing ball with his students. Both Amy Medeiros and John MacDonald speak of shortchanging themselves and their families in order to do right by their students. For each of them, teaching is a vocation. In describing what the craft does for the craftsperson, Needleman (1979) claims,

> Craft is a way of working to be alive inside my skin. It calls me to myself through my body through a set of specialized movements for each craft. All of this involves the craftsman in an exchange with the world

outside himself in which he gives his attention fully to the task at hand and receives himself. In this lies the meaning of action—I have to give outside in order to receive inside. The one without the other is meaningless. (p. 33)

No matter how great the sacrifices they make for their craft, none of the teachers would rather do anything else. Teaching makes them "alive inside their skins." Their teaching is animated and enthusiastic. Their need to forge connections is as strong as their students'. This need leads to an excitement about students and subject matter, which seems to be a precondition for effective moral education.

Connectedness: Caring, Stories, and Context. In their discussion of teaching, the teachers place great emphasis on making connections with their students. Moral education without relationship is unthinkable. All four use humor to first "reach 'em and then teach 'em" (Lickona, 1992, p. 85). In Egan's (1986) words, "A joke is not only funny; it is potentially another of those little factories of understanding, a place where understanding can be made or expanded" (p. 86). As Noddings (1992) recommends, the four teachers also connect by showing their concern. Each of them spends time with students before and after class helping them with classwork, discussing parents' and siblings' well-being, monitoring progress in nonschool activities, and chatting about weekends and vacations.

One way of making connections to students is through stories. All of the teachers have a beguiling array of anecdotes, particularly humorous ones, which they use to engage their students. These stories sometimes serve to illustrate or make concrete an abstract idea. Sometimes they bring relief or respite to the seriousness of the enterprise of learning. Gudmundsdottir (1991) refers to these stories as the vertical axis of the curriculum. During our discussions, the teachers mention that they tell stories about themselves in order to humanize and contextualize what otherwise would remain abstractions. This humanization creates its own pitfalls, however. It may cast the teachers as appealing role models for some of their students while closing them off to others. By joking that she doesn't know what a "designer" pizza costs, Amy Medeiros may set herself apart from some of her wealthier students who have never eaten in a Pizza Hut. Rebbe Kaplan's "regular guy" image endears him to the boys while alienating him from one of the observant girls, who prefers her teachers to be pale-skinned scholars rather than ruddy football players.

All four are storymakers as well as storytellers. The three humanities teachers have created strong horizontal axes (Gudmundsdottir, 1991) that form the basis of their courses. For Kaplan it is

David's complex personality; for Stratas, the expansion of civil rights; for MacDonald, the nature of the heroic. Each has crafted a curricular story that adds unity and drama to the course, in a testimonial to the power of the narrative mode (Bruner, 1986) as a learning tool.

One would expect that a mathematics teacher would rely on the paradigmatic rather than the narrative mode (Bruner, 1986). As Egan (1986) remarks, "We do not have mathematics texts rich in incident, anecdote, biography, games, puzzles, stories, magic, tricks, and so on" (p. 115). Needleman (1972) informs us that the essence of craft is in the resistance of the material to the craftsperson's hand, and mathematics would seem to be particularly resistant to the narrative mode. Medeiros, however, sought out and found a text containing the very elements that Egan says are missing in mathematics books. It is a tribute to her skill that she can weave a fabric of relationships and context throughout her prealgebra course. Relationship is essential to the narrative mode; by relating mathematics to the contents of kitchens and to camping trips, Medeiros contextualizes mathematics, making it a story of everyday life.

Each of the four teachers describes his or her own philosophy of moral education as follows:

1. It is concerned with both the individual and the community.
2. It demands high academic standards.
3. It is derived from the distinctive nature of their discipline.
4. It requires a sense of calling on their part.
5. It depends on making connections to students through caring, stories, and creating context.

The Cultural Context

Historian David McCullough (1992) writes that he has never been able to disassociate people or stories from their settings, "the background." He adds, "If character is destiny, so too, I believe, is terrain" (p. x). These teachers are affected enormously by the terrain on which they work.

Like teachers who tell stories, schools have their own stories. The stories of private schools are designed to attract a certain clientele. Parents send children to Springfield Torah Institute and to the Shaw School because they like the stories those schools tell. Some parents at Pierce, professionals and faculty members at a nearby university, have refrained from sending their children to private schools because they believe in Pierce's story of public education and pluralism. School stories represent "the kind of cultural experience that [parents] want for their children" (Henry, 1993, p. 64). Parents listen to them in order to decide whether to enroll their children. Once they send their children, satisfied parents make the school's stories their own, becoming partners in the process of education. It is a commonplace that parental involvement is important for children's academic success, that involvement is greater in the private than in the public sector where choice is not always possible (Johnson, 1990).

In the words of Rebbe Kaplan's principal, "the walls are *rebbeyim*" (Yiddish: mentors). The culture of the school can augment or undercut the teacher's message. Kaplan and Medeiros teach in schools with an ideological integrity that permeates the institutions. Shared purposes, values, and traditions build a sense of community. Smith, a public school, has looser cultural bonds, but its history as an alternative school committed to governance by faculty and to students' choice creates a degree of coherence. As Johnson (1990) observes, it is school culture with its "explicit goals and purposes that gives meaning and purpose to [teachers'] individual efforts" (p. 19). At Pierce, where students are unsure of the identity of the eponymous Franklin Pierce and where the handbook contains only the vaguest of moral messages, where there are few school rituals and traditions, Stratas is working in relative isolation. His disciplined classroom contrasts with the chaotic school cafeteria.

The Principal. Critical to the process of creating school culture is the presence of a principal with a vision, what Lanckton (1992) calls the "esteemed leader." The "esteemed leader" supports faculty members without diminishing their independence. Delineating the elements that make for a positive moral culture in the school, Lickona (1992) notes that a principal who is a moral leader is fundamental to the enterprise. According to Lickona, it is the principal who identifies the school's moral goals, who shares the moral vision with all the members of the school community: professional and support staff, parents, and students. It is the principal who spearheads the efforts to implement the mission and who serves as a model for staff, students, and parents (p. 326).

The teachers in the private schools in my study are unquestionably more complimentary about their principals than the public school teachers. Kaplan regards Dean Cahn as a role model not only for the students, but also for himself. Medeiros has enormous respect for both Mary Carparo, the middle school principal, and Barbara Burns, the head of the school. Her views on teaching mathematics to young women have been shaped by these two women: by supervision from Carparo and by having read Burns's research on mathematics and girls. The public school teachers are more likely to grumble about principals who fail to support them or who differ with them philosophically. Neither Stratas nor MacDonald considers his principal to be a role model.

Kaplan and Medeiros speak admiringly about the heads of their respective schools. Stratas is fortunate that his first principal was sympathetic and supported his efforts (his second principal all but ignores him); he admits, however, that David Stewart could not work independently of "downtown." (Stratas also was not surprised when I pointed out that the school handbook says nothing about values or character. When I asked him what moral education at Pierce means, he shrugged resignedly and said there was no consensus on the subject.) All of the principals I interview, however, expect their teachers to be role models for their students.

The ethos of the school creates the preconditions for moral education. Moral education means clear, unambiguous patterns of values and behavior. It demands a coherent school, a community that shares a vision. To implement a vision, a principal must seek out teachers with views similar to his or hers. The two independent schools I studied contain many role models: people hired expressly to reinforce the moral messages of the school. Janet Howell, the principal at Smith, was able to fill her few vacancies from a wide array of candidates. David Stewart, the principal at Pierce, had to take what "downtown" sent him. My study supports Aristotle's often-quoted dictum that morality cannot be taught without a moral community. The cultural context of the school strengthens the hand of an educator who takes moral education seriously. To use psychologist Kenneth Gergen's (1971) pithy term, the teacher's patterns and values become *salient* through repeated schoolwide exposure and an environment rich in models.

Parents. When these patterns and values are reinforced at home, no doubt they become doubly powerful. I did not investigate what went on in the homes of the students in the four teachers' classes. In discussions with 12 parents, however, (three in each of the four classes), I determined that these parents expect schools to deal with values. Certainly they are receptive to the introduction of moral prototypes into their children's classrooms, and they applaud the efforts of teachers who serve as role models. The most enthusiastic parents were those in the private schools; these parents clearly have made their schools' stories their own. In the public schools, parents were more likely to discuss the class than the school. Those whose children attended Pierce were unanimous in their appreciation of Stratas as a role model. The Smith parents praised MacDonald's expertise although they did not refer to him as a role model for their children, and they commented that their children were fortunate to have a teacher with his stellar reputation and enormous popularity.

Parents at the independent schools and the urban public school understand moral prototypes in much the same manner as do their children's teachers. At Springfield Torah Institute, the word *hero* conjures up images of the Biblical patriarchs, prophets, kings, and rabbinic scholars, past and present. For these parents, role models are essential to teaching their children how to lead Jewish lives. Parents are the primary role models for their children, but they expect the staff of the school to function as exemplars as well. At Shaw, where heroes are not part of Amy Medeiros's lexicon, parents observe that "there are no heroes today." Instead these parents speak of role models and commend Medeiros and her colleagues, who act as role models for their daughters. Parents at Pierce Middle School approve the efforts of their children's teacher, George Stratas. Arlene Short, an African-American, is grateful to Stratas for giving her daughter "heroes and role models of her kind."

Only at Smith, the suburban school, did I detect the lack of a vision of moral prototypes shared by the teacher and the parents. Of all the teachers in the study, MacDonald uses the word *hero* most naturally, uttering it unapologetically and unself-consciously. His definition may not be the traditional one; he uses it as the equivalent of Colby and Damon's "moral exemplar" (1992), a "quiet hero." By *hero*, MacDonald means someone who is committed to truth, justice, and service to others. This hero's life provides a map for socially responsible behavior. The parents I spoke to were not attuned to MacDonald's goals, despite a carefully articulated course description and an elaborate midterm progress report. One claimed to have no idea what the course was about; two were distinctly uncomfortable with the concept of *hero* or *role model*.

Desirability. Congruence between home and school is one reason that students would embrace a teacher's vision. A second reason is what Mordecai Nisan (1993) calls "desirability." In a variation of the light bulb joke, the question is, "How many psychiatrists does it take to change a light bulb?" The answer is, "One, but the light bulb has to want to change." The most coherent schools have made very clear what is desirable in ideology and praxis. Students who wish to succeed academically and socially in these milieus must accept the school's system of beliefs and behaviors, and the symbols thereof—that is, its moral prototypes. The most coherent schools in my study were the independent schools, where the ethos demands that students leave the world of popular culture at the doors or (to be completely accurate, in the case of Shaw) at their lockers. At these schools an understanding l; a trade is effected: our heroes and role models for those of the world at large.

Psychologist John Jung (1986) maintains that the literature on role models has neglected motivation as a factor in the subjects of the modeling. No matter how compelling they may be, role models cannot work their magic unless the would-be emulator wishes to emulate the model. Like the light bulb, he must want to change. In a total institution such the Springfield Torah Institute, the stakes of not adapting to the school norms are too high. After all, the primary role models are linked, directly or indirectly, to the word of God. At the Torah Institute disbelief is not an option. The pattern at Shaw is similar, but without the authority of Jewish law. Both schools are small; breaking school norms attracts attention. It is easier to escape change at Shaw, but because of the faculty's commitment to creating competent young women, academic excellence (even in male-dominated fields), risktaking, and independence generate exemplars. Computers are named for Marie Curie, Sally Ride, and Harriet Tubman. Popular celebrities, whose lives may not be exemplary, are not a part of the life of the school. Neither of the public schools has the power of the independent schools to make students want to change.

Permeable and Impermeable Boundaries. Girls who sweat on athletic fields and behind microscopes rather than blush like Barbie wannabes have become the cultural ideal at Shaw. If the school is to implement its vision, it must compete with alternative images like that of passive, self-effacing girls who are afraid to ask questions—the "good little girls" of whom Medeiros and her principal, Carparo, speak at length. Shaw therefore shuts out television images of blonde bimbos. If a school is to maintain its ideology in the midst of a host culture that transmits competing messages, it must rely on what Lightfoot (1983) calls "impermeable boundaries."

As a way of testing the permeability of school boundaries, I surveyed students from the four schools to assess their immersion in the world of television, sports, teen fashion, and popular music. The students at the middle- to upper-middle-class, suburban Smith School had the highest scores; the students at the Torah Institute scored the lowest. Yet even in the Torah Institute, which comes close to being one of Goffman's "total institutions" (that is, relatively insulated from outside influences), the students, like their counterparts in the other schools, chose exemplars from athletics.

In fact, sports references and metaphors abound at Springfield Torah Institute. Rebbe Kaplan describes the heads of yeshivot recruiting students as if they were coaches recruiting ballplayers. Students collect Rebbe cards. (Unlike rookie baseball cards, rookie Rebbe cards are inconsequential. The most valuable Rebbe cards are those that depict the most ancient of exegetes.) According to the eminent classicist Gregory Nagy, Americans idolize athletes the way the ancient Greeks idolized heroes (cited in Powers, 1993). The world of the yeshivah venerates Torah scholars just as Americans venerate athletes. In his interview with me, Dean Cahn used the image of a bodybuilder to describe how someone develops religiously and spiritually. In the yearbook, the president of the school compared running a school with running a race. Sports figures are the only media celebrities to make the hero lists of the students at Springfield Torah Institute. Rabbi Liebowitz, the Judaic studies coordinator, suggests that encouraging athletics is a way to harness the libido of young males, who are forbidden to become sexually active until marriage.

Beside athletics, another aspect of the world at large has permeated Rebbe Kaplan's classroom. When he describes heroes and role models as necessary for self-esteem—for either national pride or individual self-worth—Kaplan borrows the language of the "inside-out" school of moral education. This view is not the outlook of the traditional yeshivah educators, who believe that moral education is about training and restraint. In a "total institution" such as Springfield Torah Institute, I was surprised to find the rationale for heroes and role models couched in psychological, not functional, terms. Kaplan's struggle to deal with flawed heroes has a thoroughly contemporary flavor. Even in a "total institution," the changing notions of who is a hero apparently have left their marks.

Moral Prototypes: The Hero in Flux

I began this study by noting that formal curricula have changed in their approach to the hero. The white male-dominated textbooks and teaching materials (Blaisdell & Ball, 1915; Minnich, 1936) have been replaced by textbooks similar to those I found Amy Medeiros and George Stratas using: materials full of references to achieving women, ethnics, and people of color. The other trend I uncovered in the printed materials was a retreat from the heroic, a flight from the mythic to the comfort of the ordinary. Larger-than-life national heroes were being replaced by quiet, everyday, or local heroes (Berkowitz, 1987; Dunn, 1991; Gerzon, 1982; Giraffe Project, 1991). The term *hero* had lost its original meaning as the personification of virtue, a cultural icon of mythic proportion (Gardner, 1978; MacIntyre, 1984).

I found in these middle school classrooms what I had found in print. The "outside" had moved "inside." The concept of the hero as moral prototype was remarkably fluid; there was no consensus on its definition. In Kaplan's classroom, heroes are similar to the demigods of antiquity: Biblical and rabbinic figures of great spirituality and learning. In teaching the story of David and Bathsheba, Kaplan displeased the more traditional parents by acknowledging that the hero might have a flaw. For Stratas, the hero is of mythic proportion, but can include women, ethnics, and people of color. The hero legitimates (Berger & Luckmann, 1966) American values. In his treatment of George Washington, Stratas emphasizes the qualities admired by the young republic: humility, physical courage, and national service. He uses Washington to introduce his foreign-born students to American ideals and to integrate them into American society.

The term *hero* plays no part in Medeiros's teaching. She has fled from the hero to the relative security of the role model. MacDonald has recast the term, preferring to teach about "quiet heroes," ordinary folk who do extraordinary things. The heroes of *Walkabout* or *The Grand Babylon Hotel*, the rescuers in the Los Angeles earthquake, the boy who shoveled his neighbors' sidewalks have none of the mythic power of Kaplan's *gedolim* (Hebrew: great ones) or Stratas's George Washington. They are moral exemplars: people whose deeds inspire, but who do not serve as time-honored symbols of national values.

The word *hero* is truly a social construction of reality (Berger & Luckmann, 1966). Sociologists of knowledge (Berger, Berger & Kellner, 1973; Gehlen, 1980) identify the rise of privatism and tribalism as the inevitable by-products of modernity. Centripetal forces, which formerly bound a culture together in a Durkheimian (1956, 1973) mode, inevitably become centrifugal with the onset of urbanization and industrialization. In the United States the process hastened as the culture wars of the 1960s and 1970s eroded both religious and national authority. Attacks on authority diminished symbols and the ideals they represented. The crumbling of cultural icons is both a cause and an effect of a shift in national values. As reflected in my study, the changing notions of the hero capture the rise and fall of such icons and the virtues they represent. The movement away from objectivist or "outside-in" teaching to subjectivist or "inside-out" teaching can be understood through a framework built on the theories of the sociology of knowledge.

If one accepts as a given that different cultures may understand symbols differently, then classroom cultures can create their own definitions of the heroic. A hero in Kaplan's classroom is not a hero in MacDonald's. Not only did I find a lack of consensus on who was a hero; but also I found no agreement on the importance of heroes in contemporary society. MacDonald and Medeiros believe that society loses nothing for want of (to use MacDonald's phrase) "Heroes with a capital H." Ausband (1983), in describing a rootless America in the 1980s, claims that "we are between myths." The inclusion by some of the Smith students of animal rights activists and people living with AIDS represents the creation of new categories of heroes. We are not only between myths; we are between heroes as well.

Heroes are always linked to myth and symbol. Schutz (1962) defines a symbol as

> an appresentational reference of a higher order in which the appresenting member of the pair is an object, fact, or event within the reality of our daily life, whereas the other appresented member of the pair refers to an idea which transcends our experience of everyday life. (p. 247)

As an example, Schutz cites Jacob resting at Beth-El on his flight from Esau. There he has a dream of angels descending and ascending a heavenly ladder. The stone that he uses for his pillow becomes an altar, reminding all wayfarers and worshipers of Jacob's experience with the infinite. An ordinary stone represents a vision of the extraordinary; because of this association, it achieves an element of holiness:

$$\text{Stone (Pillow)} \longleftrightarrow \text{Altar} \longleftrightarrow \text{God's promise}$$

I suggest that much like the symbol, a classical hero, such as those proffered by Kaplan and Stratas, provides access to the transcendent. A hero provides the link between a historical personality and a virtue, thereby bridging the gap between the ordinary and the extraordinary. The razing of the altar at Beth-El would make the covenant more difficult to recollect; memory of the numinous experience eventually would be lost. An example from American history provides a parallel:

$$\text{The real Washington} \longleftrightarrow \text{The mythic Washington} \longleftrightarrow \text{Patriotism}$$

Eradication of the Washington (and the Lincoln, the Jefferson, and the like) of legend makes patriotism less accessible. Presidents' Day is a pale substitute for Washington's and Lincoln's birthdays. As Makolkin (1992) contends, nationalism is built on heroic biography.

The classical hero connects the ideal with the real, a value with the people who are encouraged to adopt that value. The symbol and the hero, the altar and the mythic Washington, inspire because of the associations evoked by each. As one of the teachers and parents in the Springfield Torah Institute told me, "Only a small segment of the population has the possibility of becoming inspired on an intellectual basis. The vast majority needs to be inspired by individuals in order to have a closeness with or love for those values." Classical heroes are bridges between the community's ideals and the members of that community. Shared ideals characterize community, so the loss of the hero may mean the loss of the community as well. Without bridges it is difficult to get from here to there.

The traditional hero most nearly resembles the *godol* of Rebbe Kaplan's classroom. Kaplan and the world in which he moves—fellow educators, parents, and students—understand the heroic to symbolize the values of spiritual perfection and religious scholarship that bind their community. For Stratas the operative values are civic duty and diversity; thus the Founding Fathers and Abraham Lincoln are big guns in his heroic arsenal. Stratas, however, is also intent on opening the pantheon of heroes to include women and people of color. His use of the heroic is much like those of the new texts I examined (Cook, 1993; Russell, 1988). He makes sure his students know about Paul Cuffe, the well-to-do African-American Quaker who chose to go to jail rather than to pay taxes that were assessed at a higher rate because of the color of his skin. They learn about Elizabeth Lucas Pinckney, the Caribbean planter's daughter who transformed American agriculture by bringing indigo to the colonies. Stratas's heroes, like Kaplan's *gedolim*, have done something extraordinary; they are on a higher plane. Both teachers use classical heroes to transmit social norms, to build collective memory, and to inspire by identification with the heroic.

John MacDonald understands the meaning of the traditional hero in much the same way. He claims that the classical hero serves a "medicinal" function, bringing solace and a Durkheimian order to society. Yet in Stratas's and Kaplan's worlds, distance confers status; it is irrelevant in MacDonald's. Distance is useful in subject-centered cultures, which praise restraint; it is an impediment in more student-centered settings, which preach self-expression. MacDonald relegates Odysseus to a postscript in his course, preferring the "quiet heroes," the people next door, to those on the distant horizon. He points out "quiet heroes" in the literature read by the students and in the daily occurrences captured by television and newspapers. "Heroes with a capital H" no longer inspire him. His choice of the hero as moral prototype is motivated by the hope of bringing out the best in his students, self-actualization through service to community.

"Heroes with a capital H" have never inspired Amy Medeiros and play no part in her curriculum. Nor do they play much of a role at the Shaw School, although the computers are named for heroic women. These girls' lives are informed by role models, not by heroes. It is no surprise that they speak about heroes in the most concrete terms, as rescuers. The heroism of a life of moral courage does not appear to be part of their worldview. The quality valued most by Amy Medeiros is competence; she presents herself as an exemplar of that value. Like MacDonald, committed to increasing her students' self-esteem, she rejects the classical hero. She is more at home with the role model, the moral prototype favored by the subjectivist, or "inside-out," school of moral education.

Moral Prototypes: The Ascendancy of the Role Model

Heroes socialize the young by reminding them of what a particular culture values; they have an aura uncompromised by time and space. Members of the group, wherever they may be, over the course of decades if not centuries, respond to the hero by recalling his or her story and the virtue that he or she personifies. The classical hero, by its very nature, is a social entity; the role model is personal. The hero functions as a symbol of society, creating culture while simultaneously legitimating it; the role model is always self-referential, self-selected, close by, bound by time and space. The root meaning of the word *inspire* is "breath." Because the role model is close, unlike the distant hero, its inspiration is often literally and figuratively the breath of the moral mentor on the protégé's face.

In their discussions with me and in their teaching, all four teachers reiterate their students' need for role models. They corroborate the literature on middle schools and on adolescent development (Carnegie Council, 1989). Without naming specific psychologists, they use psychological language, asserting how formative these years are for their students. As youths, all four had teachers who served as role models for them, pointing them toward the teaching profession.

Sociologist Dan Lortie (1975) comments on the influence of class in the decision to become a teacher. The four teachers I studied viewed teaching as conferring status. Medeiros and Stratas grew up in blue-collar or lower-class families. MacDonald's family was comfortable financially, but he and his brother were the first to attend college. For him, teaching provided a pathway to the world of books and ideas. Kaplan's family was prosperous; his father, a successful businessman. When the family became Orthodox, however, a son who aspired to be a Jewish teacher and rabbi was considered a source of prestige.

All four teachers have tinkered with their curricula to introduce their students to strong role models. Through the books the students read, the newspaper articles they discuss, and the television clips they view, MacDonald's course is designed to make students consider what motivates quiet heroes. He hopes that some of these heroes and sheroes will become role models for his students. Stratas has chosen to emphasize current events, devoting two half-periods per week to the subject. By thoughtfully selecting his news stories, such as Toni Morrison's receiving the Nobel Prize, Stratas has an opportunity to highlight positive role models for his African-American students. Medeiros has chosen a textbook that is gender neutral and full of biographies of achieving women. Kaplan can convert classical heroes into role models for his students by relying on traditional exegesis that fills in some of the detail missing in Bible stories. Abraham, the embodiment of the virtue of hospitality, can and does become a blueprint of how one behaves as a host.

Observability. Jung (1986) finds that role models require observability. The learner must have the opportunity to watch a role model firsthand. In their study of 400 rescuers of Jews during the Holocaust, Oliner and Oliner (1988) mention that the single most compelling motivation for rescuers was the influence of parents who modeled caring behavior for them. A role model's power is magnified exponentially by a cultural context that offers more opportunity to observe detail. Springfield Torah Institute, an inclusive program that allows the students to see their teachers and classmates at school, in prayer, and at play, affords innumerable opportunities for observation. When Rebbe Kaplan and I reflect on the students who are most likely to misbehave in his class, we note that they are usually students who live outside Springfield. Misbehavior in this class is relatively benign: doodling, whispering to one's neighbor, daydreaming; for some of the boys it may include poking a classmate. The "troublemakers" are those for whom the Torah Institute is not a "total institution," those who do not live in the community. For these students, Jung's factors of desirability and observability are less salient. They do not see their teachers, and are not seen, seven days a week in an institution that functions as a school, a synagogue, a community center, and a catering establishment. Shaw, like the Torah Institute, requires a long school day. Most girls participate in after-school athletics. They attend two- and three-day camping trips during the school year. Thus both independent schools afford more opportunity to observe and model than do the public schools. The public school teachers have far fewer opportunities to exert their power as models because their institutions make no attempt to be "total."

Rebbe Kaplan, George Stratas, and John MacDonald position their desks in the front of the classroom, underscoring the message, "Look at me." Amy Medeiros stands directly in front of her students, modeling competence for the girls in her class. All four teachers consciously deliver moral messages to their students. The literature on the middle school calls for teachers to become role models and stresses "the teacher as curriculum" (Stevenson, 1992, p. 22). As Rebbe Kaplan says, "I'm the little *Avraham avinu*" (Hebrew: Abraham the patriarch). MacDonald hopes he can be a "quiet hero"—that is, a role model—for his students.

In the introduction to his book, Bennett (1993) captures the essence of the teacher as role model, referring to the importance of Jung's (1986) observability.

It has been said that there is nothing more influential, more determinant, in a child's life than the moral power of quiet example. For children to take morality seriously, they must be in the presence of adults who take morality seriously. *And with their own eyes they must see adults take morality seriously* [italics added]. (p. 11)

Do Role Models Transcend Race and Gender? The four teachers ponder whether they can be role models for everyone. Only Rebbe Kaplan has his doubts. A similar question troubles actors: Can they possibly play characters with whom they have nothing in common? Can they truly get inside the skin of the other? African-American Anna Deveare Smith (1993), actress, playwright, and teacher, speaks of identity and the process of discovering America in her project *On the Road*, of which *Fires in the Mirror* is a part. (*Fires in the Mirror* is a one-woman performance in which Smith portrays both African-Americans and Hasidim involved in the events that resulted in the Crown Heights riots in the summer of 1991.) She contrasts her technique with that of persons who believe that only members of the ingroup can speak for that group. She calls that view "the self-centered technique":

Who has the right to see what? Who has the right to say what? Who has the right to speak for whom? These questions have plagued the contemporary theater. These questions address both issues of employment equity and issues of who is portrayed. These questions are the questions that unsettle and prohibit a democratic theater in America. If only a man can speak for a man, a woman for a woman, a black person for all black people, then we once again inhibit the spirit of theater which lives in the bridge that makes unlikely aspects seem connected. The bridge doesn't make them the same, it merely displays how two unlikely aspects are related. These relationships of the unlikely, these connections of things that don't fit together, are crucial to American theater and culture, if theater and culture plan to help us assemble our obvious differences. The self-centered technique has taken the bridge out of the process of creating character. It has taken metaphor out of acting. It has made the heart smaller, the spirit less gregarious, and the mind less apt to be able to hold on to contradictions or opposition. (Smith, 1993)

Those teachers who claim they can be role models for all their students refuse to believe that they are unable to build the necessary bridges; they refuse to accept a smaller heart, a less gregarious spirit, and a mind less able to deal with ambiguity.

Who Are the Students' Heroes and Role Models?

Much of the discussion about the need to provide role models or heroes for students is posited on the assumption that current exemplars for young people are inappropriate, coming as they do from popular culture. In the words of Mrs. Trustman, one of the Smith School parents, "There are a lot of things on television that kids could consider to be heroes and role models. To be frank, it's rubbish." By making a conscious effort to close off popular culture, Springfield Torah Institute and the Shaw School are trying to exclude an alternative slate of heroes and role models. Stratas and MacDonald, the two public school teachers, are much more receptive to external influences and weave television and movie references into their teaching.

Luke (1993), citing numerous sources, claims,

Much of kids' time and money, social relations and activities center around media texts such as MTV, *Beverly Hills 90210*, Teenage Mutant Ninjas, and the persons, products, and activities connected to those texts. The impact of mass media and popular cultural icons cannot be underestimated. (p. 52)

I did not find this to be the case. Few students in my study chose glamorous or celebrity exemplars. Instead they overwhelmingly chose conventional exemplars: parents, grandparents, aunts and uncles, family friends, and camp counselors. In three of the schools, students mentioned explicitly that they admired teachers (although at Shaw and Smith they were reluctant to use the term *role model*.) One tantalizing finding was that the students from the less privileged backgrounds were more likely to name teachers as role models than those from more comfortable backgrounds. Four of the eight Franklin Pierce students mentioned that teachers were role models for them. A student at the Torah Institute named a hockey coach—someone from his community, not his school. Only one student at Shaw and none at Smith referred to teachers as role models. This finding seems to corroborate Wyman's (1993) observation that "Low income and minority children are more teacher-dependent than are their white peers" (pp. 37–38).

The students' choices of exemplars resemble those of young people who have participated in past "ideal person" studies (Wechter, 1981). In these studies, children below 15 are likely to choose parents or parent surrogates. In contrast, more than half of the 16-year-olds of Prairie City who were asked to identify their ideal persons tended to choose composite or imaginary characters (Havighurst & Taba, 1949, pp. 71–72). The most socially mature, culturally aware students in my study, those at Smith, were least likely to name parents as exemplars and were beginning to create composite portraits. Twelve-year-old Sydney resembles her older counterparts in the Prairie City study 40 or 50 years ago. She says: "Maybe some of the things I do are a combination of things that I subconsciously picked up from other people."

Although feminist literature decries the lack of role models for girls (*A.A.U.W. Report*, 1992; Brown & Gilligan, 1992), I noted numerous female exemplars—parents and parent surrogates, political figures, athletes, and celebrities—on the public school students' lists. The absence of such exemplars (except for parents) among the girls at the male-dominated Torah Institute is not surprising.

When students choose athletes as role models or heroes, race seems negligible. This is not so for gender, however; no boy in my study selected a female exemplar other than his mother.

If I had stopped these students on the street or in the mall and had asked my questions about moral prototypes and people they admired, would I have received the same responses? Perhaps they chose other than celebrity heroes because they associated me with their classes, which I had been observing for six weeks or more. In my study I was struck by the amount of congruence between the moral exemplars espoused by the teachers and by their students. Rebbe Kaplan stressed the spiritual and religious giants of Jewish tradition; his students reported that they admired the same kind of people. Like their teacher, Kaplan's students also admired American political and military leaders. Amy Medeiros's watchword was competence, and her students flooded their lists with competent women: their mothers, family friends, physicians, school administrators, even their peers. John MacDonald enlivened his class with "quiet heroes," ordinary people who became extraordinary when the moment demanded transformation. His students filled their lists with similar heroes: Oskar Schindler, teachers, activists, aspiring musicians who have to face the music and practice. Although Stratas's students were reluctant to use their teacher's word, *hero*, they admired the thinkers and doers he featured in his classes: presidents and towering African-American figures like Frederick Douglass, Martin Luther King, and Malcolm X. Stratas was the teacher who hoped his students would recognize as admirable their parents, who struggled to set examples of industry, honesty, and integrity for their children. They did so.

The explanation for this congruence is not clear to me. Were the students simply adopting teacher-pleasing behaviors? Probably not at the Smith School, where autonomy and individualism are highly prized. I cannot claim that all the teachers were so influential that they unilaterally shaped their students' choice of exemplars. Stratas, Medeiros, and Kaplan enjoyed parental support for their moral prototypes. Kaplan and Medeiros had the advantage of coherent schools that reinforced their messages. All I can report is that when I interviewed them, students claimed prototypes much like their teachers'. Wechter's (1981) proviso, however, is important: Teenagers' heroes are very changeable. There is no guarantee that a similar interview six months from now would produce the same results.

The Function of Moral Prototypes in the Classroom

Yeats reminds us how difficult it is to "know the dancer from the dance" (1989, p. 222). It is similarly impossible to separate moral prototypes—heroes and role models—from the stories they tell. Moral prototypes appeal to what Schutz (1962) calls "the imagining self" (p. 241). For all of the teachers in the study, moral prototypes tell a story of potentiality, of what might be. They beckon the student-listeners to another place. The hero calls them to a more distant location; the role model's realm is closer. Like moral literature, moral prototypes are life-affirming, demanding that those who attend to their stories surpass themselves. The literature on narrative and its power to build a moral imagination (Coles, 1989; Day, 1991a, 1991b; Parr, 1982; Vitz, 1990) is as much about moral prototypes as about stories. In their appeal to the imagination, these prototypes evoke promises of transcendence.

Phenix (1974) describes transcendence as "the experience of limitless going beyond any given state" (p. 118). John MacDonald uses the metaphor of a bridge to describe his teaching. Anna Deveare Smith (1993) also refers to a bridge in describing her philosophy of acting, which allows, even encourages, an African-American to play a white Hasidic woman. Her bridge begins in wonder and leads to hope, a transcendent experience. If a role model is to wield his or her power, Jung (1986) posits the need for an attraction (wonder) and a commitment to change (hope).

All four teachers are committed to moving students beyond themselves. Moving from place to place is the essence of transcendence. This journey is depicted most clearly by Alfred Schutz (1899–1959), one of the founding fathers of the sociology of knowledge. Expanding on William James's notion of subuniverses, Schutz (1962) describes what he calls "multiple realities" (p. 207) or "finite provinces of meaning" (p. 230). The escape offered by a gripping book, a beautiful painting, an elegant sonata, a compelling daydream, or a vivid imagination is a voyage to other universes, other "finite provinces of meaning." For the teachers in my study, both the role model and the hero serve as guides to imagined worlds.

Schutz (1962) refers to imagination and dreaming as two "zones of potentiality" (p. 224). I would suggest that role models and heroes are themselves "zones of potentiality." Imagining, like the role model, is connected more closely to "the vivid present" (p. 216); dreaming occurs in a more distant realm, the realm of the mythic, where heroes dwell. Each zone has its own landscape; each has its own relationship to reality. The similarity between the role model and the hero is that both begin in what Heschel (1990) calls awe, "a sense for the transcendent" (p. 9). Heroes are images of "high transcendence"; role models, images of "low transcendence." The hero's world is more distant, less fully realized than the role model's, which begins in the everyday and with the self. The hero's world might lie in the future or in the past, in a "country of memory" (Codrescu, 1990), but in any case it is in another realm. Heroes in one "finite province of meaning" may not easily be transplanted. Schutz (1962) compares them to coins that may be legal tender in one country but not in another (p. 258). Kaplan had this experience when he tried to defend Martin Luther King, a hero from his southern boyhood, as a hero in the Springfield Torah Institute.

By demanding an escape from the self, from the "inside" to the "outside" (Codrescu, 1990), heroes require more imagination than role models. If America seems to be in flight from heroes, it may be because the world of the imagination has been replaced by instant entertainment. Myths, essential for a community's survival, die when imagination fails. As Heschel (1990) remarks, "The central problem of this generation is emptiness in the heart, the decreased sensitivity to the imponderable quality of the spirit, the collapse of communication between the realm of tradition and the inner world of the individual" (p. 159).

A Taxonomy of Moral Prototypes

I have ranked the moral prototypes used by the teachers in this study according to levels of transcendence and distance. These categories also reflect different degrees of recognition and observability. The classical hero is remote, a nationally known figure of high transcendence; the role model, reflecting personal choice and a dyadic relationship, is a figure of low transcendence. Common to all the moral prototypes is their appeal to the imagination through the stories they represent.

1.   *The classical hero*, by symbolizing the values of a given society, provides the cultural glue that links the individual to the group (Kaplan's King David; Stratas's George Washington).

2.   *The new hero* is a historic figure who represents groups that have been previously underrepresented in American life, such as ethnics, women, and people of color. Although the new heroes lack the patina acquired through time, they contribute to a group's self-esteem and add a pluralistic dimension previously missing in the depiction of the heroic (Stratas' Paul Cuffe or Elizabeth Lucas Pinckney). Both types of hero, the old and the new, embody the virtues prized by a nation at a given time. Heroes are metaphors: They reveal through allusion, not through direct disclosure. Like metaphors, they do not withstand close analysis. Theirs is a functional role, to symbolize abstractions and provide cultural cohesion.

3.   *The moral exemplar or quiet hero* is a locally or regionally known individual who displays moral or physical courage. Some quiet heroes may represent the new values about which there is some consensus, such as communitarianism or environmentalism (MacDonald's good neighbors; the Los Angeles earthquake rescuers; animal rights activists). The moral exemplar is less transcendent than the hero, and may or may not always be observed firsthand. The moral exemplar can serve as a map of an individual's moral behavior. When MacDonald tells stories about good citizens and neighbors, he does so in the hope of inspiring similar behavior in his students, who lack the benefit of direct knowledge.

4.   *The role model* is an individual who inspires through personal contact and observability. *Role model* is a morally neutral term (role models, unlike heroes can be for good or for ill). This term, the least transcendent of the four, is used by contemporary moral educators to personify the possessors of attitudes and behaviors that build self-esteem (Medeiros and her colleagues at Shaw). Of all the moral prototypes, the role model is the one most rooted in *relationship*, a word that recurs in discussions of women and morality. Therefore it is no

surprise that in their discussion of adolescent girls, Brown and Gilligan (1992) call for more strong women to serve as role models. The role model, like a mirror, helps the beholder to see the self. In the words of Adrienne Rich, role models permit the disenfranchised to see their own faces in society's mirrors.

This taxonomy seems to apply to the students' moral prototypes as well as the teachers'. Their language is as elusive as that of the adults in the study. I have reported that occasionally they refer to celebrities as heroes, but when they do so, they may be using either the language of the functional, classical hero or the rhetoric of the new hero, the moral exemplar or quiet hero, or the role model. When some of the boys in my study describe a ballplayer as "awesome," they use the reverential tones once reserved for national military and political heroes. They are resonating to the transcendent power of a symbol of grace and skill, much as the Greeks venerated their athletes. For many of those who label athletes as heroes, these figures indeed are icons, like classical heroes.

When young people confuse fame with virtue by calling entertainers heroes, like those in my study who mentioned Janet Jackson, Martin Lawrence, or David Letterman, they resemble many of the adults around them. Christopher Lasch (1978) claims that it is characteristic of the culture of narcissism to substitute celebrities for heroes. Sociologist Ernest Hakanen (1989) attempts to explain the emergence of celebrity icons as a shift in paragons; he claims that we no longer choose idols of production (nation building or industrial expansion), but instead set up idols of consumption. We substitute an Oprah Winfrey for a Henry Ford. Yet contemporary athletics and entertainment seem as much to be industries as were the arenas favored by the older military-industrial complex. (Witness the baseball strike of 1994.)

I found a far more satisfactory rationale for the shift in heroes in the tenets of the sociology of knowledge. Because American nationalism no longer can be taken for granted, American popular culture has supplanted it as a force that creates and disseminates images of powerful and achieving individuals. Through their recognizability, celebrities have the power to symbolize American values, as military and political leaders once did.

Some of the students name entertainers as heroes, but they add quickly that it is not their celebrity which appeals to them. They cite those who have associated themselves with social causes such as helping the homeless. Their interpretation of *hero* is much like John MacDonald's *quiet hero*, a moral exemplar who inspires altruistic commitment by example. Still others talk about celebrity heroes, but in fact mean role models. They study athletes or musicians for the way they execute technical maneuvers, hoping to emulate them through close observation.

IMPLICATIONS

Limitations

Although it is tempting to conclude with sweeping implications, both the author and the reader need reminders of the limitations of this study. My research dealt with four teachers teaching in four classrooms. These teachers are not typical; all four of their principals described them in superlatives. I spent only six to eight weeks in each of their classrooms; what I saw may well have been conditioned by the material they were covering at that time. Also, the chemistry between a teacher and a particular class makes for idiosyncrasy. Stratas, Medeiros, and MacDonald claimed that their classes were unusually responsive. Kaplan told me he was teaching differently with this group than with previous classes. He clearly missed the Russian newcomers, on whom he could make a greater impact; the large number of observant faculty children made him uneasy.

Another limitation in the study was my presence, which unintentionally changed the culture I was trying to record. When George Stratas commented as much to me as to the students, "Here's a word Mrs. Ingall loves—*hero*," I wondered how much I was contaminating my own data. Were my collaborators trying too hard to please? My attempts to collect data from multiple sources, to check my theories with my subjects, and to ensure a diverse sample of classrooms were methods of offsetting these limitations, but the cautions still hold.

General Implications for Reform

The need for school reform is a truism in contemporary American education. Since the 1980s an outpouring of reform documents has called for change in the way schools are organized and the way teachers are taught (Carnegie Forum, 1986; Goodlad, Soder, & Sirotnik, 1990; Holmes Group, 1986). This literature deals with technical questions such as professionalism and credentials, accountability and administration, salaries, and staffing. Far too little attention is given to the place of moral education in reforming schools and teacher education.

Implications for Practice

This study is a reminder that the essence of schooling is what happens in a classroom between a teacher and her students. It adds credence to what Stanford's Larry Cuban (1993) calls "the power of pedagogy" (p. 182), a factor that is often lost in the clamor for reform. All of the teachers in my study are gifted individuals who forge relationships through compelling narratives and the force of their personalities. Through connectedness, they can build bridges to their students, offering them opportunities for transformation. These bridges are particularly important in the lives of middle school students who are looking for models outside their families.

The study tends to support those teachers who recognize in the story a powerful force for connectedness and those theorists who advocate the use of narrative for building a moral imagination (Bennett, 1993; Coles, 1989; Day, 1991a, 1991b; Vitz, 1990). Kilpatrick's (1992) dictum, "Morality needs to be set within a storied vision if it is to remain morality" (p. 197), describes the attitude of the four teachers I studied and offers wisdom for others. Moral prototypes, whether heroes or role models, suggest that the essence of moral education does not lie in the cognitive realm that Kohlberg (1983) made so popular in the 1960s and 1970s. Moral education takes place in the emotional domain, which engages the heart more than the mind. The potentiality of moral prototypes can be found in the story. When the story works its magic, it produces what Tuvia Kaplan calls the "gleam," the bridge of understanding that connects teacher with student.

I discovered four teachers who were both storytellers and storymakers (Gudmundsdottir, 1991). When Tuvia Kaplan used the word *story* more than 80 times in our interview, I knew I was onto something.[2] The story is the vehicle for both the hero and the role model. The hero recollects the story of the group and the values that inspire, identify, and maintain that group. The classical hero tells a story honored over time; the new hero, a story with ethnically diverse characters; the quiet hero, a story of commitment to social causes. The story suggested by the role model is a glimpse of what an individual can become. In fact, students need both sets of stories, provinces of meaning, and "zones of potentiality": heroes as well as role models. Writing

---

[2] In "The Seductions of Storytelling," Buford (1996, p. 12) observes, "Implicit in the extraordinary revival of storytelling is the possibility that we need stories—that they are a fundamental unit of knowledge, the foundation of memory essential to the way we make sense of our lives."

in *Science*, Maxine Singer (1991), president of the Carnegie Institute of Washington, states:

> People have always known that heroines and heroes are imperfect. But they chose to ignore the warts so that the greatness could inspire new achievement. We are all diminished by the disappearance of heroism. Role models will be for naught if there are no heroines and heroes from whom to learn about courage, about noble purpose, about how to reach within and beyond ourselves to find greatness. (p. 249)

Rebbe Kaplan and George Stratas have it right. Role models, whose closeness and observability afford precise scrutiny of detail, teach behavior by example. Society has always depended on elders to teach young people its ways. Imitating the ways of others helps the imitators to understand their culture. The function of heroes, however, is not to teach behavior, but to make abstractions such as patriotism, love, achievement, and responsibility comprehensible. They too are essential. Without them, ideals and virtues blur. Bridges and altars collapse. Like moral art, heroes orient a culture toward a vision of how things ought to be (Gardner, 1978).

This study has implications for the administration of schools. Teachers at the Torah Institute and at Shaw enjoy enormous support from a rich school culture. It is the school that can offer opportunities for observability of role models through a longer school day, athletics, and extracurricular activities. It is the school that transmits a message of desirability: Mary Carparo's admonition, "We do not behave that way here." Finally, it is the school that wields institutional control over permeable boundaries. George Stratas and I could find no reason that the assistant principal in charge of the cafeteria allowed the world of the streets to enter the world of the school.

The principal creates the ethos of the school. Site-based management has to begin with the recognition that principals must be allowed to hire their own faculties. Principals can make a difference in creating school culture through heroes and other symbols in the creation (Wynne & Ryan, 1993). It is they who must communicate the message that teachers are expected to be moral models. Principals' failures to take a moral stand have been chronicled elsewhere. The collapse of the pseudonymous Hamilton High (Grant, 1988) was attributable largely to the moral bungling of well-intentioned principals.

The public has a right to expect administrators to be "esteemed leaders" (Lanckton, 1992) who develop coherent moral visions for their communities and function as moral models for their staff, students, and parents. They can encourage the creation of courses on heroes, such as MacDonald's Heroes and Sheroes, which help students to acquire a moral vocabulary as well as to contemplate their potential for moral behavior. They can create opportunities for their teachers to discuss what it means to be role models for their students. One of my serendipitous discoveries was that the teachers, rather than finding my presence burdensome, truly enjoyed talking about their teaching and the role played therein by moral prototypes. Perhaps school time might be better spent in more peer discussions and reflections of this type, rather than importing "experts" for teacher in-service.

Implications for Teacher Education

This study also has implications for teacher education. Even while public discussion roils over the V-word (values), institutions committed to educating teachers can ill afford to neglect the moral domain. Others (Bergem, 1990; Lanckton, 1992; Ryan, 1990) have noted the absence of serious attention to the issue of the teacher as both moral educator and moral model for her students. It is appropriate that schools of education point with pride at the rise in incoming students' GPAs. They might be advised to up the ante on values as well. Goodlad, Soder, and Sirotnik (1991) express their dismay that teacher education institutions fail to capitalize on the concept of teaching as a calling. Prospective teachers who (like Kaplan, Stratas, Medeiros, and MacDonald) understand teaching as a vocation are more likely to think of themselves as moral educators and to exercise their considerable power to shape students' values.

The subject of moral education must be addressed in Foundations courses. I am disturbed by the rhetoric of professionalization to which aspiring teachers are introduced. Calls for "mastery," "basic skills," and "competency," and the characterization of learning in terms of inputs and outputs deny preservice teachers the opportunity to reflect on their potential to inspire and transform. These courses must emphasize the importance of the connectedness that is necessary between teachers and students. Asking teachers to imitate the model of professionalism borrowed from medicine is misguided. The medical model traditionally has been based on distance between the practitioner and the patient, and this distance has led to the loss of esteem of the medical profession. Teaching is built on closeness and connection. Connectedness does not endanger authority; colleagues' and principals' professional regard for each of these teachers is admirable.

Phenix's call for a curriculum of transcendence (1974) is as compelling today as it was 20 years ago. The fact that each of these teachers, teaching vastly different subjects, makes room for "zones of potentiality" suggests that "transcendence across the curriculum" is possible. They can do so with no sacrifice of content; this fact silences those critics who claim that to expect teachers to be moral educators is to make additional demands on the overworked and underappreciated. Institutions that educate teachers must include opportunities for moral education within their disciplines. Methods courses should give fledgling teachers opportunities to learn the techniques of cooperative education. This methodology seems to provide an alternative to the narcissism that impedes the creation of community. Finally, courses in moral education should be required in schools of education.

FINAL THOUGHTS

Further study is needed on the changing nature of the hero. What are the implications of a society with shifting heroes, or without heroes at all? What developmental changes occur in children who pass into adulthood without the benefits of hero-worship as an antidote for self-centeredness? Will young women's heroes and role models continue to show less variety than those of their male peers? The contribution of popular culture, especially television, in creating heroes for young people needs greater analysis: My findings did not corroborate the gloom-and-doom portrayals of teenagers enthralled by media-created celebrities.

The notion that one's role models must reflect one's own ethnicity, race, or gender has enormous implications in our multicultural society. The current literature implies that such a match is essential, but my study raises questions about this assumption. The function of socioeconomic status and role models is also a rich vein: Are poor, urban teenagers more likely than middle-class students to turn to teachers as exemplars? Teachers' ability to generate a renewal in values may be far greater than they dreamed possible.

Other tantalizing questions arise as well. The function of "vocation" in a teacher's understanding of her work is another domain for study. How do schools of education evaluate vocation in a would-be teacher? How is vocation nurtured? Is "job satisfaction" greater for a teacher with a calling in a working-class or lower-middle-class school than in a prestigious upper-middle-class school? For a teacher who identifies herself as religious?

Finally, I have told the story of only four teachers. Other stories are left untold—stories that inspire because moral education is central to the teachers' work. The subject of moral prototypes is rich with possibilities for researchers as well as for educators and students.

Appendix

Forms and Questionnaires

Informed Consent Forms

Interview Questions for Educators

Student Interview and Questionnaire

Student Survey (Popular Culture Index)

Telephone Interview with Parents

STATEMENT OF INFORMED CONSENT

I am writing about the use of heroes and role models in middle school classes. I would like to interview you and observe your class as part of my research. There will be no compensation for your participation, which entails no foreseeable risks or discomforts, and you may discontinue participation at any time. I will give you a fictitious name in the paper and eliminate or give a fictitious name to any institution to which you refer. I hope you will allow me to include your views. I am including an abstract of my study for your information.

Carol K. Ingall

_____

I have been informed of the goals and rationale of the heroes/role models study and consent to the publication of its results.

_____   _____
Date   Subject's signature

Enc.

Consent form: Teacher

STATEMENT OF INFORMED CONSENT

I am writing about the use of heroes and role models in middle school classes. I would like to interview you about this subject as part of my research. There will be no compensation for your participation, which entails no foreseeable risks or discomforts, and you may discontinue participation at any time. I will give you a fictitious name in the paper and eliminate or give a fictitious name to any institution to which you refer. I hope you will allow me to include your views. I am including an abstract of my study for your information.

Carol K. Ingall

I have been informed of the goals and rationale of the heroes/role models study and consent to the publication of its results.

_____   _____
Date   Subject's signature

Enc.

Consent form: Principal

STATEMENT OF INFORMED CONSENT

I am writing about the use of heroes and role models in middle school classes. I would like to interview you about this subject as part of my research. There will be no compensation for your participation, which entails no foreseeable risks or discomforts, and you may discontinue participation at any time. I will give you a fictitious name in the paper and eliminate or give a fictitious name to any institution to which you refer. I hope you will allow me to include your views. I am including an abstract of my study for your information.

Sincerely,

Carol K. Ingall

—————————————————————

I have read and understood the information on the Informed Consent Form, have received a copy of the Form, and agree to participate.

———————————   ———————————————
Date   Student's signature

I have been informed of the goals and rationale of the heroes/role models study and consent to let my child participate.

———————————   ———————————————
Date   Parent's signature

Enc.
Consent form: Student

STATEMENT OF INFORMED CONSENT

I am writing about the use of heroes and role models in middle school classes. I would like to interview you by telephone about this subject as part of my research. There will be no compensation for your participation, which entails no foreseeable risks or discomforts, and you may discontinue participation at any time. I will give you a fictitious name in the paper and eliminate or give a fictitious name to any institution to which you refer. I hope you will allow me to include your views.

Sincerely,

Carol K. Ingall

_____

I have read and understood the information on the Informed Consent Form, have received a copy of the Form, and agree to participate.

_____
Date

_____
Signature

_____
Street

_____
City and Zip Code

_____
Telephone Number

Enc.
Consent form: Parent

INTERVIEW QUESTIONS FOR TEACHER

1. What does moral education mean to you?
2. How do you do moral education in your class?
3. What role, if any, do heroes and role models play in your approach?
4. What difference, if any, is there between a hero and a role model?
5. Who are your heroes and role models?
6. Do you think you are a role model for your students?

INTERVIEW QUESTIONS FOR PRINCIPAL

1. What does moral education mean to you?
2. How do you communicate your vision of moral education to your teachers?
3. How do you do moral education here?
4. What role, if any, do heroes and role models play in moral education here?

STUDENT INTERVIEW AND QUESTIONNAIRE

Name _____

1. What is a role model?
2. Think about your two best friends. Who are their role models?
3. Who are your role models? Why do you admire these people?
4. Some people use the terms *role model* and *hero* synonymously. What differences—if any—are there between role models and heroes?
5. Who are your heroes? Why?
6. A moral dilemma is a conflict between two competing "goods." For example, you may have promised a friend that you would spend time with her. Your mother wants you to use that time to visit your grandmother. Think about a moral dilemma you have recently faced. Without sharing the details of the dilemma, how did you arrive at a solution?
7. Would you look to a role model to help you solve a moral dilemma? ("What would _____ do in this situation?") Why or why not?
8. Think about the women (people) you have been studying in your English (History, Bible, etc.) classes. Are these women (people) role models for you? Why or why not?
9. Have you ever looked to these characters (people) to help you solve a moral dilemma? ("What would _____ do in this situation?") Why or why not?
10. What value has there been for you in reading books with strong women as characters (studying about George Washington, King David, etc.)?

STUDENT SURVEY (POPULAR CULTURE INDEX)

Name _____

Directions: Using the space provided, please identify the items below.

1. Stüssy

2. Doc Martens

3. Beavis and Butt-head

4. Alice in Chains

5. Charles Barkley

6. Judy Blume

7. Cindy Crawford

8. Cypress Hill

9. Shannen Doherty

10. Tony! Toni! Toné!

STRUCTURED TELEPHONE INTERVIEW
FOR PARENTS

1. Who are your child's heroes and role models?

2. What part do heroes and/or role models play in your child's schooling?

3. Try to recall a conversation with your child in which he or she discussed a school lesson or incident involving heroes and/or role models.

4. How important to you is the use of heroes and role models in your child's school?

References

The AAUW Report. (1992). *How schools shortchange girls: A study of major findings on girls and education*. Washington, DC: AAUW Educational Foundation.

Adams-Price, C., & Greene, A. L. (1990). Secondary attachments and adolescent self-concept. *Sex Roles, 22*(3/4), 187–198.

Anderson, G. (1990). *Fundamentals of educational research*. London: Falmer Press.

Anderson, W. T. (1993, May). Have we outgrown the age of heroes? *Utne Reader*, (57), 95–100.

Apple, M. W. (1990). *Ideology and curriculum* (2nd ed.). New York: Routledge.

Ascher, C. (1991). *School programs for African American male students*. New York: ERIC Clearinghouse on Urban Education.

Ascher, C. (1982). *Secondary school ethos and the academic success of urban minority students*. New York: ERIC Clearinghouse on Urban Education.

Ausband, S. C. (1983). *Myth and meaning, myth and order*. Macon, GA: Mercer University Press.

Balswick, J., & Ingoldsby, B. (1982). Heroes and heroines among American adolescents. *Sex roles, 8*(3), 243–249.

Bandura, A. (1977). Social learning theory. Englewood Cliffs, NJ: Prentice-Hall.

Bandura, A. (1986). *Social foundations of thought and action: A social cognitive theory*. Englewood Cliffs, NJ: Prentice-Hall.

Banks, C. A. M. (1993). Restructuring schools for equity: What we have learned in two decades. *Phi Delta Kappan, 75*(1), 42–48.

Banks, J. A. (1993). Multicultural education: Development, dimensions, and challenges. *Phi Delta Kappan, 75*(1), 22–28.

Barthes, R. (1977). *Image, music, text*. New York: Hill and Wang.

Beck, C. (1987). Moral education in the junior high school. In K. Ryan & G. F. McLean (Eds.), *Character development in schools and beyond*, (pp. 206–226). New York: Praeger.

Becker, E. (1973). *The denial of death*. New York: The Free Press.

Becker, H. S. (1990). Generalizing from case studies. In E. W. Eisner & A. Peshkin (Eds.), *Qualitative research in education: The continuing debate*, (pp. 233–242). New York: Teachers College Press.

Belenky, M. F., Clinchy, B. M., Goldberger, N. R., & Tarule, J. M. (1986). *Women's ways of knowing: The development of self, voice and mind.* New York: Basic Books.

Bennett, W. J. (1991). Moral literacy and the formation of character. In J. Benninga (Ed.), *Moral, character and civic education in the elementary school,* (pp. 131–138). New York: Teachers College Press.

Bennett, W. J. (1993). *The book of virtues: A treasury of great moral stories.* New York: Simon & Schuster.

Benninga, J. (1991). *Moral, character and civic education in the elementary school.* New York: Teachers College Press.

Bergem, T. (1990). The teacher as moral agent. *Journal of Moral Education, 19*(2), 88–100.

Berger, P. L. (1990). *The sacred canopy: Elements of a sociological theory of religion.* New York: Anchor Books.

Berger, P. L., Berger, B., & Kellner, H. (1973). *The homeless mind: Modernization and consciousness.* New York: Vintage Books.

Berger, P. L., & Kellner, H. (1965). Arnold Gehlen and the theory of institutions. *Social Research, 32*(1), 110–115.

Berger, P. L., & Luckmann, T. (1966). *The social construction of reality: A treatise in the sociology of knowledge.* New York: Anchor Books.

Berkowitz, B. (1987). *Local heroes.* Lexington, MA: D. C. Heath.

Blaisdell, A. F., & Ball, F. K. (1915). *Heroic deeds of American sailors.* Boston: Little, Brown and Co.

Bogdan, R. C., & Biklen, S. K. (1992). *Qualitative research for education.* Boston: Allyn & Bacon.

Bolster, A. S. (1983). Toward a more effective model of research on teaching. *Harvard Educational Review, 53*(3), 294–308.

Boston University College of Communications and School of Education (1988). *The art of loving well: A character values-based curriculum.* Boston: Boston University College of Communications and School of Education.

Brodbelt, S., & Wall, R. E. (1985). *An examination of the presentation of heroes and heroines in current (1974–1984) secondary level social studies textbooks.*

Brown, L. M., & Gilligan, C. (1992). *Meeting at the crossroads: Women's psychology and girls' development.* Cambridge, MA: Harvard University Press.

Brown, P. L. (1993, April 19). Nancy Drew: 30's sleuth, 90's role model. *New York Times,* p. 1.

Bruner, J. (1986). *Actual minds and possible worlds.* Cambridge, MA: Harvard University Press.

Bruner, J. (1990). *Acts of meaning.* Cambridge, MA: Harvard University Press.

Bullis, H. E., & O'Malley, E. E. (1952). *Human relations in the classroom course.* Wilmington, DE: Delaware State Society for Mental Hygiene.

Burrell, G., & Morgan, G. (1979). *Sociological paradigms and organizational analysis.* London: Butterworth Heinemann.

Butts, R. F. (1988). The moral imperative for American schools: ". . . inflame the civic temper." *American Journal of Education, 96*(2), 162–194.

Campbell, J. (1971). *Hero with a thousand faces.* New York: Meridian Books.

Carlyle, T. (n. d.). *Heroes and hero worship*. Philadelphia: Henry Artemus.

Carnegie Forum on Education and the Economy. (1986). *A nation prepared: Teachers for the 21st century. The report of the Task Force on Teaching as a Profession*. New York: Carnegie Forum on Education and the Economy.

Carnegie Council on Adolescent Development. (1989). *Turning points: Preparing American youth for the 21st century*. Washington, DC: Carnegie Council on Adolescent Development.

Codrescu, A. (1990). *The disappearance of the outside: A manifesto for escape*. Reading, MA: Addison-Wesley.

Colby, A., & Damon, W. (1992). *Some do care: Contemporary lives of moral commitment*. New York: Free Press.

Coles, R. (1989). *The call of stories: Teaching and the moral imagination*. Boston: Houghton Mifflin.

Cook, S. (1993). *Twentieth-century American heroes: A thematic approach to cultural awareness*. Nashville, TN: Incentive Publications.

Costantino, G., Malgady, R., & Rogler, L. H. (1988). Folk hero modeling therapy for Puerto Rican adolescents. *Journal of Adolescence, 11*(2), 155–165.

Countryman, J. (1992). Is gender an issue in math class? Perhaps it's time to change the subject. In National Coalition of Girls' Schools, *Math and science for girls*, (pp. 72–83). Concord, MA: National Coalition of Girls' Schools.

Csikszentmihalyi, M., & Larson, R. (1984). *Being adolescent: Conflict and growth in the teenage years*. New York: Basic Books.

Csikszentmihalyi, M., & McCormack, J. (1992). The influence of teachers. In K. Ryan & J. Cooper (Eds.), *Kaleidoscope: Readings in education* (6th ed.), (pp. 41–47). Boston: Houghton Mifflin.

Cuban, L. (1993). The lure of curricular reform and its pitiful history. *Phi Delta Kappan, 75*(2), 182–185.

Damon, W. (1988). *The moral child: Nurturing children's natural moral growth*. New York: Free Press.

Davis, P. (1994, January 20). Now it's Dr. Barbie. *Providence Journal-Bulletin*, p. B1, 3.

Day, J. M. (1991a). The moral audience: On the narrative mediation of moral "judgment" and moral "action." In M. B. Tappan & M. J. Packer (Eds.), *Narrative and storytelling: Implications for understanding moral development* [New Directions for Child Development] Vol. 54, (pp. 27–42). San Francisco: Jossey-Bass.

Day, J. M. (1991b). Narrative, psychology, and moral education. *American Psychologist, 46*(2), 167–168.

Dewey, J. (1974). The child and the curriculum. In R. Archambault (Ed.), *John Dewey on education: Selected writings*, (pp. 339–358). Chicago: University of Chicago Press.

Donaldson, S. K., & Westerman, M. A. (1986). Development of children's understanding of ambivalence and causal theories of emotions. *Developmental Psychology, 22*(5), 655–662.

Dotter, D. (1987). Growing up is hard to do: Rock and roll performers as cultural heroes. *Sociological Spectrum*, 7(1), 25–44.

Duck, J. M. (1990). Children's ideals: The role of real-life vs. media figures. *Australia Journal of Psychology*, 42(1), 19–29.

Dunn, L. (1991). Teaching the heroes of American history: Debunking the myths, keeping the heroes. *Social Studies*, 82(1), 26–29.

Durkheim, E. (1956). *Education and sociology*. New York: Free Press.

Durkheim, E. (1973). *Moral education: A study in the theory and application of the sociology of education*. New York: Free Press.

Egan, K. (1986). *Teaching as story telling: An alternative approach to teaching and curriculum in the elementary school*. Chicago: University of Chicago Press.

Eisner, E. W. (1985). *The educational imagination: On the design and evaluation of school programs*. New York: Macmillan.

Eliade, M. (1963). *Myth and reality*. New York: Harper & Row.

Epstein, J. (1991, April 23). Say no to role models. *The New York Times*, p. 7.

Erikson, E. (1962). *Young man Luther: A study in psychoanalysis and history*. New York: W. W. Norton.

Erikson, E. (1983). The life cycle: Epigenesis of identity/Identity confusion in life history and case history. In W. Damon (Ed.), *Social and personality development: Essays on the growth of the child*, (pp. 408–433). New York: W. W. Norton.

Erikson, E. H. (1985). *Childhood and society*. New York: W. W. Norton.

(1985). Facets: Today's kids and hero worship. *English Journal*, 74(5), 20–23.

Fears, J. R. (1990). Education and the spirit of the Constitution. In *Better schools, better lives: An invitation to dialogue*, (pp. 7–12). Boston: Boston University Center for the Advancement of Ethics and Character.

Foucault, M. (1977). *Discipline and punish: The birth of the prison*. New York: Pantheon Books.

Fowler, J. W. (1981). *Stages of faith: The psychology of human development and the quest for meaning*. New York: HarperCollins.

Fowler, L., Glover, J., & Gore, J. (1980). *A hero ain't nothing but a great big sandwich: A global perspectives experimental unit*. Albuquerque, NM: Teachers' Learning Center.

Frisch, M. (1989). American history and the structures of collective memory: A modest exercise in empirical iconography. *Journal of American History*, 75(4), 1130–1155.

Gage, N. L. (1989). The paradigm wars and their aftermath: A "historical" sketch of research on teaching since 1989. *Educational Researcher*, 18(7), 4–10.

Gardella, F. J., Fraze, F. J., Meldon, J. E., Weingarden, M. S., & Campbell, C. (1992). *Mathematical connections: A bridge to algebra and geometry*. Boston: Houghton Mifflin.

Gardner, J. (1978). *On moral fiction*. New York: Basic Books, Inc.

Geertz, C. (1973). *The interpretation of cultures*. New York: Basic Books.

Gehlen, A. (1980). *Man in the age of technology*. New York: Columbia University Press.

Gergen, K. J. (1971). *The concept of self*. New York: Holt, Rinehart & Winston.

Gerzon, M. (1982). *A choice of heroes: The changing faces of American manhood*. Boston: Houghton Mifflin.

Gilligan, C. (1977). In a different voice: Women's conceptions of the self and morality. *Harvard Educational Review*, *4*, 481–517.

Gilligan, C. (1982). *In a different voice: Psychological theory and women's development*. Cambridge, MA: Harvard University Press.

Gilligan, C. (1987). Adolescent development reconsidered. In *New directions for child development* Vol. 37, (pp. 63–92). San Francisco: Jossey-Gilligan, C., Lyons, N. P., & Hanmer, T. J. (1990). *Making connections: The relational worlds of adolescent girls at Emma Willard School*. Cambridge, MA: Harvard University Press.

The Giraffe Project (1991). *Giraffes in schools: The Standing Tall Program. Grades 6–12*. Langley, WA: Giraffe Project.

Girl Scouts of the United States (1989). *Girl Scouts survey on the beliefs and moral values of America's children*. New York: Girl Scouts of the United States of America.

Glaser, B., & Strauss, A. L. (1967). *The discovery of grounded theory: Strategies for qualitative research*. Chicago: Aldine.

Goethals, G. (1978). Sacred-secular icons. In R. B. Browne & M. Fishwick (Eds.), *Icons of America*, (pp. 24–33). Bowling Green, OH: Popular Press.

Goffman, E. (1961). *Asylums: Essays on the social situation of mental patients and other inmates*. Garden City, NY: Anchor Books.

Goodlad, J. I., Soder, R., & Sirotnik, K. A., (Eds.). (1991). *The moral dimensions of teaching*. San Francisco: Jossey-Bass.

Grant, G. (1988). *The world we created at Hamilton High*. Cambridge, MA: Harvard University Press.

Green, T. F. (1988). The economy of virtue and the primacy of prudence. *American Journal of Education*, *96*(2), 127–142.

Greene, M. (1978). *Landscapes of learning*. New York: Teachers College Press.

Gross, J. (1993, November 24). All-girl classes to help girls keep up with boys. *New York Times*, p. 1, B8.

Growing up fast and frightened. (1993, November 22). *Newsweek*, 52–53.

Gudmundsdottir, S. (1991). Story-maker, story-teller: Narrative structures in curriculum. *Journal of curriculum studies*, *23*(3), 207–218.

Hadas, M., & Smith, M. (1965). *Heroes and gods: Spiritual biographies in antiquity*. New York: Harper & Row.

Hakanen, E. A. (1989). (D)evolution of heroes: An expanded typology of heroes for the electronic age. *Free Inquiry in Creative Sociology*, *17*(2), 153–158.

Harmin, M. (1985). Value clarity, high morality: Let's go for both. *Educational Leadership*, *45*(8), 24–30.

Hartshorne, H., & May, M. A. (1928). *Studies in the nature of character: Vol. 1. Studies in deceit*. New York: Macmillan.

Hartshorne, H., May, M. A., & Maller, J. B. (1929). *Studies in the nature of character: Vol. 2. Studies in self-control*. New York: Macmillan.

Hartshorne, H., May, M. A., & Shuttleworth, F. K. (1930). *Studies in the nature of character: Vol. 3. Studies in the organization of character*. New York: Macmillan.

Havighurst, R., & Taba, H. (1949). *Adolescent character and personality*. New York: John Wiley & Sons.

Heilman, S. (1992). *Defenders of the faith: Inside Ultra-Orthodox Jewry*. New York: Schocken Books.

Henrion, C. (1992). Mathematics in a cultural and historical context. In The National Coalition of Girls' Schools, *Math & science for girls*, (pp. 130–151). Concord, MA: The National Coalition of Girls' Schools.

Henry, M. E. (1993). *School cultures: Universes of meaning in private schools*. Norwood, NJ: Ablex.

Herbst, J. (1989). *And sadly teach*. Madison, WI: University of Wisconsin Press.

Heschel, A. J. (1990). *An anthology of Abraham Joshua Heschel*. J. Neusner with N. M. M. Neusner (Eds.). Lanham, MD: Madison Books.

Hill, P. T., Foster, G. E., & Gendler, T. (1990). *High schools with character*. Santa Monica, CA: The Rand Corporation.

Holland, S. (1991). Positive role models for primary-grade Black inner-city males. *Equity & Excellence, 25*(1), 40–44.

Holmes Group. (1986). *Tomorrow's teachers: A report of The Holmes Group*. East Lansing, MI: The Holmes Group.

Hook, S. (1955). *The hero in history: A study in limitation and possibility*. Boston: Beacon Press.

Hopp, C. (1992). Cooperative small groups. In The National Coalition for Girls' Schools, *Math & science for girls*, (pp. 116–129). Concord, MA: The National Coalition for Girls' Schools.

Ingall, C. K. (1993). Bar/bat mitzvah: Policies and programs. In H. Leneman (Ed.), *Bar/bat mitzvah education: A sourcebook*, (pp. 39–44). Denver: A.R.E. Publishing.

Jackson, P. W. (1986). *The practice of teaching*. New York: Teachers College Press.

Jackson, P. W. (1990). *Life in classrooms*. New York: Teachers College Press.

Johnson, S. M. (1990). *Teachers at work: Achieving success in our schools*. New York: Basic Books.

Junell, J. S. (1969). Can our schools teach moral commitment? *Phi Delta Kappan, 50*(8), 446–451.

Jung, J. (1986). How useful is the concept of role model? A critical analysis. *Journal of Social Behavior and Personality, 1*(4), 525–536.

Kilpatrick, W. K. (1992). *Why Johnny can't tell right from wrong*. New York: Simon & Schuster.

Kohlberg, L. (1983). The development of children's orientation towards a moral order. In W. Damon (Ed.), *Social and personality development: Essays on the growth of the child*, (pp. 388–404). New York: W. W. Norton.

Lamme, L. L., Krogh, S. L., & Yachmetz, K. A. (1992). *Literature-based moral education*. Phoenix: Oryx Press.

Lanckton, A. K. (1992). *How seventh and eighth grade teachers perceive their role as moral educators*. Unpublished doctoral dissertation, Boston University School of Education, Boston.

Landau, D. (1993). *Piety and power: The world of Jewish fundamentalism*. New York: Hill and Wang.

Lasch, C. (1978). *The culture of narcissism: American life in an age of diminishing expectations*. New York: W.W. Norton.

Lickona, T. (1992). *Educating for character: How our schools can teach respect and responsibility*. New York: Bantam Books.

Lightfoot, S. L. (1983). *The good high school: Portraits of character and culture*. New York: Basic Books.

Lorenz, K. (1970). *Studies in animal and human behavior* (Vol. 1). Cambridge, MA: Harvard University Press.

Lortie, D. C. (1975). *Schoolteacher: A sociological study*. Chicago: University of Chicago Press.

Luke, C. (1993). Media and popular culture in education and society: An introduction to education studies. *Teaching Education, 5*(2), 41–56.

MacIntyre, A. (1984). *After virtue*. Notre Dame, IN: University of Notre Dame Press.

Maher, F. A., & Rathbone, C. H. (1986). Teacher education and feminist theory: Some implications for practice. *American Journal of Education, 94*(2), 214–235.

Makolkin, A. (1992). *Name, hero, icon: Semiotics of nationalism*. Berlin: Mouton de Gruyter.

Malgady, R. G., Rogler, L. H., & Costantino, G. (1990). Hero/heroine modeling for Puerto Rican adolescents: A preventive mental health intervention. *Journal of Consulting and Clinical Psychology, 58*(4), 469–474.

Maxwell, J. A. (1992). Understanding and validity in qualitative research. *Harvard Educational Review, 62*(3), 279–300.

McCullough, D. (1992). *Brave companions*. New York: Touchstone.

McEwin, C. K., & Thomason, J. T. (1989). *Who they are–how we teach. Early adolescents and their teachers*. Columbus, OH: National Middle School Association.

Mead, G. H. (1948). *Mind, self and society: From the standpoint of a social behaviorist*. Chicago: University of Chicago Press.

Merriam, S. B. (1988). *Case study research in education: A qualitative approach*. San Francisco: Jossey-Bass.

Mills, C. W. (1959). *The sociological imagination*. London: Oxford University Press.

Minnich, H. C. (1936). *Old favorites from the McGuffey Readers*. New York: American Book Company.

Morgan, C. G. (1985). The peaceful hero. *Virginia English Bulletin, 35*(2), 10–12.

Morgan, D. L. (1988). *Focus groups as qualitative research*. Newbury Park, CA: Sage.

Mosier, R. D. (1965). *Making the American mind: Social and moral ideas in the McGuffey Readers*. New York: Russell and Russell.

Moulton, M. M., & Ransome, W. (1993, October 27). Helping girls succeed. *Education Week*, 23.

Muuss, R. (1988). *Theories of adolescence*. New York: McGraw Hill.

National Coalition of Girls' Schools. (1992). *Math & science for girls*. Concord, MA: National Coalition of Girls' Schools.

Nebraska Curriculum Development Center (1968). *A curriculum for English: The hero, Units 80–84*. Lincoln, NB: University of Nebraska Press.

Needleman, C. (1979). *The work of craft: An inquiry into the nature of crafts and craftsmanship*. New York: Knopf.

Nisan, M. Torah li'shmah: A ground for motivation in Jewish education. In *Conference of the Network for Research in Jewish Education*, Chicago, 1993, June 13.

Noddings, N. (1984). *Caring: A feminine approach to ethics and moral education*. Berkeley: University of California Press.

Noddings, N. (1988). An ethic of caring and its implications for instructional arrangements. *American Journal of Education*, 96(2), 215–230.

Noddings, N. (1992). *The challenge to care in schools: An alternative approach to education*. New York: Teachers College Press.

Norman, D. (1969). *The hero: Myth/image/symbol*. New York: World Publishing.

O'Brien, J. A., & Tracy, D. M. (1991). *The effects of female mathematician role models on eighth and ninth grade first year algebra students*.

Oliner, S., & Oliner, P. (1988). *The altruistic personality*. New York: Free Press.

Parr, S. R. (1982). *The moral of the story: Literature, values and American education*. New York: Teachers College Press.

Parsons, J. B. (1986). *Fulfilling an American dream: A typology of heroes*.

Patrick, J. J., & Remy, R. C. (1991). *Civics for Americans*. Glenview, IL: Scott, Foresman.

Peshkin, A. (1986). *God's choice: The total world of a fundamentalist Christian school*. Chicago: University of Chicago Press.

Peshkin, A. (1991). *The color of strangers, the color of friends: The play of ethnicity in school and community*. Chicago: University of Chicago Press.

Phenix, P. H. (1974). Transcendence and the curriculum. In E. W. Eisner & E. Vallance (Eds.), *Conflicting conceptions of curriculum*, (pp. 117–132). Berkeley: McCutchan.

Poinsett, A. (1988). *Young black males in jeopardy: Risk factors and intervention strategies*. New York: Carnegie Corporation of New York.

Polster, M. F. (1992). *Eve's daughters: The forbidden heroism of women*. San Francisco: Jossey-Bass.

Powers, J. (1993, August 1). Why death of Reggie Lewis hurt us so. *Boston Globe*, pp. 1,14.

Purpel, D. E. (1989). *The moral and spiritual crisis in education*. Granby, MA: Bergin and Garvey.

Purpel, D., & Ryan, K. (Eds.). (1976). *Moral education: It comes with the territory*. Berkeley, CA: McCutchan.

Rabinowitz, H. N. (1978). George Washington as icon 1865–1900. In R. B. Browne & M. Fishwick (Eds.), *Icons of America*, (pp. 67–86). Bowling Green, OH: Popular Press.

Ravitch, D. (1990). Multiculturalism: E pluribus plures. *American Scholar*, *59*(3), 337–353.

Rawls, J. (1971). *A theory of justice*. Cambridge, MA: Harvard University Press.

Rigg, P. (1985). Those spunky gals: An annotated bibliography. *The Reading Teacher*, *2*, 154–160.

Rogers, C. (1961). *On becoming a person: A therapist's view of psychotherapy*. Boston: Houghton Mifflin.

Russell, S. A. (1988). *Frederick Douglass*. New York: Chelsea House.

Rutter, M., Maughan, B., Mortimore, P., Ouston, J., with Smith, A. (1979). *Fifteen thousand hours: Secondary schools and their effects on children*. Cambridge, MA: Harvard University Press.

Ryan, K. (1988). The new moral education. In K. Ryan & J. Cooper (Eds.), *Kaleidoscope: Readings in education* (5th ed.), (pp. 286–293). Boston: Houghton Mifflin.

Ryan, K. (1990). Achievement, hedonism and the teacher. In *Better schools, better lives: An invitation to dialogue*, (pp. 13–19). Boston: Boston University Center for the Advancement of Ethics and Character.

Sadker, D., & Sadker, M. (1989). *Report card #1: The cost of sex bias in schools and society*. Washington, DC: American University.

Schlesinger, A. M. (1992). *The disuniting of America*. New York: W. W. Norton.

Schutz, A. (1962). *Collected papers* (Vol. I). The Hague: Martinus Nijhoff.

Sears, R. R., Rau, L., & Alpert, R. (1965). *Identification and child rearing*. Stanford: Stanford University Press.

Seidman, I. E. (1991). *Interviewing as qualitative research: A guide for researchers in education and the social sciences*. New York: Teachers College Press.

Shakeshaft, C. (1988). A gender at risk. In K. Ryan & J. Cooper (Eds.), *Kaleidoscope: Readings in Education* (5th ed.), (pp. 461–467). Boston: Houghton Mifflin.

Shatles, D. (1992). *Infusing peaceful heroes into the communication arts curriculum*.

Shugar, C. E. (1988). In search of the modern hero. *Childhood Education*, *64*(4), 202–205.

Shulman, L. S. (1987). Knowledge and teaching: Foundations of the new reform. *Harvard Educational Review*, *57*(1), 1–22.

Sichel, B. A. (1988). *Moral education: Character, community and ideals*. Philadelphia: Temple University Press.

Simmons, C., & Wade, W. (1983). The young ideal. *Journal of Moral Education*, *12*(1), 18–32.

Simmons, W., & Grady, M. (1990). *Black male achievement: From peril to promise*. Upper Marlboro, MD: Prince George's County Public Schools.

Simon, S. B., Howe, L., & Kirschenbaum, H. (1972). *Values clarification: A handbook of practical strategies for teachers and students*. New York: Hart.

Singer, M. (1991, July 19). Heroines and role models. *Science*, *253*(5017), 249.

Smith, A. D. (1993). *Fires in the mirror* [Audiotape]. New York: Bantam Doubleday Dell Audiopublishing.

Sommers, C. H. (1984). Ethics without virtue: Moral education in America. *American Scholar, 53*(3), 381–389.

Spradley, J. P. (1979). *The ethnographic interview.* New York: Holt, Rinehart & Winston.

Stern, L. (1991). Disavowing the self in female adolescence. *Women and Therapy, 11*(3–4), 105–117.

Stevenson, C. (1992). *Teaching ten to fourteen-year-olds.* New York: Longman.

Stratemeyer, F. B., Forkner, H. L., & McKim, M. G. (1947). *Developing a curriculum for modern living.* New York: Teachers College, Columbia University.

Styer, S. (1981). *Exploring women's political careers through biographies.*

Tappan, M. B. (1991). Narrative, authorship, and the development of moral authority. In M. B. Tappan & M. J. Packer (Eds.), *Narrative and storytelling: Implications for understanding moral development.* San Francisco: Jossey-Bass.

Tappan, M. B., & Brown, L. M. (1989). Stories told and lessons learned: Toward a narrative approach to moral development and moral education. *Harvard Educational Review, 59*(2), 182–205.

Tinajero, J. V., Gonzalez, M. L., & Dick, F. (1991). *Raising career aspirations of Hispanic girls.* Bloomington, IN: Phi Delta Kappa Educational Foundation.

Tomin, B., & Burgoa, C. (1986). *A multi-cultural women's history elementary curriculum unit.* Santa Rosa, CA: National Women's History Project.

Vitz, P. (1990). The use of stories in moral development: New psychological reasons for an old education method. *American Psychologist, 45*(6), 709–720.

Wechter, J. D. (1981). *Adolescent ego ideal development and its relationship to psychosexual level.* Unpublished Doctoral dissertation, Boston University Graduate School of Education, Boston.

Wilson, J. Q. (1993). *The moral sense.* New York: Free Press.

The world almanac and book of facts. (1990). New York: Pharos Books.

The world almanac and book of facts. (1991). New York: Pharos Books.

The world almanac and book of facts. (1992). New York: Pharos Books.

The world almanac and book of facts. (1993). New York: Pharos Books.

Wyman, S. L. (1993). *How to respond to your culturally diverse student population.* Alexandria, VA: ASCD.

Wynne, E. (1986). The great tradition in education: Transmitting moral values. *Educational Leadership, 43*(1), 4–9.

Wynne, E. A., & Ryan, K. (1993). *Reclaiming our schools: A handbook on teaching character, academics, and discipline.* Merrill: New York.

Yeats, W. B. (1989). Among schoolchildren. In R. J. Finneran (Ed.), *The collected works of W. B. Yeats* (Vol. 1). The poems [revised], (pp. 217–223). New York: MacMillan.

Yulish, S. (1980). *The search for civic religion: History of the character education movement in America, 1890–1935.* Washington: University Press of America.

Author Index

Subject Index